SLAVERY, SCANDAL, AND STEEL RAILS

DISCARDED

DISCARDED

SLAVERY, SCANDAL, AND STEEL RAILS

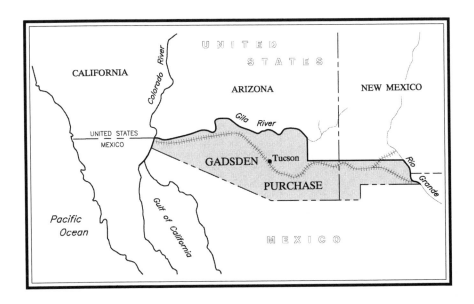

The 1854 Gadsden Purchase and the Building of the
Second Transcontinental Railroad Across Arizona and
New Mexico Twenty-Five Years Later

David Devine

iUniverse, Inc.
New York Lincoln Shanghai

Slavery, Scandal, and Steel Rails
The 1854 Gadsden Purchase and the Building of the Second Transcontinental
Railroad Across Arizona and New Mexico Twenty-Five Years Later

All Rights Reserved © 2004 by David Devine

No part of this book may be reproduced or transmitted in any form or by any
means, graphic, electronic, or mechanical, including photocopying, recording,
taping, or by any information storage retrieval system, without the written
permission of the publisher.

iUniverse, Inc.

For information address:
iUniverse, Inc.
2021 Pine Lake Road, Suite 100
Lincoln, NE 68512
www.iuniverse.com

ISBN: 0-595-32913-6

Printed in the United States of America

For Susie,
who made it possible

CONTENTS

LIST OF MAPS

LIST OF ILLUSTRATIONS

FOREWORD

This book was not intended to be a detailed look at the political or social circumstances which led to the negotiations and ratification of the Gadsden Purchase. That was done expertly eighty years ago by Paul Garber in *The Gadsden Treaty*.

Neither was this book to be a definitive history on the construction of the nation's second transcontinental railroad. That review has yet to be completed, but the foundation for it was laid by David Myrick with the publication in 1975 of the classic *Railroads of Arizona, vol. 1, the southern roads* and his earlier *New Mexico's Railroads*.

Nor was this work to be a comprehensive analysis of the historical background which resulted in the Purchase and of building the railroad along the southern boundary of the United States. Those issues have been dealt with in many previous works on the Mexican-American War and Treaty of Guadalupe Hidalgo, the Mesilla Valley controversy, the national railroad surveys of the 1850s, and the construction of the country's first transcontinental railroad in the 1860s.

Instead, this book is an attempt to be an overview, connecting the dots of history which arc across time in a continuous pattern. In this case that period stretches from the 1840s until the 1880s, and the subject is the push for, and eventual completion of, a southern transcontinental rail line.

At the same time, an effort has been made to briefly describe the human and natural characteristics of the territory acquired through the Gadsden Purchase of 1854. Several American military men, explorers, and surveyors, who had earlier passed through the region, left behind journals of their travels. Using their own words, it is these sources which have been employed to explain what they found and what the United States was acquiring from Mexico.

A similar approach was used in chronicling the construction of the Southern Pacific and Atchison, Topeka & Santa Fe railroads across the Gadsden Purchase twenty-five years later. The letters of Charles Crocker, Collis Huntington and their S.P. business partners were the foundation of this section. Starting in the

1870s, these messages, along with newspaper stories from the time, help to portray the implementation and impact of this important project, which was completed in 1881.

In telling this two-part tale, I have intentionally omitted some secondary facts and characters. While they played a role in the story of the Gadsden Purchase or the building of the railroad, in order to make the history of this period more understandable, I chose to focus only on the main events and personalities.

This book could not have been written without the support of many people. I would like to thank Sarah Clements for her research work, Jim Ayres who provided me with information on the train stop at Pantano, and Art Roman of the Deming Luna Mimbres Museum for supplying much useful material.

Among the institutions from which I received assistance were the New York City Public Library, the South Carolina Historical Society, the Bancroft Library at the University of California, the Casa Grande Valley Historical Society, the History and Archives Division of Arizona's Department of Library in Phoenix, and the Library of the University of South Carolina. The staff of the microfilm reading room of the National Archives II along with those at the Rio Grande Historical Collections and the Special Collections Library at New Mexico State University were also very helpful.

A great deal of material was gathered from the Library of Congress, the Arizona Historical Society Library in Tucson, and from the Society's Yuma branch. In addition, the City Clerk's office in each of those two communities provided important information from historic records. Most of my research time, though, was spent at the University of Arizona Library and in its Special Collections division and their research librarians offered especially useful advice.

To all of those who aided me with this effort, I say thank you. A special note of appreciation goes to the Southwestern Foundation for Education and Historical Preservation. They not only encouraged this work, but supplied financial support to help defray some of the costs associated with the research.

In addition to this assistance, I received valuable comments and criticisms on earlier drafts of this book. Those who read the original manuscript were: Howard Greenseth, Carol Juliani, Dr. James Klein, Felicia Sanders-May, and Norman Salmon. The suggestions and advice they offered, from spelling corrections to needed clarifications to unnecessary paragraphs, helped make this a much better effort. To each of them I offer my sincere appreciation.

A later draft of this book was reviewed by Bill Kalt and Pat Toth. Their comments, criticisms and opinions also improved the text enormously, and my thanks goes out to them.

The graphic design and layout of the book were done by Tom Bergin Studios. Using his painting entitled "Dawn at Picacho Peak,"©2003, Tom also came up with the spectacular cover. He additionally took the picture of me standing in front of Tucson's recently renovated historic train station. Without Tom's artistic assistance, this book would not look as good as it does.

The other photograph on the cover was taken by Carleton Watkins of the roundhouse in Yuma around 1880. This item is reproduced by permission of *The Huntington Library, San Marino, California.*

Additional photographs in the book came from a number of sources, including the Library of Congress and the National Archives II. The photograph of the Rio Grande Hotel in Las Cruces, New Mexico is used courtesy of the New Mexico State University Library, Archives and Special Collections while the picture of Tucson's original train station was supplied by Miss Roberta Niesz.

The maps were all done by Ron Beckwith, who miraculously translated my scribbles into easily understandable images. Two of the maps were variations of ones done earlier for a monograph of mine published by the Tucson Corral of the Westerners. Maps number four and seven are based on the work of the late Don Bufkin for *Too Far North: Too Far South* written by Odie B. Faulk. This 1967 book on the Gadsden Purchase was published by Westernlore Press and its proprietor, Lynn Bailey, generously allowed the use of these maps.

While my thanks goes out to everyone who helped with this effort, I cannot emphasize enough the support and assistance I received from my wife, Susie Morris. She helped with the research, proofread the manuscript, and offered advice and encouragement throughout the process. Without her, this book would simply not have been possible.

The contents of the book are, of course, completely my responsibility. If something important has been overlooked, or misstated, it is my fault alone, but I have tried to be as historically accurate as possible in telling the story of the 1854 Gadsden Purchase and the building of the nation's second transcontinental railroad through southern Arizona and New Mexico twenty-five years later.

David Devine
Tucson, Arizona
August, 2004

INTRODUCTION

Crossing the Colorado River and heading east from Yuma, Arizona, toward El Paso, Texas, a driver probably doesn't look forward to 560 miles of desolate, dreary, desert monotony. However, the automobile journey can take less than 10 hours and occasional stops in urban areas, spread out like giant pogo-stick hops across the mostly flat, dry terrain offer some relief from the sheer boredom of the trip.

Interstate 8 leaves the river behind at Yuma, a city of 60,000 people and home to both a territorial prison built in 1876 and a U.S. military pilot training program, now a Marine Corps air station, dating from 1943. The city has stretched out far beyond its original downtown river crossing location as well as the site of the first railroad bridge over the Colorado. Today it is a sprawling community of people working and living in mostly single-story frame and stucco buildings supplemented by an enormous winter population of retirees who reside in recreational vehicles and trailer courts. In its restaurants, Yuma offers some of the largest glasses of ice tea served in the country to combat the intense summer heat.

After lumbering through the Gila Mountains twenty miles east of Yuma, the motorist heads slightly northeast as the highway runs next to railroad tracks. Passing the tiny settlements of Wellton, Tacna, Mohawk, Dateland, and Sentinel, the regular spacing of these communities scattered across 60 miles of primarily barren desert land is hardly noticed by the driver as he speeds past them. He may have spotted, however, the Mohawk Mountains which have been described as a "long, narrow backbone of a range, reminiscent of a 'mohawk' haircut...".[1]

The first town of any size encountered along the route is Gila Bend, named for the huge curve once made nearby by the now dammed and dry Gila River. The small city of 1,700 residents with its handful of restaurants and service stations offers the weary motorist a short break from his trip. A side journey south can take the traveler to Ajo, a community with an enormous, now abandoned, open-pit copper mine.

Back on I-8, which goes almost directly east from Gila Bend and has separated from the railroad tracks at this point, the highway runs between some low hills. The surrounding scenery is primarily desert scrub dotting a level plain with an occasional mountain range visible in the distance. In less than an hour the driver is skirting Casa Grande, a rapidly growing community of over 20,000 people. Once encircled by enormous cotton fields which are now quickly disappearing beneath subdivision plots, the city takes its name from an ancient Indian structure which is several miles further east. Another ten miles beyond the almost 700-year old, four-story National Monument is Florence, the small-town seat of Pinal County government.

Thirty miles to the north, in an endless ocean of retirement communities and huge shopping malls, begins the metropolitan complex of Phoenix. With a population of well over 3 million in its urban area, the capital of Arizona dominates the state's politics and commerce.

Back to the south, northwest of Casa Grande is Maricopa. This tiny community is wedged between two Indian reservations, each of which offers a casino to the tourist. Near a discount shopping mall to the south of Casa Grande, I-8 is absorbed into Interstate 10 and the roadway swings down toward Tucson.

Once again small settlements spring up with regularity along the highway. The farming communities of Eloy, Picacho, and Red Rock hug the road, as do interchange services and an odd assortment of recently-installed immense and whimsical playground-like metal sculptures which litter a large vacant parcel of property for sale.

By this time, the main line of the Union Pacific Railroad has reappeared next to the highway. Before the company was taken over in 1996, for almost 120 years these tracks were part of the Southern Pacific Railroad Company system. If the traveler is lucky, he may spot a six-times-a-week Amtrak passenger train using the line, but it is more likely he will see one of the sixty freight trains which pass through every day.

Near the tracks at this point, the singular shape of Picacho Peak sticks up into a usually crystal blue, warm desert sky. This was the site of Arizona's only Civil War skirmish and today around the low mountain's base, among the saguaro cactus, souvenir shops, RV park, and ostrich farm, cattle can sometimes be seen grazing on the open range. Within thirty minutes after this the driver is entering the urban mass of Tucson, a metropolitan area which covers hundreds of square miles and is approaching a population of one million.

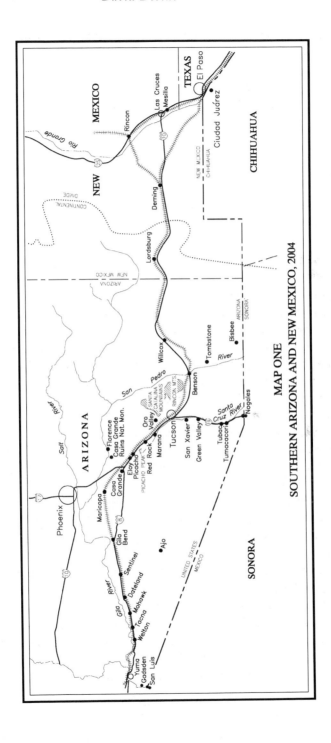

MAP ONE
SOUTHERN ARIZONA AND NEW MEXICO, 2004

Resort hotels lie in the foothills of the majestic Santa Catalina Mountains while traditional motels line many of Tucson's major streets. Fast-food places by the hundreds, excellent Mexican food establishments, and almost fifty Chinese restaurants are available for a meal. Two traditional newspapers, the *Arizona Daily Star* and *Tucson Citizen*, are published locally, and seemingly omni-present gas stations with mini-marts attached can be used to fill up the car and its driver simultaneously so the trip is not unnecessarily delayed.

Twenty-five percent of metro Tucson's population is Mexican-American. In addition, thousands of Mexican citizens toil for low wages as maids, roofers, and farm laborers. In recent years the crossings of the nearby desert international boundary by some of these people has resulted in hundreds of deaths due to exposure along with the formation of unauthorized American militia groups intent on stopping those illegally entering the United States. Local Mexican-Americans like to remind others, though, that because of the 1854 Gadsden Purchase, the border crossed them, they didn't cross the border.

Returning to the highway, electronic message boards warn the swift-moving motorist of upcoming problems while other signs point toward Interstate 19, the 65-mile road to Nogales and the border with Mexico. This southbound highway passes both operating open-pit copper mines as well as more Indian gambling and entertainment centers. It also goes by the quietly dignified mission of San Xavier del Bac as well as the historic church at Tumacacori and the artist colony of Tubac.

Back on I-10, just east of Tucson the motorist drives by an exit close to which the ruins of the abandoned railroad station of Pantano still silently lie. Then the road descends into the San Pedro River basin near Benson, a community of 4,000. The river is a narrow stream lined with lime-green cottonwood trees and the driver sees mountain peaks scattered across the landscape, with the Rincon range rising mightily to the northwest. To the south is the famous but small old silver mining town of Tombstone, and another 25 miles further is Bisbee with its now mostly unused copper mines.

Going eastward from Benson, although interrupted once by a rocky, hilly area, I-10 is primarily flat as it swings to the north toward a usually dry desert lake bed before passing the agricultural town of Willcox with a population of 3,100. After this the highway turns due east again and soon the traveler enters New Mexico, still speeding along at 70 m.p.h. or more through the low hills found along the state-line.

The level desert floor quickly returns, interrupted only by an occasional fire-works stand and the cities of Lordsburg with 3,000 people and Deming with 11,000 residents. In Lordsburg is found a historic two-story adobe building named after the town's earliest residents, while Deming boasts a popular local history museum. Between these two communities the highway has crossed the continental divide, but it is only apparent because of a roadside sign. For long stretches in New Mexico the railroad tracks again parallel I-10.

The motorist quickly reaches Las Cruces, which was founded in 1849 and today is home to more than 60,000 and also the site of New Mexico State University. Nearby Mesilla is a small Mexican-style, mostly adobe town of 2,000 centered around a peaceful plaza surrounded by tourist shops.

The highway has headed almost straight east since leaving Arizona but at Las Cruces it turns due south. In less than an hour the driver crosses into Texas, with I-10 running for a few miles next to the Rio Grande as it flows through El Paso. The city has more than 560,000 residents closely connected with their 1.2 million Mexican neighbors in Cuidad Juárez on the south side of the international border.

Looking back on the trip, the driver may recall the dull sameness of the desert scenery, broken only rarely by agricultural activity. The random location of north-south running mountain ranges and the scattered sites of communities along the highway may also have left a slight impression. In general, though, it is mostly a fast journey through a flat, forgettable landscape that is remembered.

Except, perhaps, if the driver looks at a map of the area and notices how the southern boundary of New Mexico goes directly west from El Paso before taking a slight turn southward and then heads west again. This arrow-straight line continues into Arizona to the border city of Nogales, where it unexpectedly angles northwest, running until it hits the Colorado River several miles south of Yuma.

The traveler could scratch his head over why the international line with Mexico didn't simply go due west from El Paso. He may wonder why the bend was put in the border, preventing the United States from having any access onto the Gulf of California. He might laugh at the long-told explanation that after leaving the Nogales area in the summer heat of 1855, the thirsty survey crew locating the boundary decided to head for the nearest cold beer stop. That was in Yuma, but they missed their mark by about 20 miles.[2]

That explanation, of course, is only a humorous antidote, not real history. This is the story of how that border line was actually decided upon through the background, negotiations, and ratification of the Gadsden Purchase in the 1850s. It involves the secret messages, political intrigue, and pre-Civil War sectional splits in the country over slavery which resulted in a treaty which its namesake ultimately rejected.

This story also includes why and how the railroad tracks which the Purchase was intended to accommodate weren't installed until twenty-five years later. The hardball business dealings between railroad rivals, the expected financial bonanza the tracks were expected to bring to the region, and the internal disputes and disagreements between officials of the Southern Pacific Railroad Company are all part of the legacy of the southwestern United States.

The two stories of the building of the country's second transcontinental rail line and the treaty with Mexico which was negotiated to let that happen play a very important role in the history of southern Arizona and New Mexico. It has been 150 years since the Gadsden Purchase was completed, and in that time the area has traveled a long way.

CHAPTER ONE

"Let us not fail to pay a tribute to the high and distinguished services of Col. Gadsden, of South Carolina"

It was a dream long before it was practical. The idea of spanning the continent with railroad tracks was first conceived during the 1840s while the United States was still in its physically formative stage. It was sought, depending upon the source, to improve trade with China, or to enhance the business prospects of southern states, or to increase the military capabilities of the country, or for a myriad of other reasons. Regardless of the rationale, the belief that an American railroad had to be built from the Atlantic to the Pacific was widespread.

Beginning in the 1830s, economic rivalries among southern cities and between different sections of the country led to numerous proposals for laying tracks from Atlantic coastal communities west to the Mississippi River.[1] Among those advocating for these routes was James Gadsden of Charleston, South Carolina.[2]

Born in May of 1788, Gadsden was the third of sixteen children.[3] He graduated with honors from Yale College in New Haven, Connecticut, and at age eighteen entered into business in his home town. After war with Great Britain broke out in 1812, Gadsden received an appointment as a Lieutenant in the Corps of Engineers and served in Canada and New York.

At the end of the hostilities, Gadsden assisted General Andrew Jackson "to examine and report on the military defenses of the Gulf of Mexico frontier".[4] The future President considered his young associate a skillful engineer and a man of integrity, and thought it important he be encouraged to remain in the Army.[5] Gadsden was then promoted to Captain in 1818 and later to Colonel while serving again under Jackson in Florida. But after ten years of military service, Gadsden eventually left the Army because of political intrigue in the United

States Senate which denied him a promotion to Adjutant General. He believed Senators such as Thomas Hart Benton of Missouri opposed his appointment because of their disputes with South Carolinian John C. Calhoun who was Secretary of War, and this snub was one Gadsden would never forget.

Settling near Tallahassee, Gadsden became a planter, an occupation he did not enjoy. While in Florida, in 1824 Gadsden was also a member of the first Legislative Council and then three times unsuccessfully sought election to represent the territory in Congress, but he refused to campaign for the position, thinking it an undignified thing to do.

In the 1830s Gadsden temporarily returned to his home state to work as an engineer on a survey for a rail line which was proposed to connect Charleston with Cincinnati and Louisville.[6] While that project was not implemented, he later moved back to his home town permanently and, with the support of Calhoun, who by then was in the United States Senate, in 1840 Gadsden became president of the financially troubled South Carolina Railroad Company. In that position he oversaw the extension of the company's tracks from Charleston to Columbia at a cost of $2.3 million. Upon the completion of this effort in 1842, he was toasted for the accomplishment at a dinner marking the occasion.[7]

Even earlier than that, Gadsden had become a major spokesman for running rails all the way west to the Mississippi River. He and some of his contemporaries believed that to compete with the growing commercial importance of New Orleans, southern Atlantic coastal cities had to have western train routes. They thought these communities needed to try and redirect business away from the Louisiana port and toward Memphis or another point on the Mississippi more accessible to them by rail.[8]

Transportation by rail, though, was still in its infancy then, having originated in the United States in 1830. There were only 2,800 miles of track in the country by 1840, and the next decade would see another 6,000 miles added.

Southern states, however, lagged behind their northern neighbors in the laying of rails. This was one reason why Gadsden and a few other southerners considered it essential to extend tracks from their coastal communities all the way west to the Mississippi River.

Over time, the even more daunting idea of linking the entire continent together by a railroad stretching from the Atlantic to the Pacific began to develop, and one of the first to propose the concept of tracks to the west coast was Asa Whitney. A New York merchant who had spent time in China, Whitney in 1844 started advocating for a transcontinental rail line. In January of 1845, he presented the proposal in a memorial to the Congress of the United States.[9]

A few months later, people in Memphis called for southern and western leaders to attend a convention in their city to discuss regional development issues. James

Gadsden was among the hundreds of delegates sent to the gathering from more than one dozen states, and he was appointed a member of the "Committee on Railroad Connection of Southern Atlantic Ports with the Mississippi River". Gadsden was entrusted with giving the group's recommendations, and in his report outlined the need for several southern train routes to the Mississippi River.[10]

In a letter written in September of 1845, Gadsden labeled the idea of extending rail lines to the Mississippi River a "Great Work".[11] He also thought the recent Congressional action to annex Texas into the Union, a move he had personally supported, would have very important consequences for extending the line even further west. "This work now acquires additional interest from the recent annexation of Texas," he wrote, "and the probability that the much advisable route for a railroad from the Atlantic to Texas and the Pacific will be via the Carolina, Georgia, and Memphis route."[12]

Gadsden was in part pushing the need for additional southern railroads because he saw it as a way for Charleston to become more commercially viable. During a speech delivered in early 1846 he pointed out that his home town had fallen economically behind. To improve, he said the city had to diversify its agricultural economy, and would do so because of a "system of railways opening to southern enterprise the rich valley of the Mississippi."[13] Expanding on that idea, he wrote Calhoun, "We need only railways to the Valley of the Mississippi to realize all our fond & confiding predictions as to the future prosperity and growth of this city [Charleston]."[14] Later, Gadsden would look even further west, calling for the eventual construction of a railroad from ocean to ocean.

The divisive issue of slavery in the south, however, was certain to play a role in any Congressional decision about a proposed railroad to the Pacific. Unlike the privately funded railways east of the Mississippi which Gadsden was initially promoting, the transcontinental line west of the river was conceived by most people as a national work to be paid for partially by federal taxpayers. Plus, since it would cross public land, Congress would have to approve the right-of-way. This meant a coalition of southern and northern politicians might have to come to an agreement on the route and how it could be financed. Thus, slavery and its possible expansion westward could be a factor considered by Congress in making its decision about the route of a transcontinental railroad.

Despite that, the slave-owning Gadsden was being singled out for praise by many southerners because of his tireless railroad efforts. One journal commented: "Whilst upon the subject of southern railroads, let us not fail to pay a tribute to the high and distinguished services of Col. Gadsden, of South Carolina. He has been the life of all these movements, and their pioneer. With extraordinary practical ability and indomitable perseverance, his services can never be estimated too high. Devoted to the cause of the State and of the South, he is ever ready to sacrifice himself in their service."[15]

While southerners were still talking about their regional railroad future, by February of 1846 Asa Whitney had prepared another memorial to Congress which outlined the reasons a far northern railroad linking the two coasts was essential.

To develop a trade route to China which could access its incredibly large population while implementing a transportation system that would definitely be faster to the far east than that available to the sea-faring British, Whitney proposed building a railroad from the shores of Lake Michigan. Crossing the Mississippi River at Prairie du Chien in Wisconsin, the line then headed west to the Pacific Ocean at the mouth of the Columbia River. Neither Whitney nor anyone else had very detailed information about the geography or hydrology of much of this expansive stretch of land, but nevertheless he assured Congress the railroad was feasible to build.

Once this project was completed, Whitney said, the continent could be crossed in eight days. He believed rail and ship traffic all the way to China might be accomplished in thirty days from the east coast of the United States instead of the five or more months it took by water alone. This, he thought "must revolutionize the entire commerce of the world; placing us directly in the centre of all, and all must be tributary to us, and, in a moral point of view, it will be the means of civilizing and christianizing all mankind."[16]

To pay for this enormous undertaking, estimated to cost $50 million and take 15 years to complete, Whitney petitioned Congress to grant him a strip of land 60 miles wide along the entire route of his proposed railroad. As the tracks were laid, he assumed development and agricultural activity would follow on the vacant land. He would then sell the property to raise the construction capital required to keep the work going. At the end of the project, any monetary balance remaining was to be used to reward his efforts.

The initial political reaction to the entire proposal was generally negative, but with Whitney's persistent lobbying efforts, the idea eventually gained numerous backers and several states sent resolutions to Congress in support of the concept. Many southerners, not surprisingly, were much less favorable. They thought the project would lead to their economic ruin and that New Orleans or Memphis should be the eastern starting point of the transcontinental tracks instead.

Some from northern states joined in with this criticism, calling Whitney's 1846 idea too expensive and too far north to be kept open during the winter months. After considering the concept, a divided Congress did nothing about it.

One of the factors which made a Congressional decision on the issue so difficult during the 1840s was the physical configuration of the country. While the 1803 Louisiana Purchase had almost doubled the nation's size, the western border of the United States remained far from the Pacific coast. It wasn't until 1845 that Texas became a state and the next year, when the Oregon Country was added, did the United States finally have access to the Pacific Ocean. Further south, though, the coastal lands of California and vast unexplored stretches of the continent's interior were still part of Mexico.

That fact, however, didn't stop James Gadsden from proposing to build a U.S. rail line through another country. In his report of February 1846 as President of the South Carolina Railroad Company, Gadsden suggested two possible routes crossing Mexican territory to the Pacific. The first, which had originally been conceived by someone else a few months earlier, cut across Texas to the port city of Mazatlán; the other went further north along the Red River heading toward San Francisco.[17]

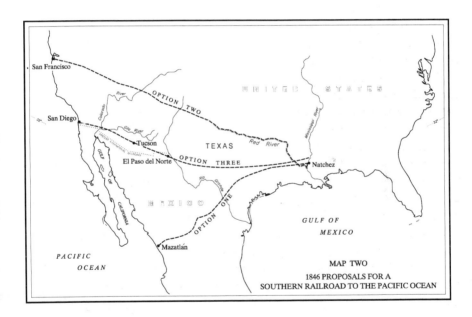

MAP TWO
1846 PROPOSALS FOR A
SOUTHERN RAILROAD TO THE PACIFIC OCEAN

An alternative southern path to the Pacific was also proposed around this same time. It would pass through south Texas and then generally follow the 32nd parallel of north latitude near the Gila River to the Colorado River and go on to San Diego. All of the land along this route west of Texas, of course, was also part of Mexico.

J. D. B. DeBow, editor of the New Orleans publication, *The Commercial Review*, took note of that latter possibility. Even given that, he rallied instead behind the cause of a railroad from Charleston to Mazatlán, arguing it was the best choice of any proposed route.

The primary difficulty with this concept, DeBow conceded, was that much of the required land was in Mexico, but the United States was then at war with its militarily-weak southern neighbor. Assuming the U.S. would triumph in this struggle, thus allowing it to construct a railroad to Mazatlán, DeBow in 1847 urged that during peace negotiations, "The right-of-way for a railroad through such region of Mexico to the Pacific...should by all means be exacted."[18] To put it even more bluntly, he continued, "<u>Let us demand the right-of-way from Mexico</u>."

A major problem with this potential southern railroad line, however, as well as the alternatives suggested by Whitney, Gadsden, and others, was that very little information existed concerning what topography and natural features were found in the western regions of the continent. Most of the territory beyond the Mississippi had not been explored, mapped, or even seen by Americans, so all of the bold statements and assertions of fact by proponents about railroad construction costs and feasibility were really just wild speculations and uninformed guesses. Reliable information and verifiable financial estimates would have to be determined by people who would actually visit the proposed transcontinental routes.

CHAPTER TWO

"Unless this should get a value as a highway between the two oceans"

The beginning of the conflict with Mexico in 1846 required the United States military to cross and explore the territory west of Texas. This enormous expanse of land had been visited previously by only a few Americans, but because of the war and the need to hurry troops to California, reconnaissance of potential overland routes to the Pacific coast was essential.[1]

Although not officially stated as a policy, the westward-moving soldiers and the survey party which accompanied them would also have the opportunity to observe routes which might eventually accommodate a southern transcontinental railroad. In addition, they would have the chance to describe the unknown desert land, its native peoples, and its exotic plants for those living east of the Mississippi River.

To get to southern California in order to occupy it for the United States, two groups set out from Santa Fe, New Mexico, in the fall of 1846. The first, consisting of 300 cavalry dragoon members of the U.S. Army of the West, was led by General S.W. Kearny and left on September 25th. They would take the quickest route possible, following the Rio Grande south and then heading west along the Gila River until it joined the Colorado River. From there they would proceed overland into California.

Three weeks later, a second group departed Santa Fe on their way to California. This was the famous "Mormon Battalion", hundreds of volunteer male members of the Church of Jesus Christ of Latter Day Saints accompanied by a few women and children. Under the direction of Lieutenant-Colonel Philip St. George Cooke, one of their goals was to locate a wagon trail to the west coast. To do this they would swing far south of the Gila River and cut across the

Mexican state of Sonora, then follow the San Pedro River north, visit the small village of Tucson, and return to the Gila before heading for California.

On their journey west, the battalion would take with them six large ox-drawn wagons, numerous wagons pulled by mules, and a few private vehicles for the women and children. Also going along were twenty-eight head of cattle and enough flour, sugar, and coffee for sixty days, salt pork for thirty, and a twenty day supply of soap.[2]

The thirty-seven year old Cooke was a West Point graduate and stood an imposing six feet, four inches tall.[3] Two of those accompanying him were Henry Standage and Samuel Rogers, both members of the Mormon faith. Each of these three men would write journals of the trip which described in some detail their experiences and hardships.

On November 13th the troop turned southwest from the lower Rio Grande. The next day, Standage recorded, "Our rations now have become so short both beef as well as other things that the Col. has ordered an old white ox to be killed that has been drove in a team something like 1200 miles [from Council Bluffs, Iowa], and has given out by the way."[4] By the 15th the weather had turned very cold, bringing snow and rain, and the meat from the white ox was "really the poorest beef that can be imagined and not only is there a lack of fat, but it is covered with sores caused by the blows received from day to day in order to get the poor thing along through the deep sands."[5]

The battalion had to be very careful about where it went through this unexplored territory since food and water were needed for both men and animals. Thus, searching out and finding watering holes and grassy pasture land was critically essential.

Around the middle of November, Cooke had to choose between a route straight west to the San Pedro River across unknown territory thought to be a prairie, or one which went further south. Hoping to find water along the way, he chose the latter, but wrote of the shorter desert cutoff: "It is probable that between 80 and 100 miles may be saved, and some bad road avoided. It is only necessary for a small experienced party, well provided with water, (with Indian guides, if practicable) to explore the prairie, and discover the watering places."[6] He also noted of this potential route, "If the prairie, to the north, is open to the San Pedro, and water can be found, that improvement will make my road not only a good but a direct one from the Rio Grande to the Pacific."[7]

Both the desert cutoff and San Pedro River routes through the area are shown on a map of the region prepared after the battalion's march.[8] Over the next decade, the desert alternative would take on great significance to southern railroad supporters because of its direct line west. Then, thirty-five years later, it would basically be this shortcut to Cooke's wagon road which track layers would actually follow through the dry country of the Arizona territory.

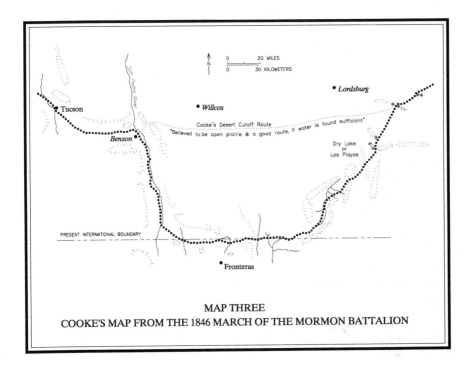

MAP THREE
COOKE'S MAP FROM THE 1846 MARCH OF THE MORMON BATTALION

By the middle of December, Cooke had another decision to make about which path to follow. One possibility could take him far around Tucson, a garrison town of a few hundred Mexican soldiers and civilians, but it would be 100 miles farther than the direct route toward the settlement. Cooke chose the shorter way, writing of the town and its inhabitants: "We will march then to Tucson. We came not to make war against Sonora, and less still to destroy an unimportant outpost of defense against Indians. But we will take the straight course before us and overcome all resistance."[9]

On December 16th, the American troops moved into Tucson and found that it had been deserted by its Mexican defenders. Of the village Rogers said only: "The town is built in the Mexican style…Here are some fine farms. The people seem more intelligent than at Santa Fe."[10] Standage added of those locals who remained behind when the Mexican military departed, "We were kindly treated by the people of Touson [Tucson] who brought Flour, Meal, Tobacco, Quinces to the camp for sale and many of them giving such things to the Soldiers."[11]

Facing the prospects of a long 75-mile march without water to the Gila River, Cooke rested the battalion for a day before setting out from Tucson. Rogers wrote of the route north, "Continued in the same direction over these dry, dusty and level plains, covered with bushes armed with thorns…".[12] Standage commented that he was "almost choked with thirst" through this stretch of desert, but eventually water was found.

By December 21st, the battalion had reached the Gila River near which Cooke exuberantly estimated were living between 15,000 to 20,000 Pima and Maricopa Indians. Rogers' impression of this experience was: "Camped among scores of Pima Indians, who had meal and corn and beans for sale. I traded an old shirt for some beans. These Indians are large, robust and healthy."[13] In addition he noted, "They have also watermelons; the land appears very dry and barren." Finally he wrote, "Their blankets made from cotton raised by themselves are of excellent quality."

Christmas Day passed without notice by the three men, and the battalion proceeded west, crossing the Colorado River on January 11th, 1847. By the 29th they had reached San Diego, having covered 1,125 miles on foot in 102 days.

In a letter written in December of 1847, Cooke recalled that from the San Pedro River valley: "It is then about 48 miles to Tueson [Tucson], a town of about 500 inhabitants with a fort and garrison…From Tueson it is some 75 miles to the Gila. It is a level plain, generally of clay, where my wagons and footmen (water being very scarce) passed at the rate of about 30 miles a day."[14] Then he noted of part of the trail the battalion had blazed between the Rio Grande and Gila River, "The route from Tueson passes through a country abounding in exceedingly rich gold mines."

Gold would be the reason some people would soon follow Cooke's wagon road. Within three years after the march he led, Americans were streaming to California, inspired by the discovery of gold. For those who wished to take a southern route to the coast, and avoid the mountains and inclement weather of the northern trails, Cooke and the Mormon Battalion had shown the way.

****

It was the need to get fighting men from Santa Fe to California as quickly as possible that sent General Kearny and his troops to the Gila River in 1846. Among those under his leadership was a fourteen-man topographical unit commanded by First Lieutenant William H. Emory. An 1831 graduate of West Point and a veteran of survey work between Canada and Maine, Emory hailed from Maryland's Queen Annes County on the eastern shore of the Chesapeake Bay. Among his friends at the military academy had been Jefferson Davis, future United States Senator from Mississippi, Secretary of War, and President of the Confederate States of America.

On their way to California, Emory and his survey crew would collect information about the territory being traversed with the instruments in their possession: two chronometers for time keeping, two sextants for determining latitude and longitude, and a barometer for measuring atmospheric pressure and estimating elevation.[15] But since the troops were moving as fast as they could on horseback and on foot, the result of Emory's efforts was more personal observation than actual detailed survey. The record of the journey, however, would for several years be the best available description of the territory through which the men traveled.

Along the way to the Pacific, both Emory and Captain Abraham R. Johnston of the First Dragoons would write detailed descriptions of the more than two-month trip. The journals, though, would not be published until 1848, thus making their findings unavailable to decision-makers in Washington for some time.

Eleven days after leaving Santa Fe, by early October Kearny's troops met Kit Carson, who was heading east toward Washington, D.C. The famous guide told them that the Mexicans had surrendered California. Upon hearing this news, the General sent two hundred of his men back to Santa Fe, and the just over 100 remaining continued west.[16]

Also going with them would be Carson, who had been persuaded to forsake his family in the east and join the group for a return trip to California. Of this decision, Johnston wrote, "It requires a brave man to give up his private feelings thus for the public good; but Carson is one such! honor to him for it!"[17]

The going was slow, Carson telling the troops almost immediately, "At the rate we are traveling, we will not get to Angelos [Los Angeles] in four months."[18] Within a few days, the soldiers and their animals had reached the Gila River and Emory noted: "Its section, where we struck it, 4,347 feet above the sea, was 50 feet wide and an average of two feet deep. Clear and swift, it came bouncing from the great mountains which appeared to the north about 60 miles distant."[19]

During their journey along the river, the men found numerous Gila trout along with blue quail, and signs of beaver, deer, wolf, bear, plus a lot of tarantulas. Cottonwood, sycamore, walnut, and other trees were plentiful in this area, and during the day in the mountains the temperature was 70 degrees, but at night it would fall below freezing.

By October 20th, the troops had encountered some Apache Indians, and Johnston wrote: "They are partly clothed like the Spaniards, with wide drawers, moccasins, and leggings to the knee; they carry a knife frequently in the right legging, on the outside; their moccasins have turned up square toes; their hair is long, and mostly they have no head-dress…they have some guns, but are mostly armed with lances and bows and arrows."[20]

Both soldiers wrote of the often difficult terrain they were crossing at this time. Emory's journal from October 26th states: "Soon after leaving camp, the banks of the river became gullied on each side by deep and impassable arroyos [washes]. This drove us insensibly to the mountains, until at length we found ourselves some thousand feet above the river, and it was not until we had made sixteen miles that we again descended to it. This distance occupied eight and a half hours of incessant toil to the men, and misery to our best mules…The men named this pass 'the Devil's turnpike' and I see no reason to change it."[21]

By the first of November the two men were remarking on the appearance of cactus plants, especially the giant saguaro. A few days later, needing mules to replace those that had died on the exhausting trip, some were obtained from local Apaches. In exchange for each animal, the Indians were given a blanket, some cloth, a knife and a looking glass. Johnston noted of this trade, "Animals are cheap to people who steal all they have; and they have very little use for them, except to eat, as their country is too rocky to need their animals much to travel about."[22]

One of the Indians bartering with the Americans was described by Johnston in some detail. She was an old woman wearing fancy clothes and holding what could have been valuable nuggets. "A squaw had some crystals of metal of yellowish color, but rated them too high to purchase," he wrote.[23] Continuing, Johnston commented: "There is a fine silver mine, it is said, on the San Pedro. The old squaw came into camp arrayed in a light gingham dress, trimmed with lace, no doubt the spoil of some Sonora damsel, who had put all her industry upon this, her fandango dress."

About this same time, Emory commented: "The Gila now presents an inhospitable look; the mountains of trap [dark-colored igneous rock], granite, and red sandstone, in irregular and confused strata, but generally dipping sharply to the south, cluster close together…The valley, not more than 300 feet across from base to base of these perpendicular mountains, is deep…".[24]

A few days later, after crossing the junction of the Gila and San Pedro rivers, the troop emerged onto the flat plain of the Sonoran desert. As they did, the men would become the first outsiders in 70-years to encounter the magnificent Indian ruins which would one day be called "Casa Grande".

Emory wrote of the central structure of the site: "It was the remains of a three-story mud house, 60 feet square, pierced for doors and windows. The walls were four feet thick, and formed by layers of mud…".[25] As to who had built it, Johnston said that General Kearny was told by a Pima Indian who lived near what was then known as the "Casa de Montezuma": "It was built by the son of the most beautiful woman who once dwelt in yon mountain; she was fair, and all the handsome men came to court her, but in vain; when they came, they paid tribute, and out of this small store, she fed all people in times of famine, and it did not diminish; at last, as she lay asleep, a drop of rain fell upon her navel, and she became pregnant, and brought forth a boy, who was the builder of all these houses."[26]

According to Johnston, the generosity shown by the mythical woman continued among the local Indians. When Carson asked to buy bread, the reply was, "Bread is to eat, not to sell; take what you want."[27]

Both the Captain and Lieutenant Emory were lavish in their praise of the thousands of Pima and Maricopa Indians living near the Gila. The Apaches were their only enemies, the Americans were told, but other than that they "were at peace with all the world".

In describing the personal appearance of these native people, Johnston wrote: "The long hair of the men of the Pimos and Coco Maricopas is remarkable, reaching to their waists; they put it up in twist, and coil it over their heads at times, at others it hangs down the back; it is cut straight across the forehead in men and women, and protects their eyes from the sun. The men and women both have long hair, but the men the longest…".[28]

About Indian clothing Emory stated: "The dress of both nations [Pimas and Maricopas] or bands was the same. That of the men a breech cloth and a cotton serape of domestic manufacture; that of the women the same kind of serape pinned around the waist and falling below the knees, leaving the breast and arms bare."[29]

Of their dwellings, Johnston said: "The houses of these Indians are all built alike: a rib work of poles 12 or 15 feet in diameter is put up, thatched with straw, and then covered on top with dirt, in the centre of this they build their fires; this is the winter lodge: they make sheds with forks, and cover them with flat roofs of willow rods for summer shelters."[30]

Animals which the Indians possessed included chickens, dogs, horses, mules, and oxen. To water their crops, according to Emory, the tribes utilized an elaborate irrigation system in their desert surroundings. "We were at once impressed with the beauty, order, and disposition of the arrangements for irrigating and draining the land," he wrote. "Corn, wheat, and cotton are the crops of this peaceful and intelligent race of people…".[31]

As they traveled along the mostly dry Gila River, the troops traded with the Indians. At one stop Emory commented: "The [soldiers'] camp was soon filled with [Indian] men, women, and children, each with a basket of corn, frijoles [beans], or meal, for traffic. Many had jars of the molasses expressed from the fruit of the pitahaya [saguaro cactus]. Beads, red cloth, white domestic, and blankets, were the articles demanded in exchange."[32]

While both writers praised these Indians, Emory was especially enthusiastic in his comments. "To us it was a rare sight to be thrown in the midst of a large nation of what is termed wild Indians," he said, "surpassing many of the christian nations in agriculture, little behind them in the useful arts, and immeasurably before them in honesty and virtue."[33]

Once they had descended from the mountains and were on the desert floor, the U.S. troops made good time, sometimes covering over 20 miles or more in a day as they passed numerous Indian communities. Of this route Johnston predicted: "Its resources will not be called into play by our people…unless this should get a value as a highway between the two oceans—a thing no doubt perfectly favorable, if a man of capital and energy should undertake to open a route between Galveston and China."[34]

The Library of Congress

THE GILA RIVER NEAR THE GREAT BEND (circa 1855)

To work the land as the Indians did, Emory thought slaves would make no sense from an economical standpoint. "No one who has ever visited this country," he offered, "and who is acquainted with the character and value of slave labor in the United States, would ever think of bringing his own slaves here with any view to profit, much less would he purchase slaves for such a purpose."[35]

On November 15th it rained for only the second time since the group had left Santa Fe seven weeks before and General Kearny ordered a rest day. By the 19th, the Americans awoke in the desert to find half-inch thick ice around them and very cold air.

After eventually crossing the Colorado River, the troops learned of the recapture of California by Mexican soldiers. General Kearny decided to move westward as quickly as possible with his one hundred or so men, hoping to catch the enemy by surprise. The Mexicans, also referred to as Californians, learned of the Americans approach and established themselves at the Indian village of San Pascual along the road to San Diego.

By early December, the U.S. soldiers were nearing San Pascual, and Johnston wrote in his journal: "We ate heartily of stewed and roast mutton and tortillas. We heard of a party of Californians, of 80 men, encamped at a distance from this; but the informant varied from 16 to 30 miles in his accounts, rendering it too uncertain to make a dash on them in the dark, stormy night; so we slept till morning."[36]

In the early hours two days later, the Americans, with Captain Johnston leading the advance guard, charged the Mexicans. The battle was fought in part with lances and Emory saved Kearny's life when the General was about to be stabbed by one of the enemy. In the end, eighteen Americans and two Mexicans were killed, but it was the latter that retired from the battlefield.[37]

Johnston's journal, which had chronicled a journey of more than two months through territory previously unknown to Americans, concludes with these words: "The foregoing is a literal copy of the rough notes of my late aid-de-camp, Captain A.R. Johnston, 1st dragoons, who was killed at daybreak on the 6th December, 1846, in an action with the Californians at San Pasqual. S.W. Kearny, Brigadier General."[38]

CHAPTER THREE

"The most feasible route from the Rio Grande to California"

The Army of the West under General Kearny quickly controlled California. Other American troops invaded and occupied part of central Mexico. Despite these battlefield successes, in the United States public support for the war was flagging. An initial burst of enthusiasm had been followed by the realization that the territorial expansion motives of President James Polk and others behind the war effort were morally questionable. It also became apparent that despite U.S. military superiority and the chaotic governmental situation in Mexico, the fighting would not be over quickly and this led to a growing demand to end the hostilities.

One American who opposed the conflict was James Gadsden. Originally a supporter of the war, by early 1847 Gadsden had turned against it, fearing it would harm the U.S. economy and that some members of the Polk administration wanted to annex all of Mexico. To end the fighting, he suggested to South Carolina Senator John C. Calhoun that a new border be established along the 32nd parallel of north latitude, calling it "the most natural boundary & best calculated to preserve peace between the two contiguous powers."[1]

Some time later, Gadsden would elaborate on this proposal, insisting that natural features, but not a river, were needed to separate the two countries. Pointing to the Sierra Madre as a possible border, he wrote Calhoun that those mountains were, "the great natural barrier which should be placed between the Anglo Saxon & Spanish Race...".[2]

Recognizing the growing discontent with the war, at the urging of Secretary of State James Buchanan, President Polk sent Nicholas Trist south to negotiate a settlement. Departing Washington, D.C. in April of 1847, Trist left with specific instructions about what the terms of peace should contain.

The American draft treaty called for a new boundary between the two countries to run up the middle of the Rio Grande from its mouth. Then the border was to head quickly west before turning north to intersect the Gila River over one hundred miles east of its junction with the San Pedro River. From there the line would follow the Gila to the Colorado River and into the Gulf of California.[3]

Under this proposal, which paid Mexico $15 million in five equal annual installments, both upper and lower California, along with much other territory, would be deeded to the United States. Also included in the original draft agreement was a requirement that U.S. citizens be granted the eternal right of free transport by any means possible across the Isthmus of Tehuantepec in southern Mexico. Some Americans were looking at this 125-mile wide strip of land between the Gulf of Mexico and the Pacific Ocean as an economically more viable transit route than a transcontinental railroad for shipping goods from the east coast of the United States to California and China.

In the cover letter accompanying this initial proposal, Buchanan revised two of its conditions. He informed Trist that an offer of up to $30 million in ten installments could be made. Buchanan also said that retaining lower California in the final agreement was not to be considered a deal-breaker. If it were dropped, however, the price should be lowered to $20 million. He additionally insinuated that including the right of passage across the isthmus was not mandatory, but that the U.S. would pay $5 million more if it were included.

The man sent with these instructions to negotiate an end to the war had been born in 1800 and spent much of his childhood in New Orleans. At age seventeen Nicholas Trist was invited by Thomas Jefferson, an old friend of his grandmother, to visit him at Monticello.[4] Later, after attending West Point but not graduating, Trist would become the former President's student, unofficial private secretary, and eventually one of the administrators of Jefferson's will.

By 1828 the six-foot tall, rail-thin Trist had been appointed a clerk for the State Department in Washington, D.C. This would be followed by service as secretary to President Andrew Jackson and appointment as American consul to Havana in 1833. Trist would stay in Cuba as a diplomat and farmer for twelve more years. Then, at former President Jackson's request, he became deputy to Secretary of State Buchanan. It was from this position that Trist was picked to go to Mexico.

Upon arriving in that country, and after a cease fire was put in place, Trist opened peace talks in late August of 1847. His Mexican counterparts, though, immediately balked at the proposed American boundary line, including the border advanced to separate Texas from Mexico. They wanted it farther north at the Nueces River and not the Rio Grande, an idea the somewhat sympathetic Trist did not reject out of hand. His superiors in Washington, however, found that proposal totally unacceptable and Trist's position on the issue intolerable.[5]

Even though they were being badly beaten on the battlefield, the Mexicans with whom Trist was dealing took a stubborn stand in the negotiations. One issue they brought up was the possibility of barring slavery from any territory ceded to their northern neighbor. In reply, Trist informed them, "The bare <u>mention</u> of the subject in any treaty to which the United States were a party, was an absolute impossibility; that no President of the United States would dare to present any such treaty to the Senate [for ratification]."[6]

Mexican officials also strenuously objected to how much territory they were being asked to cede to the United States. One negotiator indicated his nation could relinquish some property, but that California was not for sale. Plus Trist was told: "If, however, we [the United States] insisted upon more, the war must go on. Their reverses would probably continue. Well, if it must be so, it could not be helped; but at least we should have to content ourselves with possessing no other title to any of their territory than that by conquest, in all its nakedness, and subject to all the odium and to all the insecurity that inseparably attach to it."[7]

While in early September of 1847 the negotiators for Mexico were seeking to limit the amount of land they lost, two months earlier the United States government had decided it needed somewhat more. First Lieutenant, now Major, William H. Emory had returned from California to Washington D.C. by July. He contacted the Secretary of State about the difficult terrain along the eastern portion of the Gila River which his survey crew and General Kearny's troops had marched through the previous year.

Emory had deduced that near the 32nd parallel, which was some fifty or so miles south of the Gila River and also just below the line of Lt. Col. Cooke's proposed desert cutoff route, the mountain chains in the area flattened out. Thus, instead of containing towering peaks, massive ridges, and deep valleys, this land formed an extended level area reaching from Texas to the Gulf of California. Emory concluded, therefore, "It is possible to pass through the mountain system, in this region, near the parallel of 32°, almost on the level of the plateau…".[8]

The importance of this discovery for a railroad to the west coast was not lost on Buchanan. It would mean the Rocky Mountains could be avoided in laying tracks to California. Thus, based on Emory's information, and prior to the start of peace negotiations in Mexico, on July 13th of 1847 Buchanan sent Trist a letter. He suggested an important modification to the originally proposed boundary line. The Secretary of State wanted "to run it along the thirty-second parallel of north latitude from the Rio Grande to the middle of the Gulf of California."[9] Achieving this, Buchanan believed, "presents a favorable route for a railroad to the Pacific", but he directed the change was not to jeopardize the negotiations.

Six days later, after talking to Emory personally and in order to re-enforce how vital this change was considered, Buchanan wrote Trist another letter. While reiterating that this alteration should not kill the peace treaty, Buchanan emphasized, "It is deemed of great importance that you should obtain this modification, if it be practicable."

For various reasons, including that Mexican officials had intercepted the first message and read it, Trist did not receive either of these letters until two months later, the second not until September 27th.[10] It was then too late for the proposed change to be included in the initial round of negotiations, but those sessions had ended in failure anyway. By the time Trist had Buchanan's letters, the armistice was over, and American troops had once again taken to the battlefield, capturing Mexico City on September 14th.

A few weeks later, President Polk decided that Trist's earlier actions regarding where the Texas border might be located along with his handling of other treaty issues could be tolerated no longer. In early October he had Buchanan send a letter recalling the negotiator, and the message was repeated on the 25th of that month.[11]

Both communications were handed to Trist on November 16th and he felt a replacement would soon be appointed.[12] That, however, didn't happen. In addition, upon learning of Trist's fate, Mexican officials became very concerned about the prospect for ending the war. It was obvious to them that some Americans wanted to take over all of Mexico, but they knew Trist did not share that view.

By December 4th, Trist was still in Mexico when a reporter for the New Orleans *Delta* talked to him. The two men knew each other, and Trist told the journalist he was contemplating disobeying his recall orders from Washington. To this the newspaperman replied: "Mr. Trist, make the Treaty. Make the Treaty, Sir!"[13] Two days later, Trist sent Buchanan a very long letter, informing him of his decision to stay and complete his assignment.

When he saw Trist's 61-page communication, Polk was furious. Writing in his diary he commented: "His dispatch is arrogant, impudent and very insulting to his Government, and even personally insulting to the President...I have never in my life felt so indignant...".[14]

Of course, at that point these Presidential sensitivities were of no concern to Trist. Beginning in early January of 1848 he resumed treaty negotiations. The issue of the Texas border was quickly resolved in favor of the United States. West from there, however, the Mexicans would not agree to a new border along the 32nd parallel. As Trist explained later, although he insisted on the new line, the Mexican response was such that "it constituted an insuperable obstacle to the negotiation of a treaty...".[15] Then he added: "This was the case, even if the difference between the territory which that line would give us, and that comprehended in the [original] boundary...should be ever so inconsiderable. It mattered not whether it was ten miles or ten feet in width, the effect would be all the same: to render a treaty impracticable."

In consolation for this loss, Trist optimistically added a section to the draft treaty. It stated that if it became "practicable and advantageous to construct a road, canal, or railway, which should in whole or in part run upon the river Gila, or upon its right or its left bank, within the space of one marine league from either margin of the river, the governments of both republics will form an agreement regarding its construction, in order that it may serve equally for the use and advantage of both countries."[16]

While the Mexicans had not yielded on the 32nd parallel border question, they did concede that the new boundary line would include San Diego within the United States. They refused, however, to consider an American request for a right-of-way across the Isthmus of Tehuantepec since that permission was then in the hands of a British company. The Mexicans also insisted that the treaty include a provision for protecting settlers living south of the new international border from raids by Indians originating in what would become territory of the U.S.

To accommodate this last point, Article XI was inserted into the proposed treaty. It required the American government to forcibly restrain these raids by "savage tribes", and "when they cannot be prevented, they [Indians] shall be punished by the said government, and satisfaction for the same shall be exacted…".[17] Trist justified this requirement by noting that it was simply an expansion on conditions which already existed between the two countries. In addition, using language which was unusual for an American diplomat, he stated these stipulations were mandatory "to any who take the proper interest in their [Mexican] security; in a word, to any one who has the feelings of a Mexican citizen…".[18]

The negotiations, which had been conducted outside of Mexico City, were concluded successfully and a document was finalized on February 2nd, 1848. The treaty of Guadalupe Hidalgo, named after the town where it was signed, would transfer almost 600,000 square miles of territory to the United States. This enormous addition to the country would eventually contain the states of California, Nevada and Utah, most of Arizona, and parts of New Mexico, Wyoming, and Colorado.

Trist had limited the amount to be paid by the United States to $15 million since lower California was not included in the deal. What he and his Mexican counterparts did not know when they approved the treaty, though, was that only a few days earlier gold had been discovered in upper California. The cherished metal was found in such quantities that it would start a huge rush of people across the continent seeking their fortunes. Some of those who would go west during this period were later to play very important roles in the development of the first several transcontinental railroad lines.

Upon completion of the treaty negotiations, one of the Mexican officials involved commented to his American counterpart, "This must be a proud moment for you; no less proud for you than it is humiliating for us."[19] To this Trist replied, "We are making <u>peace</u>. Let that be our only thought."

The treaty which was sent north for ratification conformed in most major respects with the draft Buchanan had given Trist before he departed the United States. It would also end the military hostilities and the American occupation of Mexico. Despite that, Trist was not happy with the document, saying later he was "intensely ashamed" of its terms and calling the war "an abuse of power on our part".[20] In explaining himself, he said he would have yielded more often to Mexican demands, but knew this would have resulted in a document unacceptable to the administration and Congress in Washington.

When the treaty reached the White House on February 19th, Polk still held Trist in contempt, but the President also foresaw the enormous impacts the treaty would have upon the United States. Writing prophetically he commented, "There will be added to the U.S. an immense empire, the value of which 20 years hence it would be difficult to calculate…".[21] Thus, he didn't let his personal feelings for Trist stand in the way of sending the document to the Senate for approval, and this was quickly done with some modifications suggested.[22]

In the course of its ten-day debate on the treaty, the Senate did alter the original document to some extent with seven mostly minor amendments. One proposed change which wasn't accepted would have prohibited slavery from the new territory to be purchased from Mexico. That proposal was soundly defeated by a vote of 38 to 15.

An effort to increase the amount of land area to be obtained by the United States also failed. Offered by Senator Jefferson Davis of Mississippi, this change would have drawn the boundary line hundreds of miles further south, but the idea was overwhelmingly rejected.

On March 10th, 1848, the Senate approved the revised treaty by a vote of 38 to 14. It was sent back to Mexico for adoption, along with a warning from Secretary of State Buchanan of what would happen if it weren't accepted. Recognizing that threat, by the end of May the Mexican Congress had ratified the document, and the size of the United States was increased substantially. At the same time, the American government would be legally and financially responsible for Indian raids into Mexico from north of the new border.

It was then up to surveyors from both countries working under the direction of two appointed Boundary Commissioners to establish the new line between the nations. The Polk administration named a Commissioner, but he died before being confirmed by Congress. It then appointed another man who, along with chief surveyor A.B. Gray from Texas and Major William H. Emory as astronomer, oversaw the delineation of the border from the Pacific Ocean to the

Colorado River in cooperation with their Mexican counterparts. This project was completed by February of 1850 when the crews, planning to meet again along the Rio Grande on November 1st, adjourned their work.

The earlier election of Zachary Taylor as President, however, meant that another Commissioner would eventually be named to the politically appointed position. The new administration picked a replacement, but John C. Frémont decided to assume a seat representing California in the United States Senate instead. Thus, it wasn't until June of 1850 that John Russell Bartlett became the fourth American Commissioner appointed to be responsible for the survey which would establish the new boundary line between the U.S. and Mexico.

The Library of Congress

JOHN RUSSELL BARTLETT

Born in the United States but raised in Canada, Bartlett worked as a young man in retail and banking in Providence, Rhode Island.[23] He was a member of the state's historical society, and later served as corresponding secretary for the New York Historical Society when he moved there and became a bookstore owner.

During his time in New York City, Bartlett help found the American Ethnological Society and published three books, including *Dictionary of Americanisms* in 1848. The next year he returned to his home state and sought appointment as United States Minister to Denmark. Instead of receiving that position, because of his political connections he was chosen for the $3,000 a year job of heading the United States Boundary Commission, a role for which he had little qualification except for his interest in Indians.

Bartlett filled staff positions for the survey effort based more on political patronage than professional experience, and he filled a lot of them. He had twice as many people working for the Commission as did his predecessor. His own brother was appointed to purchase equipment for the group, and ended up buying supplies which included four iron boats, vessels which were never used.

Bartlett also employed a wide range of artists and scientists to accompany the expedition. His primary goal seems to have been to comprehensively document the border area and only secondarily to finalize the new boundary line.

After learning of the extent of the staff on the revised Commission, surveyor Gray concluded derisively, "The party consisted of some forty assistants, and at least one hundred other persons, comprising tailors, bootmakers, saddlers, stonecutters, carpenters, blacksmiths, botanists, geologists, &c., four-fifths of whom might have been dispensed with…".[24]

These members of the Commission, along with a military escort of 85, sailed to New Orleans in August of 1850. From there they made their way into the interior of Texas, and arrived at the remote border city of El Paso del Norte in the middle of November. They would be met a few weeks later by their Mexican associates under the leadership of General Pedro Garcia Condé.

Bartlett's journal of his time as Boundary Commissioner is full of detail about the people and places he was to visit over the next two years. El Paso del Norte, he wrote, was centered around a plaza and had a population of about 5,000 who lived in single-story adobe homes. The two to three foot thick mud brick walls were whitewashed and windowless on the exterior, but had muslin or white cotton covered openings onto an interior courtyard. The floors of these homes were of mud, concrete, or brick.

Agriculture in the area consisted of raising wheat, maize, onions, pumpkins, apples, quinces, pears, and peaches. Grapes were also grown, but Bartlett was contemptuous of the locally produced wine, calling it mediocre and saying it caused "a severe headache".

To secure needed supplies, the isolated residents of El Paso del Norte had to pay substantially. As Bartlett noted, "At present they obtain every thing that can be transported thither by wagons, though, of course, at a greatly enhanced cost."[25]

Across the Rio Grande from the Mexican community was a tiny American settlement in Texas. One day it would take the name El Paso, while El Paso del Norte would become Cuidad Juárez.

Some forty miles away was the small Mexican town of Mesilla. Bartlett was told its population was nineteen hundred and it had been recently founded by people not wanting to live in the United States. Because of disputes with Americans moving into the area and claiming land which had once been part of the Republic of Texas, many local inhabitants wanted to leave the United States. Bartlett wrote sympathetically that these people, "to avoid litigation, and sometimes in fear for their lives, abandoned their homes, and sought a refuge on the Mexican side of the river."[26]

Given that alleged history, the Boundary Commissioner believed if the new border resulted in their being on the American side of the line, these people would completely abandon the new town of Mesilla. That, however, would not prove to be necessary because of an extremely controversial compromise Bartlett reached with General Condé.

When the two men met in late 1850, a problem with the boundary line as described in the treaty of Guadalupe Hidalgo quickly became apparent. The wording of the peace settlement was based on an inaccurate map of the area, so the actual physical location of El Paso del Norte was not properly described. Condé insisted this error meant that the new east-west boundary line should be forty instead of eight miles north of the Mexican town. Bartlett, who had been told by the administration in Washington to be conciliatory in his dealings with his associate, eventually conceded the point. In exchange, he obtained an agreement for a distant north-south jog in the border to be further west than supposedly called for by the treaty.

In April of 1851, when this compromise was actually marked on the ground by the establishment of the initial eastern point of the new boundary between the two countries, the people in the small town of Mesilla rejoiced. They had remained in Mexico, and according to Bartlett, "The event was celebrated by firing of cannon and a grand ball, which many from El Paso [del Norte] attended."[27]

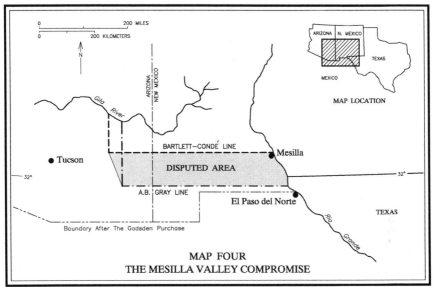

MAP FOUR
THE MESILLA VALLEY COMPROMISE

After Bufkin

In addition to following his instructions to be accommodating in his dealings with Condé while also allowing Mesilla to remain in Mexico, Bartlett believed that at its western end the new compromise boundary line would bring some rich mining areas into the United States. At the same time, he thought the loss of what became known as the Mesilla Valley was not very important and wrote, "We have a similar valley on our side of the Rio Grande, as well situated and equally productive."[28]

It wasn't agriculture, of course, which held most people's interest in the Mesilla Valley. Instead, a pair of factors made securing the area for the United States imperative to many of those involved. One was the demand by surveyor Gray and other Americans working for the Commission to uphold generally accepted surveying standards. This meant the physical reality of where El Paso del Norte was found on the ground should determine the border, not its location on a faulty map. The other important factor was the perceived unique availability for an economical transcontinental railroad route through the lost territory. Combined, these issues resulted in huge criticism of Bartlett's compromise.

Chief surveyor Gray had been detained in San Diego in 1850 and then returned to Washington, D.C. where he became gravely ill. Thus, he didn't rejoin the Commission in Texas until July of 1851. A few days after arriving he learned of the Mesilla Valley boundary settlement between Bartlett and Condé and vigorously protested it. He refused to sign their agreement, assuming that would nullify the entire compromise. As he understood the peace treaty, his signature was required to validate any joint decision made concerning the document. As a result, if he didn't approve the Bartlett-Condé compromise, Gray believed it would be voided.

The importance of the 6,100 square mile Mesilla Valley, Gray explained in great detail, was to accommodate the route of a southern transcontinental railroad. While this territory had agricultural value, it was as a pathway to the Pacific that primarily interested him. The easy grades across the area made it an ideal railroad route in Gray's opinion. He summarized this view by writing, "I believe the disputed district will be found to embrace the most accommodating gateway over the Rocky Mountains, and the most feasible route from the Rio Grande to California."[29]

While he lobbied over the importance of the Mesilla Valley for railroad building, Gray recognized that even with his version of the treaty boundary line there were still two substantial mountain barriers along the Gila River which would have to be crossed. Despite that, Gray thought the engineering challenges of implementing a railroad through this area could be met if the Bartlett-Condé agreement were nullified.

Bartlett, naturally, took a vastly different view of a railroad route through the area, and of the compromise itself. Settling the issue as he did was the right thing to do, in his opinion, and Bartlett thought the consequences for a railroad were not the most important factor in making that decision. Besides, even though he wasn't very clear on the topic, Bartlett by 1854 apparently had concluded the territory involved with the compromise wasn't sufficiently large enough to provide an unobstructed railway line to the west coast anyway.

In his two volume memoir of his service as Boundary Commissioner, Bartlett devotes an entire chapter to what he entitled, "Adaptation of the Country for a Railway."[30] He provides quite specific suggestions about how a rail line could be built through the general area, but disregards whether it would be on the Mexican or American side of the border. "After crossing the Rio Grande," he writes, "…there is an open country for more than one hundred miles. Some mountain ranges are then to be passed, through easy slopes or defiles, and in no case by surmounting them. In fact, so gradual are the ascents and descents, that they are scarcely perceived. After they are passed, broad, open, and level plains occur, where for miles very slight embankments or excavations will be required for the construction of a road."[31] Once the route passed the San Pedro River, the Commissioner concluded, "We shall have an uninterrupted plain of about two hundred and fifty miles to the Colorado."[32]

Even though Bartlett thought the Mesilla Valley unimportant for an American railroad route to the Pacific, many members of Congress were highly critical of his agreement with Condé. At the same time, people interested in a southern transcontinental railroad were furious with the loss of the Valley. According to one historian, people who disagreed with the American Commissioner's action "seemed to suspect that Bartlett's compromise with Condé was a case of a New England Yankee blithely disregarding the needs of Texas and the South for a way to California…".[33]

Despite the political furor, the administration of President Millard Fillmore, who had assumed the office upon the death of Zachary Taylor in July of 1850, backed Bartlett in his dispute with surveyor Gray. For one thing, the compromise would lower the number of Indians in the United States, thus reducing the potential for violations of Article XI of the Treaty of Guadalupe Hidalgo. The administration ordered Gray to approve the agreement, which he refused to do, and he was therefore relieved of his duties. Eventually, Major Emory was appointed to the post of chief surveyor.

While Emory disliked the compromise, he didn't think that a transcontinental rail line through the area would be jeopardized by the loss of the Mesilla Valley. As he wrote some years later, "The line agreed to by him [Bartlett] was no worse than that claimed by his adversaries."[34] Explaining this conclusion, Emory continued, "It was ignorantly represented that while Mr. Bartlett's line lost the route for the railway, the other line secured it." Disputing that opinion, Emory stated emphatically, "The practicable route so adjudged by myself, and by other officers who retraced my steps and re-surveyed this country, is to the south of both these lines of boundary claimed under the treaty of Guadalupe Hidalgo."

To settle the Bartlett-Condé boundary dispute in the field, Major Emory approved the compromise with the reservation that it was the line agreed to only by the two Commissioners. Once that issue was resolved in August of 1851, work on the border survey continued. However, because of illness, the need to obtain more supplies, and a general wanderlust to explore the country he was in, Bartlett spent much of his time over the next 18 months away from the survey crews. Instead, with some assistants he would journey though northern Mexico, documenting what he saw. These travels wouldn't help establish a new border, but they would provide him with the narrative for the 1,000 page memoir he would publish within a few years.

By June of 1852, Bartlett was in California along the Colorado River at the American military outpost of Fort Yuma. Commenting on the future prospects of the region, he predicted that a "considerable town" would be built "if a railway should ever pass here".[35] Sometime later, the settlement of Colorado City would be established across the river from the fort. Eventually its name would be changed to Yuma, and with the arrival of the railroad in 1877, its commercial importance would increase significantly.

Crossing the barren desert along the Gila River east of the Colorado in the middle of June, Bartlett made note of the high temperature. He gave much more attention, though, to the saguaro cactus, describing in great detail this majestic plant which was so unusual to a New Englander. "The forms it assumes are various;" he wrote, "sometimes rising like a simple fluted column, although more frequently it is furnished with several branches, which, after leaving the main trunk, turn gracefully upwards and rise parallel with it. Sometimes the branches are singularly contorted; but usually, their disposition is symmetrical, and the appearance of the whole plant has been, not inaptly, compared to that of a giant candelabrum."[36]

On July 16th, 1852, Bartlett was in Tucson, well south of the new international boundary line but the largest settlement in the area. While the town, which had been founded in 1775, once had a population of one thousand, only a few hundred remained at the time of Bartlett's visit because of Apache raids. Bartlett commented on the place: "The houses of Tucson are all of adobe, and the majority are in a state of ruin. No attention seems to be given to repair; but as soon as a dwelling becomes uninhabitable, it is deserted, the miserable tenants creeping into some other hovel where they may eke out their existence."[37]

The local attraction to Bartlett and others who passed through Tucson at this time was a pair of giant meteorites, the larger of which was in the military garrison, the other serving as an anvil in a blacksmith shop. Five-feet long and weighting about 1,400 pounds, the bigger meteorite, according to a drawing, had the shape of an arch.

In the Santa Cruz River valley nine miles south of Tucson, Bartlett visited the mission church of San Xavier del Bac. He described the adjacent Indian village as "truly a miserable place, consisting of from eighty to one hundred huts, or wigwams, made of mud or straw…".[38]

The almost 60-year old mission itself, though, was an entirely different matter. "In the midst of these hovels," Bartlett wrote, "stands the largest and most beautiful church in the State of Sonora. It is built of brick on the summit of a low hill, and has two towers and a dome…It is elaborately ornamented inside and out…The interior is gaudily painted; and from the profusion of gilding, one might suppose the Mission to have possessed a gold placer. Around the alter, and in the niches, are many wooden statues, from the size of a foot to that of life…".[39]

After leaving Tucson, Bartlett would continue to roam the countryside, writing of what he saw. Meanwhile, the survey work was being done by others. Finally, however, the Commission's cost of $500,000, which was five times the original estimate, combined with the effort's slow progress and the controversial Mesilla Valley decision, caught up with its leader. By the end of 1852, Congress had cut off funding for the work, and Bartlett was relieved of his duties. Eventually, Major Emory was appointed to finish the project, which was finally accomplished in 1853.[40]

But Bartlett left a lasting legacy behind. Not only had his writings and drawings captured the character of the desert land he traveled through, but he also helped establish a new international border despite creating the Mesilla Valley controversy. The southern railroad, he thought, could still be accommodated. Besides, he argued, the compromise was reached based on other considerations and was the right thing to do under the circumstances.

Surveyor A.B. Gray, however, considered the Mesilla Valley essential for the railway project. The Texan also saw enormous repercussions if the compromise, and Bartlett's handling of the entire boundary survey effort, were allowed to stand. He wrote: "The evil consequences of this unfortunate mismanagement have been felt too sadly by many, and much remains yet to be disentangled. Trouble and confusion, waste of public money, delays, national difficulties, and privations have all grown out of it."[41]

While those two argued over how critical the Mesilla Valley actually was, Major Emory had, even before the treaty of Guadalupe Hidalgo was finalized, offered his own opinion. To build an American railroad through the general area, he had concluded that more land to the south of the new boundary line would have to be acquired.

CHAPTER FOUR

"If necessary a further purchase of land from Mexico should be made for the right-of-way"

The belief that even more Mexican territory would be needed to permit the construction of a southern transcontinental railroad was initially not shared by many. That issue was only a minor technicality when compared to the tremendous railway opportunities provided by the land acquisition obtained by the United States under the Treaty of Guadalupe Hidalgo. Thus, within less than a year of the peace settlement, numerous factions were making a case why their route across the continent to the west coast was the best choice.

The perceived enormous economic benefits for the terminal points, as well as the land along the entire line connecting them, were considered extremely desirable. The two cities where the tracks would start and stop, one near the Mississippi River and the other on the Pacific Ocean, seemed guaranteed of monetary and status rewards. It was also assumed that commercial advantages in agriculture, industry, mining, population growth, and community development would follow the tracks. The section of the country which prevailed in securing the first line, whether north, central, or south, was therefore believed certain to have business advantages over their regional competitors.

In July of 1849, the New Orleans-published *DeBow's Commercial Review* summarized the case for the eight leading candidates for the transcontinental railroad, four of which were at least partially on foreign soil, the others contained entirely within the United States. In this latter category, the first went from Galveston on the Texas coast to the American community of El Paso and then along the Gila River before heading to San Diego. *The Commercial Review* criticized this option as starting too far south, stating, "A work so stupendous must be the common work of America, and for that it ought, as nearly as possible, to be <u>central</u>."[1]

The second possibility was a route from St. Louis to San Francisco, the option pushed by politician Thomas Hart Benton of Missouri. Among the advantages of this alternative, he said, were: "The western wilderness, from the Pacific to the Mississippi, will start into life under its touch. A long line of cities will grow up. Existing cities will take a new start."[2]

The third choice was Asa Whitney's original 1845 proposal which ran from near Chicago on Lake Michigan to the mouth of the Columbia River. However, given the territorial changes which had occurred because of the war with Mexico, by 1849 Whitney was proposing that a branch of his northern road should also go to San Francisco.

The final alternative according to editor DeBow ran from Memphis to Santa Fe, New Mexico. From there the tracks would head south to the Gila River, follow it to the Colorado River, and then go on to San Diego. While acknowledging that some reconnaissance work had been done along the western portion of this route by Major Emory and others, the publisher concluded more detailed information about this isolated desert territory was needed.

As a corollary to this last option, the article listed another possibility which in large part was located on Mexican soil. It basically followed Lt. Col. Cooke's proposed cutoff trail that ran directly east from Tucson and was found some distance south of the Gila River. The article stated this line could run "to the southward of the Gila, and intersecting that river at a considerable distance from its source; the road is supposed to be good—through an open prairie—if water can be had. It deserves exploration."[3]

As he preached compromise about any final decision among these choices, DeBow also said, "As a Southron, we confess a deep and abiding interest in these schemes to connect the two oceans. Our own cities must revive under their influence, and commerce visit again and rule in her wonted marts."[4] The editor then asked what had held back the business development of Richmond, Charleston, Savannah, and Mobile. Answering his own question, he wrote, "The operation of our federal system has built up New York, and centered in it nearly all the foreign trade of this nation, which is conducted with the produce of southern climes."[5] Thus, DeBow believed building a southern transcontinental railroad might help economically rejuvenate cities in the South while also leveling the commercial disparities between the regions of the country which had resulted because of national policy decisions.

Which railroad route, though, should be chosen to do this? Trying to establish some basis for judging the main options, DeBow listed two criteria which he felt must be met by any railroad route under consideration. First, it had to be entirely on American territory and secondly, it should be as central as possible.

Based on those two assumptions, the editor by this time preferred a route from Memphis to either San Diego or San Francisco. He believed that both the proposed line starting in St. Louis, along with Whitney's idea, were "so mountainous as to be almost impracticable."[6] He pointed to the central location of Memphis, noted the city's easy river access, and also argued that the slavery question should not be an issue in deciding the route of the railroad.

While DeBow may have advocated national unity in answering the question of where the transcontinental railway should be located, regional interests in the country did not cooperate. In hopes of promoting itself as the eastern end of the great project, the civic leaders of St. Louis held a National Railroad Convention in October of 1849. A total of 889 delegates attended from thirteen of the country's 30 states, but the vast majority were from Missouri, Illinois, Indiana, and Iowa.[7]

One of the primary topics facing the delegates at this gathering was whether to recommend the host city as a terminal point for the railroad project. Disagreements over that subject split the convention, and in the end, the conclusion was to endorse one central path heading east from the Pacific which would eventually divide into three branch lines running to Chicago, St. Louis, and Memphis.[8] A philosophy of slicing the national railroad pie to try and please everyone had thus been established, a pattern which would continue among some project proponents over the next decade.

A few days after the St. Louis meeting was adjourned, almost 400 delegates from fourteen states gathered for another convention in Memphis. This time, however, most of the men were from Tennessee and Mississippi. Originally scheduled to be held in July, this conclave had been postponed due to an outbreak of cholera in the city.[9]

In promoting attendance, Memphis boosters declared that their city held the most advantages as an eastern terminus of the transcontinental railroad. They pointed out that southern cargo ships would have to use steam power to go up the Mississippi River to St. Louis, but that northern vessels would be able to float downstream to their community.

Once the Memphis Convention was convened, delegates from Texas pushed the El Paso to San Diego choice, concluding, "If necessary a further purchase of land from Mexico should be made for the right-of-way."[10] Others attending the meeting, though, thought too little information existed about any of the possible transcontinental routes since not much was known concerning the vast territory recently acquired from Mexico. They advocated the U.S. Army survey the various alternatives to allow Congress and the President to have reliable and consistent data on which to base an informed decision. In the end, the convention's committee on resolutions recommended that surveys be performed "and then the route chosen which appeared the best—that being the best road which was easiest of access, best for national defense, most central, convenient and cheap."[11]

The entire delegation attending the convention went even further, expressing a preference for a specific line for the transcontinental railroad. It "should be built by a route from San Diego via the Gila River, El Paso, the northeastern boundary of Texas between 32 and 33 degree," they said, "and reach the Mississippi between the Red and the Ohio" rivers.[12] Memphis, of course, was the leading community to fit that final description.

Before adjourning, those attending the meeting heard from Asa Whitney. Stressing the commercial need for a transcontinental railroad and not advocating any particular route, in his speech Whitney did disparage the Gila River proposal. The delegates also wanted to hear from Mississippi Senator Jefferson Davis, but he declined the opportunity, citing fatigue.

The outcome of the convention was summarized by *The Commercial Review* in a report prepared by a committee headed by editor DeBow. It outlined the great barriers which would have to be overcome to implement any transcontinental project, stating, "It is four times the length, on the shortest route, of any [rail]road as yet constructed in this or any other country. Its path is interrupted by obstacles of the most stupendous character, mountains, gorges, rivers, deserts. Immense tracts for hundreds of miles of the country through which it must pass are hopeless and sterile wastes. In scarcely any portion of its giant length have advanced the traces of civilization or even population."[13]

The commercial advantages of the project, however, were simply too great to ignore. In addition, the alternative to a potential week-long train trip across the continent was a dangerous six-month cross-country journey graphically described in the report as: "The emigrant's wagon must rattle over crags and mountains and through inhospitable wildernesses, for wearisome months and with innumerable hardships, after the frontiers of the States are passed. Or if the routes by the Isthmus [of Panama] or of Cape Horn be selected, then a dangerous and protracted navigation of the ocean for 5,000 to 18,000 miles must be compassed…".[14]

According to DeBow, the next step which needed to be taken was to select one of the leading candidates for a transcontinental railroad. Because it was "several hundred miles shorter than any other route, and can be built for greatly less expense,"[15] the editor's preference was that a line near the Gila River was definitely the one to choose. If that were done, his report suggested northern states would benefit greatly because the route would open up the commercial markets of the south to them instead of simply having the tracks run from one northern destination to another.

But the national split shown by the differing recommendations from the 1849 St. Louis and Memphis conventions reflected the sharp divide which existed between northern and southern railroad interests. Both wanted the first line through their part of the country and would do what they could to insure that happened.

As supporters of the various routes promoted the benefits of their own choices, they also emphasized the negatives of the other options. Both Whitney's proposal and Benton's St. Louis to San Francisco line, many southerners claimed, would be almost impossible to build because of the mountainous terrain and the enormous cost involved in bridging and tunneling through western ranges. Even if that could happen, it was argued, the tracks would be snow bound for several months each winter, making commerce problematic.

According to northerners, the territory from El Paso west along the Gila River and all the way to the coast was a wasteland. It not only couldn't provide the materials like wood and water needed to lay tracks, but communities would never spring up near the line since agriculture was impossible in the intense desert heat.

Underlining all of these arguments was a dispute over the expansion of slavery. If the railroad route went along a central or northern path, the increased population which was expected to follow it might tip the balance of political power more in favor of nonslaveholding states. On the other hand, the selection of a southern route would increase the possibility that new slave-supporting states could be created out of the recently acquired U.S. territories in the southwest.

It was therefore clear that the decision about the location of the first transcontinental rail line could have implications far beyond the route itself. As one author noted: "If, say, the first railroad to the Pacific and probably the only one the nation would build for a generation should follow a southern route, southern territories would in all probability be settled earlier than more northern ones and would earlier become states. They would in all probability be settled largely by Southern people and would be slaveholding. Upon arriving at statehood they would send senators and representatives to Washington who would help to defeat measures hostile to slavery."[16]

The other available choices, however, would have the opposite effect according to this writer. "If, on the contrary, the first railroad to the Pacific should follow a northern or central route, the more northern territories would first develop into states; and they would be settled principally by people from the free states or Europe, would be nonslaveholding, and would contribute to majorities in Congress hostile to slavery."[17]

Given those two distinct possibilities, it wasn't surprising that neither Congress nor the nation could decide on a plan for building the first railroad across the country. Not only were vital issues involved, such as the expansion of slavery, but reliable information about the estimated cost, difficulties of construction, and actual advantages of each proposed route simply didn't exist.

Despite that, proponents of the various routes kept pushing their favorites. On July 4th, 1852, a railroad convention was held in Little Rock, Arkansas, with delegates from five southern states attending. They cited the recent California gold rush as one of the reasons a transcontinental railway was badly needed. To achieve the goal of reaching the west coast, the delegates to this convention agreed that Memphis should be the starting point, but from there they suggested a new route, one which would follow the 35th parallel to Albuquerque, New Mexico before heading to the Pacific. While this path had earlier been considered too difficult to build because of the mountainous terrain, the convention concluded that, "Late information induces the confident belief that a pass across these mountains has long been traveled, having but few and trifling obstacles, and thus shortening, by several hundred miles, the distance to California by any other known route."[18]

About the same time, Congress was presented a memorial from engineer and architect Robert Mills. After careful study from topological, climatic, and cost viewpoints, he recommended that two tracks should run west. One would go from St. Louis, the other from Memphis. These lines could converge in Texas, proceed via the Gila River route to San Diego, and then go up the coast to San Francisco.

Mills concluded of his proposal, "By this route we shall get rid of all the mountains north of El Paso del Norte, and the interruptions of the winter frost, to say nothing of the superior agricultural character of the country along and on each side of this central route."[19]

In February of 1853, Congress was also sent a memorial in support of a transcontinental railroad by the legislature of New Mexico. These territorial officials, who represented an area north of the Gila River which stretched all the way west to the Colorado River, suggested that any possible cross-country route had to pass through their territory. They offered four reasons why that should be so, including the central location of New Mexico and the low cost of construction since the tracks could be laid "on a very direct line, without crossing a single elevation which would require an inclined plane or a tunnel."[20] In addition, the petition added, the route would never be snow bound and would also have access to an abundance of coal for locomotive fuel.

Simultaneously, Congress was receiving a lot of advice about, and recommendations for, other proposed railroad lines to the west coast. Combined with the controversy over the possible expansion of slavery which a southern route might achieve, this left the national politicians in a predicament, so, not unexpectantly, they did very little of substance besides constantly talking about the project.

During this continuing debate in the early 1850s over the future route of a transcontinental railroad, the Gila River option had assumed great importance for southerners, who also recognized that northern economic and abolitionist forces were aligned against them. As one South Carolina politician accurately predicted, "I believe there is a concurrent opinion that the Gila route is best; but…it will not be adopted."[21]

The concept that the Gila River route was the best choice had been stressed in a July 6, 1852, speech by Congressman V.E. Howard of Texas. He pointed out that this road would open up vast mineral wealth for exploitation, would be useable all-year round, would expand trade with Asia, and would be much cheaper to build than any other alternative. However, some of the land needed to construct this railroad, Howard argued, had been given away by John Russell Bartlett when he agreed to the Mesilla Valley compromise. "All accounts tend to prove that Mr. Bartlett has surrendered the best route for the [rail]road," Howard said.[22] "He has given up to the Mexican Government public land sufficient to construct the road to the junction of the Colorado and Gila."

Not only was Bartlett vehemently criticized by Howard and other southerners for his actions, but some of them saw the motives of a plot behind what he had done. If the Mesilla Valley wasn't available for railroad construction, the southern route would not be as advantageous as possible and a central or northern route was more likely to be selected. The decision of Rhode Island Yankee Bartlett could thus end up thwarting the dreams of many in the south.

After returning to the United States from his wanderings in Mexico, the former Boundary Commissioner addressed these suspicions. He quoted James Gadsden of South Carolina as saying that he, Bartlett, had been instructed by officials in Washington "to run it [the boundary line] if possible, as to exclude us [the South] from the [railroad] route secured under the Treaty."[23] Then he reiterated the entire allegation as, "I so far forgot the duties of my position as to be swayed, in determining the position of the boundary line, by a desire 'to exclude the South' from the route thereby obtained…".

Bartlett adamantly denied that he or his superiors in the administration were involved in a northern conspiracy to stymie southern interests. He also said investigations about the practical railroad routes in the area had shown that "for nearly 200 miles, or about one-half the length of the Gila, that river was unapproachable, owing to its elevated mountains…".[24] Given that circumstance, the Boundary Commissioner concluded any tracks laid in the area needed to run through Mexican territory west of Texas.

Bartlett, however, advocated another possibility, one which had been advanced earlier by Major Emory. If additional property from El Paso del Norte to near the San Pedro River was obtained from Mexico, the advantages of the land's level topography could be realized. Bartlett believed that only a ten to twenty mile-wide strip of additional desert would be needed to accomplish that goal.

In the spring of 1853, Bartlett critic and southern railroad promoter James Gadsden was selected to go to Mexico to acquire more territory for the United States. He had stepped down as President of the South Carolina Railroad Company in 1850,[25] and the next year had contemplated leading a group of southern farmers and their slaves westward. He hoped the expedition might open a possible route for a railroad to the Pacific coast while at the same time introduce slavery into California.[26] That plan, however, was not realized, but when Gadsden went to Mexico as American Minister, he would obviously still have the interests of the south, the expansion of slavery, and the possibility of a southern transcontinental rail line in mind when he entered into negotiations.

CHAPTER FIVE

"A very good—perhaps the best—route for such a railroad"

It wasn't only to obtain more territory for a transcontinental railroad that the 65-year old Gadsden was sent to Mexico by the administration of new president Franklin Pierce. Also to be considered were the issues of Indian incursions south of the border along with possibly addressing American rights to the Isthmus of Tehuantepec.

Nominated in 1852 on the 49th ballot by the Democratic Party as a compromise candidate, Pierce was seen by his supporters as a congenial man who didn't have much of a political record which could be attacked. Even though from New Hampshire, the newly-elected President selected a sectionally diverse cabinet, naming Jefferson Davis of Mississippi his Secretary of War and northerner W.L. Marcy the Secretary of State.

While disputes with Mexico may not have been at the top of the U.S. foreign policy agenda at the time of Pierce's inauguration on March 4, 1853, events quickly intervened. By March 13th, the Governor of the New Mexico territory, William Carr Lane, had unilaterally declared that the controversial Mesilla Valley was part of the United States.

A former eight-term mayor of St. Louis, Lane was a self-described impulsive man who had been appointed territorial governor in 1852.[1] He labeled boundary commissioner John Russell Bartlett a "fool and knave" for his compromise over the Mesilla Valley, and after traveling with local volunteers to the disputed region early in 1853, Lane proclaimed it would be part of the United Stares until the issue could be permanently resolved. He based his decree on six assertions, including that the Bartlett-Condé agreement was not a final settlement of the matter, that the Mexican government could not protect inhabitants of the area from Indian raids, and that many people in the region wanted to be U.S. and not Mexican citizens.[2]

In a written reply, the Governor of the Mexican state of Chihuahua, Angel Trias, said that Lane would not be allowed to take the area by force. He pointed out the long-term possession of the territory by his country, the wishes of most of the people to remain part of Mexico, and Lane's lack of authority to act on behalf of his own federal government.

Governor Trias was ordered to send troops to the valley by President Antonio López de Santa Anna, and 1,000 soldiers went prepared to fight over its control. As one Mexican newspaper commented, "If just because Mexico is weaker than the United States, we should submit to the most exaggerated pretensions, our country would be unworthy of the name nation."[3]

Upon receiving Trias's letter, and also hearing stern words from American diplomats in Mexico City, Lane backpedaled. He decided the whole situation should be resolved by his superiors in Washington, passed the matter on to them, and was soon removed from his office.

Lane's initial proclamation, however, forced the Pierce administration to act. The boundary dispute caused by Bartlett's Mesilla Valley compromise needed to be resolved and more land, if possible, obtained to accommodate a southern transcontinental railroad. The disagreement over American rights to the Isthmus of Tehuantcpec was also still festering, and there remained unresolved issues covered by Article XI of the 1848 Treaty of Guadalupe Hidalgo concerning compensation resulting from Indian raids into Mexico.

Within three years of the Treaty's approval, it had been estimated that $10 million a year for at least a decade would be needed by the United States military to forcibly prevent Indian incursions south of the border.[4] Based on that economic analysis, American officials in Mexico were instructed to seek a release from the provisions of Article XI in exchange for several million dollars to be paid to the Mexican government. The negotiations, however, had not been finalized by the time Pierce moved into the White House.

At the same time there was growing international disagreement over rights to the Isthmus of Tehuantepec. After some Americans acquired permission to build a railroad across the isthmus in 1849, the following year a New Orleans-based company was formed to implement the idea. Part of the project was to include development of the 300-mile wide strip of land which came with the rights to the isthmus granted by the Mexican government.

By 1851, however, public opinion in Mexico was heavily opposed to the possible American colonization of this region which cut through the very heart of the country.[5] In response, the Mexican Congress nullified the New Orleans company's rights to the isthmus and they were told they would be physically prevented from proceeding with any work on the project.

Fearing the reaction of its militarily-superior northern neighbor, Mexican officials did not rule out the possibility of renegotiating terms for permitting construction of a railroad across the isthmus. The American government refused this offer, proclaiming instead that the provisions contained in the original agreement were still valid. In addition, the New Orleans company filed a $5.3 million claim against Mexico and also threatened to send men to the area to seize the isthmus. Complicating matters further, by February of 1853, the Mexican government had granted permission to a second American company to build a railroad across the isthmus, resulting in two U.S. firms simultaneously claiming rights to the passage.

Thus it was left to new President Pierce to deal with three major issues with Mexico. These were: the need for more land to build a southern transcontinental railroad which would also settle the Mesilla Valley controversy, raids south of the border by Indians, and the problematic isthmus dispute.

Pierce could have used military force to resolve these questions by simply sending the U.S. Army south again and requiring the Mexican government to sell more territory while forsaking Article XI of the Treaty of Guadalupe Hidalgo and recognizing American rights to the isthmus. Instead he chose diplomacy and selected James Gadsden of South Carolina to go to Mexico City to try and negotiate an agreement.

Originally hesitant to take the job because of family obligations and his advancing years, at the urging of Secretary of War Davis, Gadsden was named Envoy Extraordinary and Minister Plenipotentiary to Mexico in May of 1853.[6] He received a salary of $9,000 a year, and was given fairly detailed instructions by Secretary of State Marcy before leaving for his foreign post.

Marcy told Gadsden he was to address the "unsettled state" of affairs between the two countries, a job which would be difficult because of the "hostile feelings engendered by the late war with Mexico [which has been] embittered by the severe wounds inflicted on her national pride…".[7] Despite that, the Secretary wrote Gadsden, "It is the earnest wish of this government to cultivate friendly relations with that Republic," and indicated the United State would be liberal in its dealings with her southern neighbor.

In his long letter of instructions, Marcy also discussed the isthmus, Indian, and railroad issues. Of the possibility of laying tracks along the Gila River route he wrote: "A better knowledge of the country in the vicinity of the Gila has demonstrated the great difficulty—not to say, impossibility—of constructing a railroad along its banks…yet a very eligible route for such a road is found at a further distance…on the Mexican side of the line but not on the American side of it."[8]

National Archives II

JAMES GADSDEN

In general terms, Marcy directed Gadsden to seek a change in the international boundary which would run directly west from El Paso del Norte, cut south, then go on to the Gulf of California. If that was not possible, the new Minister to Mexico was to seek a border which would go from Texas to the San Pedro River and then head north to connect with the Gila. "It is believed that if the United States could acquire this latter line," Marcy wrote, "they would then have within their territory a good route for a railroad." That, he told Gadsden, was the "sole object" the administration had in wanting to alter the existing border.

The Secretary assumed Mexico would appreciate the concerns the United States had for building a railroad through the area. "She ought not to suspect any sinister design on our part," Marcy said, "for she must know that such a road will be a very expensive work which our government would not patronize, nor our citizens embark their capital in to the amount of many millions, if in any part of the way it were to run through a foreign territory."

While admitting he wasn't familiar with the region, Marcy said he had been told the sought-after land was unpopulated, and added, "Nor is it at all inviting to settlers". Thus, he concluded the property could be acquired for "a moderate sum" of money, but indicated the United States would be "willing to pay liberally," although he did not specify an exact amount.

Having sailed on August 1st of 1853 aboard a steamer from New Orleans bound for Vera Cruz, and after arriving in Mexico City, one of Gadsden's first orders of business didn't deal with negotiating a change in the border. Instead, he had to address rumors of an American military invasion of the country. On the 31st of August he was sent a letter by Manuel Diaz de Bonilla, the Mexican Minister of Foreign Relations, stating that he had "received information through a trustworthy channel that a military division of the United States, consisting of two thousand troops is moving toward the frontier of this Republic for the purpose of occupying a part of its territory…".[9]

Gadsden replied the next day. Referring to on-going Indian raids in the area, he explained that these soldiers were merely marching to the border "so as to strengthen [the] ability to preserve order on the frontier: and to aid in the fulfillment of other obligations imposed by the Treaty of Guadalupe."[10]

While this incident may have been a false alarm about an American military incursion into Mexico, an event in November was not. On the 15th of that month, Bonilla notified Gadsden he had heard that two ships left San Francisco bound for the Mexican state of Sonora on a filibustering [non-governmental military invasion] expedition. The ships, according to the Minister of Foreign Relations, carried in total over 200 armed men along with several pieces of artillery.[11]

Gadsden responded by requesting that U.S. naval vessels in the Pacific act "against all attempts at invasion of the Territory of Mexico."[12] One of the ships was stopped, but the other eluded authorities and sailed for lower California. There, according to a message from the American Minister, those involved with the filibuster attempt had captured and occupied, "La Paz, the Capital of Lower California; and where, it is supposed, the party will await reinforcements; and mature their plans for consummating their original designs against the State of Sonora."[13]

By early December, Gadsden could report that the renegade Americans had evacuated La Paz and, showing his national bias, incorrectly assumed, "Sonora is probably by this time in occupation of the filibusters: for there is certainly a sympathy among the citizens of that State in favor of these expeditions."[14]

Not being fully informed about the particulars of this illegal military incursion by American citizens into Mexico, Gadsden had no way of knowing the expedition's leader was William Walker. His goal was the creation of the "Republic of Lower California" which was also to include the Mexican state of Sonora. To accomplish that, Walker implored his mercenary soldiers: "When you meet the enemy, let the holiness of your cause, move your arms and strengthen your souls. When you strike at a Mexican foe, remember that you strike at an auxiliary of the Apache, at an accessory to the murder of innocent children, and the rape of helpless women."[15]

The attempted incursion south of the border, though, was a total failure. After the Mexican military drove Walker's men from La Paz, the Americans retreated to Ensenada on the west coast of lower California. From there they tried to invade Sonora overland, an action which ended in defeat and surrender in the spring of 1854.

While government officials in Mexico City complained to Gadsden about this American invasion of their nation, they were also objecting to constant Indian raids from the north. Under Article XI of the Treaty of Guadalupe Hidalgo, the United States was either to stop these attacks or pay the victims compensation for their loses. Neither of those steps, though, had been taken.

On October 18th of 1853, Bonilla sent Gadsden a communication "calling his attention to the extensive and disastrous depredations continually committed against the frontier departments of this Republic since the year 1848 by the barbarous tribes living in North American territory…".[16] The Minister of Foreign Relations requested that the United States assume its military and financial responsibility under the 1848 Treaty when he wrote, "All that Mexico can do is to ask that it be enforced, satisfaction being given for the injuries already caused by failure to observe it and a repetition thereof being avoided."

At the same time, because he had not received any definite word from Washington as to how much money he could offer to settle the boundary dispute matter, Gadsden had little progress to report toward negotiating a new treaty. But he had personally concluded the United States would need a revised border at least as far south as the 31st parallel of latitude. He was also hoping for a "natural line" between the two countries since he was convinced the new boundary had to be established using geographical features such as mountains and deserts. As he wrote: "It is an old national maxim which all history has confirmed that rivers and valleys unite a people, mountains and unpassable barriers separate."[17]

As he awaited additional instructions from the Pierce administration, Gadsden also speculated on long-term boundary issues between the two nations.

He believed that eventually the entire Rio Grande valley had to be under the control of only one government. Therefore, he assumed that either west Texas would again become part of Mexico, or the Mexican border states of Tamaulipas, Nuevo Leon, Coahuila, and Chihuahua would in the future be added to the United States through revolutions or additional purchases.[18]

Of more immediate concern, however, was how much should be paid for any boundary change he was able to secure. That amount still had not been made clear to Gadsden by the State Department, but once he arrived in Mexico and saw the bankrupt condition of Santa Anna's government, he quickly concluded they would demand a very high sum.

While the Mexican President had initially agreed in late September of 1853 to negotiate a new treaty, it was over two months later before serious discussions concerning a revised border actually began. The delay in part may have been caused by Gadsden's obvious contempt for Santa Anna, while from their perspective the Mexicans saw the American Minister as arrogant and inflexible.

Finally, after a period of procrastination, on November 30th, 1853, Gadsden was sent a letter stating that Santa Anna had appointed a three member commission headed by Bonilla to negotiate a new treaty to resolve the major issues between the two countries. This was done, the Minister of Foreign Relations wrote, because the Mexican President had "taken into consideration the very urgent request made to him by His Excellency [Gadsden] relative to the portion of land needed by the United States for the construction of a railroad on the northern frontier…".[19] Based on that decision, December 5th was set as the date the discussions would finally begin.

Bonilla's flowery language in conveying the message that Santa Anna had decided to move forward on drafting another treaty was an attempt to hide the real reasons the Mexicans agreed to negotiate. The dictator's government was broke and needed cash quickly in order to pay its army to subdue brewing rebellions against it. They were also under the mistaken impression the U.S. would provide almost any amount of money in exchange for the land needed to build a southern transcontinental rail line. In addition, it was fairly obvious that if a new agreement weren't reached, the United States could simply take the territory with its superior military strength. Thus, the Mexican President wanted to make a deal.

A few weeks before he received the message from Bonilla signaling that serious talks could finally begin, Gadsden was still awaiting directions from Washington on what actual terms to seek in a new treaty. In some desperation, on November 3rd he had sent Marcy a letter stating: "I was much disappointed at not having heard from the Department of State by the last steamer. I am not able therefore to report any further progress on a Treaty of adjustment of differences…".[20] Then

Gadsden continued by highlighting one of his major concerns: "As the pretensions of the [Mexican] Supreme Government are very extravagant…my apprehensions are as to an issue <u>on the amount to be paid</u> and therefore was I the more desirous of receiving your views as to this subject…".

Within two weeks after this letter was forwarded, Gadsden finally obtained instructions from Washington on what specific terms the new treaty should encompass. Christopher Ward of Pennsylvania, a member of the Democratic Party National Committee, had been sent south with a secret message from Secretary of State Marcy. This lengthy communication was considered so important that Ward had to memorize it in total to insure a written copy could not fall into Mexican hands and thus jeopardize the negotiations.

When Ward met with Gadsden on November 14th, he conveyed the Secretary's message. The Minister was to secure a revised boundary along one of six alternate lines, all but one of which contained American access to the Gulf of California.

The first option, the one much preferred by President Pierce, began south of the mouth of the Rio Grande and proceeded west before heading north to again run along the same river. From there it went west, generally along the 31st parallel, and terminated by including lower California within the United States. Fifty million dollars was to be offered for this new border.[21]

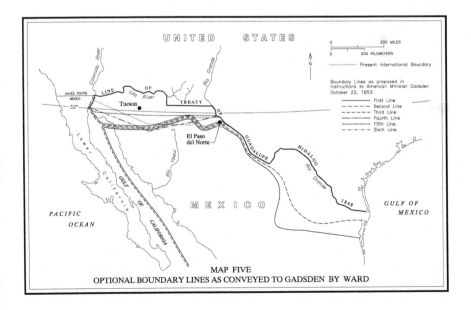

MAP FIVE
OPTIONAL BOUNDARY LINES AS CONVEYED TO GADSDEN BY WARD

The second possibility was similar to the first, but excluded the lower California peninsula. Not more than $35 million was to be paid for this alternative according to Marcy.

Thirty million dollars was to be offered for the third option. It began along the Rio Grande south of El Paso del Norte and cut almost straight across to the Gulf of California. It also included lower California within its borders.

Each of these first three possibilities were to be paid for in ten equal installments. Since twenty million dollars was to be offered for the fourth option, it would only take two annual payments. This line was the same as the third, but excluded lower California.

If none of these substantial boundary changes were possible, Gadsden was informed that "the object of the negotiation will be to get an eligible route for a railroad from the Rio Grande to California."[22] To do this, Marcy encouraged him to seek a line between the 31st and 32nd parallel of latitude which would include both access to the Gulf of California and "would throw within the limits of the United States a very good—perhaps the best—route for such a railroad." Fifteen million dollars would be provided for this territorial revision.

The final alternative was a modification of the fifth option but left out American access to the Gulf completely. Once the line running from Texas reached the 111th degree of longitude, it was to turn northwest and go on an angle to the mouth of the Gila River along the Colorado. Although acceptable, Marcy said this route was clearly the least desirable.

In addition to a revised boundary line, whichever was finally agreed upon, the American Minister to Mexico was also to obtain a release from all Indian raid claims which had resulted because of Article XI of the Treaty of Guadalupe Hidalgo. It was these two issues only, Ward was instructed by the Secretary of State, that Gadsden had to settle in a new agreement.

Ward, however, had other things in mind. At the time of his appointment as diplomatic messenger, he was working for the New Orleans-based American firm which alleged it still had rights to build a railroad or canal across the Isthmus of Tehuantepec. Thus, while no mention of the isthmus issue had been made by Marcy in his secret communication, Ward intentionally mislead Gadsden and told him the new treaty had to include financial compensation for his isthmus client.[23]

Since his directions to the American Minister were all verbal and there was no way of checking them for accuracy, when Ward insisted the agreement stipulate a large monetary settlement for the New Orleans company, Gadsden could not know of the subterfuge. Intuitively not trusting the messenger, however, Gadsden required Ward to put his instructions in writing, which was reluctantly done, and this would later prove very politically embarrassing to President Pierce.

Ward also insinuated to Gadsden that without the isthmus concession, the United States Senate was unlikely to ratify any new treaty with Mexico. Based on that advice, and Ward's falsified message, Gadsden included the issue in the treaty discussions.[24]

At his first meeting with the three appointed Mexican officials held on December 10, 1853, Gadsden presented them with a draft treaty. Prior to that date, Santa Anna had made it clear the talks would be based only on the minimal amount of land actually needed by the United States for a southern railroad. From the beginning, therefore, it was apparent the U.S. would not obtain access to the Gulf of California. Gadsden believed one reason for Santa Anna's refusal to consider selling more land was the Walker filibustering incursion into the country which had occurred only a few weeks earlier.[25] Other possible explanations include the bitter dislike of Santa Anna and Gadsden for each other, the Mexican desire to maintain a land bridge between lower California and the state of Sonora, and Santa Anna's personal desire to minimize the amount of property sold.

In looking back at the negotiating process years later, the Mexican President also referred to the difficult situation his government found itself in. It was so militarily weak, Santa Anna said, it had to reach an agreement. Gadsden made it very clear, he stated, that the Americans were going to obtain the territory they needed for a railroad "one way or another".

In more colorful language, the dictator would write of this veiled threat along with the loss of a vast amount of his nation which had resulted from the 1848 Treaty of Guadalupe Hidalgo. "The government at Washington, with knife in hand," Santa Anna offered, "was still trying to cut another piece from the body which it had just horribly mutilated, and threatening another invasion. In the deplorable situation of the country, it seemed to me that a break with the colossus would be a foolish act; and I adopted the course which patriotism and prudence counseled, a pacific settlement."[26]

Santa Anna noted that other than the fertile Mesilla Valley, he had been told the land to be ceded to the United States "'was rocky mountains inhabited by Apaches, who, according to their custom, make war continually upon the adjacent departments'."[27] He also pointed out that Mexico was selling a thin sliver of land for the same amount of money which it obtained for "THE HORRIBLE SACRIFICE OF HALF THE TERRITORY OF THE REPUBLIC," under the terms of the 1848 treaty.

In addition to these reasons, Santa Anna mentioned the need for his government to raise cash. Difficult times, though, were nothing new for the Mexican leader. Having first assumed the presidency in 1833, he was well known in the United States for his role at the Alamo. After being exiled for awhile, he returned as President between 1841 and 1844, but was driven from power again. He served his country by leading its troops during the Mexican-American War, and then became President once more in 1853.

"I should have preferred to reply to them, as at other times, with my sword," Santa Anna wrote in typical fashion of dealing with Gadsden and the United States. Despite that strident attitude, in the end he decided to negotiate, even though he thought the treaty would be "one of the great sacrifices which I have consecrated to the welfare of my country."[28]

By the third negotiating session on the 22nd of December, Bonilla suggested a change to the originally proposed revised boundary line. Even though he considered this might only be a temporary resolution of long-standing territorial issues, the next day Gadsden agreed to the recommendation with some minor modifications. Then in reply to an idea from the Foreign Minister, Gadsden proposed an acceptable offer to entirely terminate Article XI of the Treaty of Guadalupe Hidalgo and combine into one amount the payment for both the claims for Indian raids filed under it along with the price of the territory to be transferred.

On Christmas Eve, the negotiators discussed the isthmus situation. Gadsden wanted the rights of the original, New Orleans-based American company to build across the land recognized, but Bonilla refused. Instead, he suggested that any financial claims the firm might have against the Mexican government be assumed by Washington, an idea which was adopted, and the company was specifically named in the treaty. Based on that, the major disputes between the two countries had been resolved by the sale of enough land to accommodate a southern transcontinental railroad and payment for Mexican claims for Indian attacks and American claims over the isthmus issue.

To finalize the treaty, Gadsden offered $12 million but Bonilla demanded more. In the end, $15 million was to be paid for both the territory and settlement of the Indian claims. Another $5 million would be set aside by the U.S. to pay for any outstanding American claims against Mexico, including by the identified company involved with the isthmus. Finally, the treaty was to include a provision that each country would use its military forces to halt lawless invasions of the other.[29]

Having reached an agreement, the new treaty was finalized and signed on December 30th, 1853. Gadsden was pleased with the result, in part because territory containing vast mineral wealth was to be added to the United States. The final outcome of the negotiations, he also thought, was honorable and just for both sides. The American Minister asked that the terms of the treaty be kept secret until the document was ratified in Washington, and then left Mexico to return to the U.S. via steamer.

Even as Gadsden was on his way back to the United States, some American newspapers began reporting rumors of a possible agreement. According to the *New York Daily Times* on January 9th, 1854, however, "The President and Cabinet positively deny that any treaty whatever has been received from Mexico."[30] In their defense, speedy communication with Gadsden was obviously impossible so officials in Washington couldn't know what had taken place in Mexico City. The article did, though, allude to a "secret agent" being sent south, mistakenly saying this official had nothing to do with the negotiations.

On the 10th, the *Times* went even further with its report denying the existence of a proposed treaty, labeling stories about its completion "Humbug". "The President, [Secretary of State] Mr. Marcy, and the other members of the Cabinet, say unreservedly, not only that there is no such treaty in existence," the *Times* wrote, "but that they have no knowledge of any new treaty having been negotiated with Mexico…".[31] Then on the 11th the newspaper wondered if a treaty would be possible at all, pointing out the strained personal relationship between Santa Anna and Gadsden.

The next day the American Minister to Mexico landed at New Orleans aboard the steamship "Texas" with the treaty in hand and sent its contents on to Washington. Although stating it might not have all the exact details of the agreement, the local *Daily Picayune* proclaimed: "In selling the disputed territory of Mesilla the Mexican Government has sold an embarrassment. In freeing himself from the 11th article of the treaty of Guadalupe, Mr. Gadsden has got rid of an onerous duty; but in abolishing this dangerous article Señor Bonilla has closed the door against American intervention…".[32]

By January 17th, even the *New York Daily Times* was acknowledging that a new treaty had been negotiated. The next day the newspaper speculated on why Santa Anna, a man who had earlier promised to die rather than give up another square inch of Mexican territory to the U.S., would make such a deal. "In the first place he will obtain money from the United States to sustain an army," they wrote, "which of course will do his bidding so long as his means of paying them hold out."[33] Then the newspaper listed several other reasons the Mexican dictator would have agreed to the treaty. "He will make a very good argument, too, on the ground that the Northern boundary line was really in dispute between us," the *Times* said, "that the territory he has ceded away was overrun and desolated by the savages, and therefore, useless to Mexico and that the railroad which we will probably run through the territory, and the American settlements likely to spring up along the line, will afford to Mexico an impenetrable defense against the Indians."

Chicago's *Daily Tribune*, though, was not impressed by Gadsden's efforts. After summarizing the contents of the agreement, it concluded of the $20 million to be spent under the terms of the proposed treaty: "Pretty good pay, when it is considered that at least 30,000,000 of acres of the whole [new territory] is as sterile as can be imagined, and not worth that many cents. The whole matter, however, is arranged so to secure a Southern route, through American territory, for the Pacific Railroad."[34]

Not surprisingly, the view of most southerners was very favorable toward the agreement. The Richmond *Enquirer* offered its support, writing: "The distinguishing merits of this treaty are, first, that it adjusts all the disputes between the United States and Mexico, and thus cements the amicable relations of the two governments; secondly, that it removes every inducement to filibuster invasions of Mexican soil; thirdly, that it secures the only safe and practicable route for a railway to the Pacific; and lastly, and chiefly, it gives the South a chance for two or three more slave states."[35]

The *Charleston Daily Courier* fully agreed, heaping lavish praise on both the treaty and the American negotiator. They suggested the new territory be called "Arresonia" [possibly meaning "little spring"] and have a South Carolinian as its first territorial governor in order to honor Gadsden.[36]

Despite the glowing southern praise for the treaty, future approval of the agreement by the United States Senate appeared politically uncertain. According to the *New York Daily Times*: "The Gadsden treaty is getting in bad odor. Many Senators think he is giving too much money for too little and they want to go down to latitude twenty-seven...".[37] The newspaper concluded that because of this, "It looks now as though there might be a strenuous opposition in the Senate to the ratification of the Gadsden Treaty."[38]

Its rival newspaper, and avid opponent of the agreement, the *New York Herald* went even further. On January 20, 1854, it predicted: "The President has called the Cabinet together on the Gadsden treaty...From what I know of their opinions, and those of a majority of the Senate, Santa Anna can not get over ten millions of dollars for what land he offers. It is now very doubtful whether the President will send it to the Senate, it being a second edition of N. P. Trist's abortion."[39]

CHAPTER SIX

"Here is your country for a railroad"

Two months before James Gadsden arrived back in the United States, he had obtained Mexico's diplomatic permission for a U.S. reconnaissance of the territory dealt with by the new treaty. As part of a Congressional mandate to collect topographical and other information on the leading candidates for an American transcontinental railroad route, Gadsden had secured approval for a survey party to cross through the northern Mexican border states generally along the 32nd degree of latitude.

Given Mexico's consent, on the 18th of November of 1853, Secretary of War Jefferson Davis sent orders to Lieutenant John G. Parke of the U.S. Army's Topographical Corps in San Diego. Davis instructed Parke to survey a potential railroad line from the Pima villages on the Gila River through Tucson and then to the San Pedro River. From there the route was to follow the shortest and most practical path to just north of El Paso.

This was just one of several transcontinental railroad surveys Davis directed to be completed. Early in 1853, in an attempt to actually get something done about building the cross-country line, Congress approved $150,000 to have numerous topographical reports compiled and the results compared. Over the objections of some elected officials who questioned the government's right to be involved with the project at all, the Secretary of War was authorized "to employ such portion of the corps of topographical engineers, and such other persons as he may deem necessary, to make such explorations and surveys as he may deem advisable, to ascertain the most practicable and economical route for a railroad from the Mississippi River to the Pacific Ocean...".[1]

Capitol Hill had been haggling for years over which transcontinental route was the best choice, and the bickering and disagreements resulted in nothing of substance being accomplished. Despite that, there were obvious incentives to proceed with planning the project. The west coast of the country had to be militarily defended and the allure of enormous trade with China, which Asa Whitney had first dangled in front of the American public in 1844, was still economically enticing.

There were also very important budgetary reasons for the federal government to get involved with building the railroad. When compared to the cost of ship voyages via Panama or around Cape Horn, train travel would save an estimated $63 million in annual transportation costs related to sending military men, materials, and the mail to California.[2] In addition, the time to get from coast to coast would be reduced from many months by ship to around one week by rail.

Before transcontinental tracks could be laid, however, a final Congressional choice of route had to be made, and that meant specifics of the various options were desirable. To obtain better information, crews from the Army's Topographical Corps were sent into the field by Secretary Davis. These surveys were to be done rapidly, so in reality they were more of a general reconnaissance than an actual survey.

Each of these efforts was to take special note of mountain passes and bridge sites since those two factors would greatly influence the feasibility of implementation and the cost of laying track. The surveyors were also to record careful notes concerning "the amount and location of timber, building stone, coal, and water which might be used in constructing and operating a railroad. Great importance was attached to the geology, soil, meteorology, and vegetation of the regions traversed, since they were indications of prospective ability to support a population. On the more northern routes great efforts were made to learn the depths of snow in the mountain passes in winter."[3]

Davis had several distinct possibilities to select from in ordering the surveys, and he chose the most likely, and politically popular, candidates. The first was to generally follow Whitney's proposed northern route between the 47th and 49th parallels of latitude. The second survey line, Thomas Hart Benton's favorite, would run near the 38th degree from St. Louis to San Francisco, with an auxiliary east of the Rockies following a line further north. The third choice traced the 35th degree of latitude through Albuquerque to Los Angeles. The final option was the 32nd parallel alternative which would proceed from east Texas to El Paso del Norte, then go south of the Gila River and on to San Diego.

The implementation of this last survey was broken into three sections, with Lt. Parke in charge of the portion from the Pima villages along the Gila River all the way to El Paso. Since in late 1853 this territory was still part of Mexico, and treaty negotiations over transferring it had yet to be completed, the diplomatic permission for the work obtained earlier by Gadsden would come in handy.

Despite the Mexican government's approval of the mission, however, in December, Davis informed Parke of Walker's recent filibustering expedition into Mexico, calling it "lawless conduct on the part of our misguided citizens."[4] The Secretary of War warned the Lieutenant that this action "may excite a feeling among the Mexican people, which would render it unsafe for your party with its military escort to make its appearance among them," but left it to Parke's discretion as to whether or not to proceed.

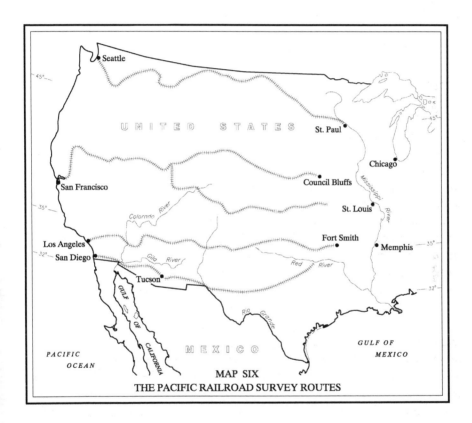

MAP SIX
THE PACIFIC RAILROAD SURVEY ROUTES

Hailing from Pennsylvania, Parke was a 26-year old graduate of West Point and a four year member of the Topographical Corps at the time of his assignment. With about $5,000 at his disposal and a contingent of fifty-six men, ignoring the potential danger spelled out by Davis, he decided to move forward and departed San Diego for Fort Yuma on the Colorado River in January of 1854. By February 13th, the men were at the Pima villages and from the 16th of that month, when they left the Gila River behind, to their March 21st arrival at El Paso, Parke maintained a diary of the journey.

In the desert south of the Gila River, Parke noted a lack of water and grass for the party's animals, which resulted in much travel by night to reduce exertion. He also observed a low mountain which he called "El Picacho", writing that this twin-peaked ridge rose abruptly out of the surrounding plain and that it "looms up, with its well-defined and angular profile, a most prominent landmark."[5]

On February 20th, the men were approaching Tucson. Parke and an associate rode into town to explain what they were doing in the area, to offer their credentials from the Mexican government, and to be shown the two famous meteorites earlier mentioned by Bartlett. He called the community: "A one-storied flat-roofed adobe town of about six hundred inhabitants, whose sole pursuit is agriculture; the much dreaded Apaches having interfered greatly with their pastoral occupation."[6]

The temperature the next morning was near freezing, and Parke described the Santa Catalina mountains, which rise to above 9,000 feet in elevation north of Tucson, as "high, rugged, and with numerous spurs, extending eastward to the San Pedro."[7] The men marched directly toward that desert stream, which was "about eighteen inches deep and twelve feet wide, and flows with a rapid current," arriving on a cold, damp day.[8]

East from the river was a vast natural gap, framed by mountains on both north and south, which generally followed the line of Lt. Col. Cooke's cutoff route first proposed in 1846. "We had a perfectly smooth road over a reddish soil," Parke wrote on February 28th, "covered with grass, and devoid of trees with the exception of a few scattering palmettos, down to the Playa, which at present is a hard, smooth, and apparently level area of about fifteen miles in length by nearly ten in width, without a particle of vegetation, it being the perfection of sterility."[9]

Because of a complete lack of water for their animals, the men began a search the next day at 1 a.m. After more than twelve hours and twenty-three miles of marching over rough terrain cut by dry washes, they did find some. Farther east, the land leveled out once again, and as the men moved forward on March 6th, one of the teamsters with the survey party commented on the table-top flat territory, "Here is your country for a railroad."[10]

At a spot ninety miles west of El Paso, Parke decided to deviate slightly from his orders. He could follow the level plain directly to Texas, but would do so without water, so decided to head for the small Mexican town of Mesilla instead. On the way there, two soldiers were sent across the international border to nearby Fort Webster to inform the post commander of the survey party's movement through the area. They returned, however, to report: "Instead of finding a flourishing post, garrisoned by three companies, as was expected, they found not a soul and the post in ruins, most of the buildings burned to the ground, and the remaining ones sacked—all a perfect wreck."[11] The Indians who had only recently destroyed the fort were gone, and Parke concluded: "We must be more cautious and circumspect in our movements hereafter. To be in such close proximity to Indians and not see any of them, indicates clearly that all is not right."

By the middle of March the survey crew was safely at Mesilla, which was described as "a very thriving and busy place, and has a rapidly-increasing population."[12] Presumably unknown to Parke, or the Mexican population of the town, by this time Gadsden had arranged for the community to become American, and the United States Senate was beginning to debate the proposed treaty which would accomplish that objective.

After having traveled for five weeks across 373 miles of desert from the Pima villages on the Gila River all the way to El Paso del Norte, Parke summarized his findings. He noted there was a lack of both lumber and water, the latter being available in only nine spots along the entire line. The Lieutenant believed, however, that by digging shallow wells that problem could be overcome and recommended an experiment be conducted to see if it were possible. As to the feasibility of building a railroad through the territory he and his men had explored, Parke stated, "By observations made on the ground, it was found perfectly practicable to construct a line of grades answering the purposes of a railway communication along or near the route traveled…".[13] Later, when Parke's findings were combined with those of the other teams surveying the 32nd parallel option, the result was apparent: This was indeed country through which a year-round railroad could be easily built.

The conclusions of Parke's work, along with the reports from all the other transcontinental railroad surveys, were eventually sent to Secretary of War Davis for evaluation and a recommendation. At the same time, a Texas company was taking preparatory steps for possibly building a privately financed cross-country railroad along the 32nd parallel and had hired surveyor A.B. Gray to examine the route.

Gray was working for the Texas Western Railroad, a company founded in February of 1852. It had been chartered to build a line across the state but its owners had even greater ambitions and were thinking of laying tracks all the way to the Pacific Ocean. The firm, however, was on very shaky financial ground. Not knowing that, one journal at the time wrote of their plans to build across Texas and possibly keep going all the way west to the coast: "We cannot see then how a company possessing such a munificent donation [of land granted by the state of Texas] and such privileges can fail to succeed. This division of the Pacific route will unquestionably be built."[14]

Anticipating the successful completion of Gadsden's negotiating efforts over revising the international border, the Texas Western company chose Gray to investigate their potential path to the Pacific. Not only was he known as the man who had pointedly criticized Bartlett over the Mesilla Valley compromise, but the surveyor had other credentials for the job as well. Born in Virginia in 1820, Gray assisted with surveys of the Mississippi River delta and then enlisted in the Texas navy. Around 1840, he was appointed a member of the boundary commission which delineated the new border between the Republic of Texas and Mexico, after which he worked for the U.S. War Department in exploring the Lake Superior region.

While described as fearless and energetic, Gray shared a few traits with his nemesis from the North, John Russell Bartlett. He sometimes made foolish decisions which endangered those under him; plus he liked to wander over the country he was suppose to be surveying. He also had a streak for the finer things in life, as one of his companions from the 1854 trip chronicled when the men reached the Gulf of California.

"Gray made a little exploration on his own hook along the shore," this author wrote, "and returned to camp with his neck handkerchief full of soft shelled crabs. He knew well what they were, being from Norfolk, Virginia. He commenced to comment over our fare and said what a pity it was that we did not have some butter and a frying pan; what a famous meal we would have on soft shell crabs fried in butter."[15]

This description of the expedition leader was written many years later by Peter R. Brady, a frontiersman who accompanied Gray on his surveying trip for the Texas Western Railroad. Originally from Washington, D.C., Brady said he graduated from the U.S. Naval Academy in 1844 at age nineteen and then spent time as an officer serving in the Mediterranean. By 1846, he was a lieutenant with the Texas Rangers in the war with Mexico and afterwards stayed in the state. Based on his experience, Gray appointed Brady a captain of his reconnaissance party.

The total group consisted of only nineteen men, mostly Texans, all of whom were comfortable in the rugged and unknown territory they would be crossing. Departing San Antonio on January 1, 1854, one night on their way west the men came across an escaped slave dressed in "rags and tatters". When they found him wandering in the Texas desert, according to Brady, the man was, "A lean, poor, starving, runaway Negro, who staggered and reeled as he came forward to the light of the camp fire."[16]

The next morning, having eaten as much as he could, the man explained that despite being married with two children, he had fled from his master in Arkansas about four months earlier. He was headed on foot to Mexico where he would be free and along the way had used a stolen shotgun to kill rabbits, birds, snakes, or steal food. Eventually, though, just as the countryside became more barren, he ran out of ammunition, once forcing him to eat spoiled meat from a dead steer. He was starving to death when he came across the survey party, who called the man, "Charles Augustus".

Brady wrote of him: "When I looked at that Negro and thought what he had endured to secure his liberty it brought strange thoughts to my mind...He had been told that by traveling west he could soon reach Mexico, where he would be free...There were no settlements on the road, nothing to live on, a desert uninhabited country, but that was so much better for him. There was no danger of his being arrested and carried back into slavery. He would risk it...for the sake of his freedom. What a precious boon liberty must be."[17]

In order to collect a $50 reward for returning runaway slaves, one of Gray's men talked of turning the man over to the sheriff when the survey crew reached American El Paso. For that reason, even though they were in the middle of Indian country, Charles Augustus decided to run away once again. Having been appointed cook for the party, one night he baked a huge stack of bread and the next morning was gone with the food. Also missing were Gray's much-prized thoroughbred mare, a saddle, and firearms.

After arriving in El Paso shortly thereafter, Gray learned that Lieutenant Parke was residing nearby, having just completed his reconnaissance work for the Secretary of War. The two met and discussed Parke's findings and he gave Gray a cistern barometer with which to measure altitude.[18] Based on his own earlier experience with the Bartlett-led boundary survey, and after hearing from Parke, Gray decided to go further south in looking for the most practical rail line through the region.

Before his survey party departed for the west coast, however, Gray went off to Santa Fe on business while his men stayed behind and had a two week drunken and gambling escapade. They eventually left El Paso to the sound of church bells on Easter morning, and the men split up in order to better explore the territory below the border.

The routes the men were following were well south of the new border with Mexico as negotiated by Gadsden and also far below the path the railroad would apparently take through the area. Since that line had already been researched by others, Gray was exploring for alternatives. As they moved further west, the two crews eventually reunited and returned to the known railway route through the territory. Then Gray once again divided the men into two groups, one going along the 32nd parallel of latitude, the other heading farther south.

East of the San Pedro River, like Parke, Gray noticed both a lack of water and the absence of trees. He also noted that a little rock blasting and excavation could be needed to build a rail line through the area, but only one bridge to cross the San Pedro would be required.

Brady recounted an event which occurred in this general vicinity that summarizes the terror of the times. Around April 25th, the men spotted the trail of some 200 Apache Indians, and the naive Gray decided to pursue them. Brady said of this decision, "[Gray] was as innocent of there being any danger as the babe unborn."[19]

After the Apaches became aware of being followed, they approached the Americans, and Brady went out to meet them. One of the Indians was impassioned, yelling and screaming at them to leave. Brady further explained: "He picked up a stone in each hand and rushed to the front within a few yards of where I stood, and placing the stones on the ground before him, with an angry voice and excited gesture, swept both hands and arms around and told us that the country was all theirs and that we must turn around and go back."[20]

Brady indicated the survey party was on its way to California and couldn't turn back. It started to rain, but talking between the two sides continued. While the vastly outnumbered survey crew had Sharp's rifles [longarm weapon with 0.44 or 0.52 caliber] with which to fight, the Apaches were armed mostly with bows and arrows or lances. Eventually the Indians departed, saying they only fought Mexicans, that Americans were their friends. The group was headed, one of them announced, to a nearby ranch to kill the Mexican man and take the women and children captive. "All this country," an Apache proclaimed to the surveyors, "was theirs and the Mexicans should not live there."[21]

That night it snowed, and the next day the Americans ran into Mexican troops from Tucson and informed them of the Indian plan. Soldiers were sent to help at the ranch, and an hour later a bloody battle was fought at which the survey crew was present. Brady wrote that Mexican cavalrymen were: "Lancing and killing the rascals, picking them up on the point of their lances and lifting them off of their feet. Their allies, the Tucson Apaches, were butchering and mutilating those who were left wounded behind. No cry of mercy was given and no quarter was shown. The carnage was awful. They killed and butchered as long as there was an Apache left in sight…".[22] Then Brady nonchalantly commented, "We soon saw that we could be of no help to the Mexicans at the ranch helping to kill the wounded, so we returned to our camp to finish our lunch which had been so rudely interrupted."

Having lanced to death many of the Indians, the Mexicans proceeded to cut off the victims' ears and tie them together in order to verify how many had been killed. The grisly "record" was described as 2 1/2 to 3 feet in length and looked like dried fruit on a string. In the end, Brady concluded, "There were also other evidences of the atrocities committed, which I will not mention here, to show that the troops from Tucson were not a very tender hearted set and could come as near holding their own as the Apaches themselves."[23]

After that deadly encounter was over, Gray decided to explore an optional railroad route west from Tucson. This line could possibly serve as an alternative to the one already surveyed by Parke and others that ran almost directly north from the tiny community. "Having previously examined the Gila river to the junction [with the Colorado]," Gray wrote, "I was desirous to know the nature of the country near the head of the Gulf [of California], and to see if a line could not be carried from the Santa Cruz valley, on a direct course to Fort Yuma; or at any rate, to a point on the Gila below the great bend, which would shorten very much the route by way of the Pima villages."[24]

Going through the desert some 130 miles west of Tucson, Gray wrote that the mountains in the area: "Derive their name from the vast deposits of red oxide and green carbonate of copper found among them, and which the Indians have made use of to paint (ajo) themselves with. These mines are unquestionably of great value, and must become important, more particularly from their being situated in the neighborhood of the contemplated railway."[25]

The Texan had other reasons for being interested in this potential mining area. According to Brady, Gray sent him to these mountains to fetch some ore samples to take to San Francisco for analysis. "He had been promised the necessary capital to assist in the development of any mines which could show any merit," Brady wrote, "and which lay on the American side of the [new] boundary line."[26]

Gray concluded that a rail line running from Tucson in an almost straight westerly direction toward the Colorado River would be 70 miles shorter than the route via the Pima villages on the Gila River. He thought this alternative could be built without difficulty and would provide easy access to the rich mineral wealth in the area which would one day become the open-pit copper mining community of Ajo.

Despite that suggestion for the railroad route, in his journal Gray also discussed the agriculture of the Pima and Maricopa Indians who lived along the Gila, and one of their crops attracted most of the Texan's attention. "The cotton…" he said, "though cultivated by the Indians in the most primitive manner, exhibited a texture not unlike the celebrated Sea Island cotton. Its fiber is exceedingly soft and silky, but not of the longest staple. Large tracts of land on the Gila and in other portions of this district, appear to possess the same properties of soil; and where, I have no doubt the finest cotton will soon be extensively raised and brought to its highest state of perfection by proper cultivation."[27]

Farther west, as the men approached the junction of the Colorado and Gila rivers from the south, Brady wrote: "It was heavy traveling and there were lots of animals scattered along the road where they had died from exhaustion and then dried up like mummies. On this stretch of desert there had been neither ravens nor coyotes to devour them."[28] The men knew, though, that they had to keep going in the late-spring heat of 1854. "About 1:30 p.m., through the shimmering of the burning sand under us and the rays of the torrid sun dancing and trembling in the glare and the wind like a blast from a furnace," Brady said, "away off to the northwest we could descry a strip of green. We all knew what that was, it was the cottonwood timber of the Gila [River] bottom. Oh, glorious sight."[29]

Upon reaching their destination, Gray's men ate a hearty meal of pork, bacon, beans, bread, and coffee supplied by the soldiers stationed at Fort Yuma. Brady noted at the time: "There were no settlements on the Arizona side of the Colorado. Nobody lived there but the Yuma Indians. There were no stores and no whiskey, not a drop to be had for love or money."[30] After several days of rest, from the desolate outpost of the fort located on the eastern border of California, the survey crew would proceed on to San Diego, arriving in June.

Gray submitted his final report on the expedition to the Texas Western Railroad Company eight months later. As part of his analysis he estimated how much it would cost to build a railroad from El Paso to the junction of the Colorado and Gila rivers, a spot he considered to be "navigable waters of the Pacific". The total price to cover this distance of 578 miles, he thought, would be $8.5 million, with almost $6 million of that being used for iron rails. Because of the level terrain, the expense of grading the entire route would just be a few million dollars, and only a $50,000 bridge over the Rio Grande and a $6,000 one across the San Pedro River would be necessary. The flat topography also meant that no costly tunnels would need to be drilled anywhere along the line.[31]

The surveyor also calculated that the railroad in this area would need 75 first-class steam engines, at an estimated cost of $10,500 each, along with 1,000 freight and baggage cars. In addition, 100 passenger cars would be required, as well as depots, machine shops, and other miscellaneous buildings. The total cost for these, Gray thought, should be under $3 million. Thus, adding in $2,000,000 for contingencies, he concluded the total route from El Paso to the Gulf of California could be built and equipped to operate for just over $16 million, or $28,000 per mile, an exceptionally economical price.

Gray and his men had traveled through an inhospitable desert country, searching for the most practical route for a railroad crossing, even though all of the territory they had explored between Texas and California was still in Mexican hands. While traveling southwest of Tucson, though, the Americans met with a Dr. Spencer to discuss mining in the area. After the conversation, Brady wrote in his journal that the jurisdiction of the area could be about to change since, "Spencer had heard from Mexico that the Gadsden Treaty only awaited the approval of the United States Senate and the President to become a law…".[32]

CHAPTER SEVEN

"The President's treaty has been repudiated and rejected"

Ratification in the United States Senate of the treaty negotiated by Gadsden was far from certain. Its approval might be thwarted by a combination of abolitionists, who feared the creation of additional slave states, with expansionists lusting after even more Mexican territory. This pair of interests could be supplemented by those who demanded protection for the American company which actually had Mexican permission to build across the Isthmus of Tehuantepec. These groups, and the public in general, would then be further inflamed by the press coverage of some northern newspapers which were adamantly opposed to the treaty as a financial boondoggle.

The *New York Herald* was one of several leading publications which strenuously urged rejection of the document. After the contents had become known, the paper accused Jefferson Davis of being behind the whole thing in order to enrich himself.[1] It claimed he owned property along a possible southern transcontinental route which would quadruple in value if the project were built.

The *New York Daily Times*, however, took a different stance, generally supporting the measure. Shortly after the terms of the treaty became public, their Washington correspondent speculated on its chances for passage. "A very strong influence is at work to prevent the ratification of any such treaty with Mexico as that which it has commonly been supposed Mr. Gadsden brought home with him," he wrote, "and which gives us only a very small strip of Mexican territory."[2] Then he continued, "The ultra Southern interest insists on territory enough to make another Slave State, as an offset to California; but I still incline to the opinion, from what I can learn, that if the treaty comes to the Senate it will be ratified."

Whether the treaty would even be sent to the Senate at first was in doubt. President Pierce was not supportive of the agreement since it pointedly favored one of the two American companies competing for construction rights across the Isthmus of Tehuantepec and he wanted to reject the entire document outright.

The President's cabinet was divided on the issue, with Secretaries Davis and Marcy urging it be submitted to the Senate; also pushing Pierce to send the treaty forward was Senator Thomas Jefferson Rusk of Texas. The President finally relented, and on February 10th, 1854, he sent the Gadsden Treaty to the Senate for its consideration.

Pierce, however, recommended three changes be made to the document. First, he thought both the United States and Mexico should be equally responsible for opposing Indian raids along the new border. His second proposed alteration would remove any specific reference to the New Orleans-based company which had been inserted at Ward's insistence. While supporting settlement of American financial claims against Mexico, the President did not want the isthmus issue singled out in the treaty. Finally, Pierce sought to dilute the wording concerning filibustering expeditions by Americans into Mexico.

It wasn't until March that Gadsden's treaty would be considered by the full Senate, and its timing couldn't have been much worse. The Kansas-Nebraska Act, which established both those territories and allowed them to determine their own position on slavery, was also being debated prior to its passage in late May. Abolitionists thus saw the acquisition of even more southern land as just another step toward the eventual creation of additional slave states.

On March 9th the Senate asked that the President provide them with the written directions under which the treaty had been negotiated by Gadsden. They also wanted to see the correspondence between the United States and Mexican ministers and "all instructions, verbal or otherwise, given to any agent, and the name of such agent, and the report (if any) of such agent."[3] The role of Ward in the negotiations had obviously become known to some Senators and they wanted to look into it. Complying with their request, Pierce responded with the documents on March 21st.

Senate consideration of the treaty was supposedly being conducted in executive session to insure secrecy and prevent public disclosure of the proceedings, but based on leaks from those involved in the debate, the press was publishing a running commentary on what was happening. The *New York Daily Times* wrote that the Presidential material concerning Ward's involvement received by the Senate created much excitement because "they are believed to be prejudicial to the previous prospects of ratification."[4]

That possibility, however, was inconceivable to the *Times*. They offered the front page opinion that it could "scarcely imagine a more short-sighted policy than the rejection of this treaty would be."[5] Santa Anna, the paper believed, needed money and was going to acquire it from somewhere. If it didn't come from the United Stares, he could get it from abroad. "If he should obtain it from England or France," the *Times* wrote concerning financial support for the Mexican leader, "of course one of the prominent conditions would be that we should be excluded from transporting troops or munitions of war across Mexican territory." If that was to occur, the newspaper feared, the existing lack of U.S. military defense of the west coast could be very costly. "How long would it be in that case, if war should occur," they asked, "[that] we should lose California and Oregon?" Calling the protection of those distant lands the "weak point in the Union," the *Times* thought the only realistic alternative was to ratify the treaty negotiated by Gadsden.

A few days later the *Times* reported on a speech by Senator James Shields from Illinois. He argued the treaty should be defeated since the money to be given to Santa Anna's government would assist "a blood-thirsty tyrant, capable and guilty of almost unheard of cruelties…".[6] While acknowledging this human-rights perspective was interesting, the newspaper continued to support the document because the most likely option was to again wage war to resolve the outstanding issues between the two countries. The *Times* preferred negotiations to bloodshed and concluded, "We are bound to accept the condition of things as we find them," but it wrote of the treaty, "Still there is now great reason to fear its rejection."

By this time the duplicity of Ward in influencing the negotiations had been fully revealed to the Senate. Pierce conceded that Ward did "not convey a correct impression of my 'views and wishes'," concerning the isthmus issue, and he emphasized that the entire topic was not intended to be included in the negotiations with Mexico.[7] Then the President very generously added, "While the departure of Mr. Ward under any circumstances, or in any respect, from the instructions committed to him is a matter of regret, it is just to say that, although he failed to convey in his letter to General Gadsden the correct import of remarks made by me anterior to his appointment as special agent, I impute to him no design of misrepresentation."

The impact of the startling disclosure of Ward's role in the negotiations, however, was to place the entire treaty in extremely serious trouble. The political repercussions of his isthmus scheme were quickly shown in a number of failed votes in the Senate, where a two-thirds majority was needed to adopt motions on the treaty. On April 4th, an attempt was made to change the boundary line to the 31st parallel, a move which would have given the United States access to the Gulf of California. This motion, though, only received 21 of the forty-one votes cast and therefore failed.[8] Tellingly, it showed an almost even split of Senators, thus casting the future of the entire treaty in substantial doubt.

The next day another effort was made to begin the boundary at its western terminus along the 31st degree of latitude, but then jog it slightly north farther east. This change would also have given the U.S. a port on the Gulf, but it was overwhelmingly defeated.[9]

Given the failure of sufficient Senators to approve anything concerning the agreement, the *New York Daily Times* concluded after the April 5th vote, "The Gadsden Treaty has had a narrow escape from destruction...".[10] It also reported that those Senators leading the early push for passage had stepped aside, to be replaced by Rusk of Texas.

The *New York Herald* took a completely different view of the proceedings. On April 6th it wrote: "A large number of Senators desire a natural boundary between the United States and Mexico—such a one as cannot lead to any future misunderstanding, and also a port on the Gulf of California...Unless the first mentioned amendment with regard to the natural boundary is made, the treaty will be rejected, and the chances are that it cannot be licked into such shape as will command the necessary two-thirds vote."[11]

That same edition of the newspaper also carried a dispatch from Mexico City dated March 16th. It stated, "Everybody here is waiting for the ratification of the treaty...because without the 'collateral aid' derived from it, Santa Anna will never be able to carry out his designs." The article indicated plans for spending at least part of the money had already been made, with $400,000 going to purchase military arms, another $800,000 for use to encourage Spanish colonization of the country, and a similar amount to retire a small portion of the nation's enormous debt.

On April 11th, the *Public Ledger* of Philadelphia offered the opinion that, "The Gadsden treaty will, in all probability, receive its final death-blow in the course of this week, unless it can be so amended as to satisfy that portion of its friends who are opposed to it only as regards the measure of the [land] grant and the sum to be paid for it."[12] Then, criticizing the choice of Gadsden as negotiator and calling the territory to be acquired without value, the newspaper said, "The friends of the Southern Pacific Railroad are the only bona fide supporters of the treaty, and it might just as well be called a 'purchase of the right-of-way for a railroad to the Pacific' as by any other name."

The previous day Senator Rusk, whose main interest was in securing a southern route for the railroad, had attempted to move the ratification process forward. He offered an amendment which changed the boundary line so that it ran 150 miles west from the Rio Grande, then turned south for thirty, and headed directly west again. This motion was adopted by a vote of 32 to 14.[13]

Two days later, Rusk altered his own international boundary. He proposed keeping the same border west of the Rio Grande, but when the line reached the 111th degree of longitude, it would angle off, "to a point on the Colorado River twenty English miles below the junction of the Gila and Colorado Rivers...".[14] The impact of this change would be to reduce the amount of territory granted to the United States while also maintaining the denial of U.S. access to the Gulf of California, one of the main objectives of Santa Anna. By a vote of 30 to 13, this motion was adopted.

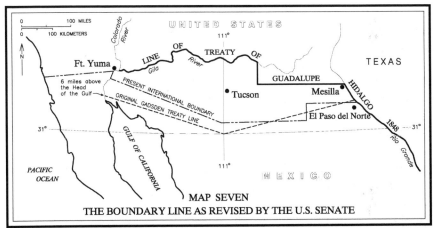

MAP SEVEN
THE BOUNDARY LINE AS REVISED BY THE U.S. SENATE

After Bufkin

Rusk then moved to eliminate from the treaty the American promise to assist in reducing Indian raids into Mexico, a motion which was unanimously passed. As a substitute, new wording was overwhelmingly adopted which simply nullified Article XI of the Treaty of Guadalupe Hidalgo.[15]

Next the Senator from Texas successfully sought to reduce the amount of $15 million to be paid for the acquired territory. He also wanted to completely eliminate the $5 million slated to be set aside for the United States assumption of claims by American citizens against Mexico, including that of the New Orleans company with original permission to build across the isthmus. The price for the property was thus set at $7 million, no mention was made of American claims, and this motion was approved by a vote of 30 to 13.[16]

The Senate then proceeded to also remove the anti-filibustering article of the proposed agreement, but it did reject an effort to strike out references to two portions of the Treaty of Guadalupe Hidalgo which simply urged negotiations prior to any future military conflicts between the two countries. After completing its work on April 12th, the legislative body adjourned, having vastly altered Gadsden's treaty.

Almost all that was left of the American Minister's efforts was the purchase of enough property to build a southern railroad, a land acquisition which would also settle the Mesilla Valley controversy. Despite that, at least it appeared that sufficient Senators supported the revisions to insure ultimate passage of the document. The changes which had been made, however, were reportedly unacceptable to either President Pierce or Santa Anna.[17]

On April 17th, an attempt to insert an amendment into the treaty which would bind the United States government to recognize and protect the rights of the second American company that had eventually secured Mexican permission to build the isthmus project was considered and narrowly defeated. Thirty-four Senators did agree, though, to make some additional minor modifications in the location of the boundary line, but they refused to increase the amount to be paid to $10 million.[18]

Having concluded its consideration of the treaty, a vote of final ratification was held. The result showed 27 of 45 senators in favor, which was three short of the number needed for approval. The Gadsden Treaty, as substantially revised, was therefore rejected by the United States Senate.

Most of the eighteen Senators in opposition were anti-slavery members from the North, while three were against it because it did not recognize the rights of the second American company to build across the isthmus. Another two opposed the treaty since they wanted even more territory to be acquired, including access to the Gulf of California.

According to the *Texas State Gazette*, defeat of the agreement was the "most disastrous blow the South in general and Texas in particular had received at the hands of Congress in fifty years."[19] In contrast, the *Public Ledger* of Philadelphia thought: "The long agony is over. The Gadsden Treaty has been rejected, and that subject, which has caused so much anxiety and trouble…is set to rest."[20] Then the newspaper added derisively, "Now that the Gadsden treaty is dead and gone, the Southern Pacific Railroad will have a hard road to travel."

The *New York Daily Times*, of course, took a different perspective on the outcome. It noted that during the Senate's debate of the treaty, President Pierce had insinuated that if it were rejected, he might use military force to seize the Mesilla Valley.[21] Instead of war, the *Times* believed Pierce would appoint someone else to try to negotiate a new agreement with Mexico, but it also suggested the defeated treaty "may be resuscitated".

That possibility was extremely important to those interested in pushing the southern transcontinental railroad route. Participants at the "Southern and Western Commercial Convention" held in Charleston, South Carolina, from April 8th to the 15th, 1854, let it be known how vital the project was to them. This group included some Senators from the South who amazingly missed the final vote on the treaty because they were attending the convention.

James Gadsden spoke to this gathering and criticized the role of northerner John Russell Bartlett in helping to instigate the Mesilla Valley controversy. He also offered the opinion that news dispatches being distributed at the meeting conveyed "the astounding fact that the most imposing and violent opposition to the treaty is, that it covers the proper ground for a railway, and requires an addition of territory, which may encourage Southern emigration and occupancy."[22] The Minister to Mexico was correct, although he didn't come right out and say so: it was mostly anti-slave Senators who were trying to defeat the treaty because they feared it would create more slave-supporting states.

Upon weighing the consequences of their action overnight, on April 18th the United States Senate agreed to reconsider the rejected agreement. The *New York Daily Times* noted that only two or three votes had to be changed to secure ratification and remarked, "The friends of the treaty have strong hopes of accomplishing this."[23]

After taking a few days off from its debate, on April 25th the Senate resumed discussion of the treaty. It once again slightly altered the boundary line which had been accepted earlier and also raised from $7 to $10 million the amount to be paid for the territory.[24] Seven million of that would be provided to Mexico immediately upon ratification of the agreement, with the balance to be given once the new boundary line had been surveyed and established on the ground.

The Senators additionally included a clause in the document which recognized the rights of the second American company to build a railroad across the isthmus. By inserting the statement: "The United States may extend its protection, as it shall judge wise, to it [the isthmus project] when it may feel sanctioned by the public or international law,"[25] the U.S. government was astonishingly offering its military assistance to a private company doing business in a foreign country.

Based on these changes, the Senate approved the treaty by a vote of 33 to 13 with most of the opposition still coming from anti-slave members. The return of Senators from the Charleston convention along with addressing the isthmus issue were the two major factors in altering the outcome. The final result showed Ward's efforts in Mexico had completely backfired. Instead of having his client covered for financial damages, their competitors were specifically offered American military protection for constructing the isthmus project.

The inclusion of the second American firm in the treaty, however, did not result in anything. The company never built a railroad across the isthmus, and in 1937 the provision was terminated by a new agreement between the United States and Mexico. As President Franklin Roosevelt said then, "This article of the Treaty of 1853, while of potential value at the time it was negotiated, has never operated and has no present-day use…".[26]

At the end of the Senate's 1854 deliberations, the entire agreement bore little resemblance to the one concluded by Gadsden. While the route for the railroad was retained and the Mesilla Valley controversy settled, jurisdiction over only 29,640 square miles of territory, or 9,000 fewer than had been agreed upon during the original negotiations, was transferred. Mexico was provided no help with Indian raids, or against American filibusters. The monetary claims arising from Indian attacks into Mexico from the United States had been dropped completely from consideration, but U.S. military protection was offered to the American company involved with the isthmus project. Finally, the total price was reduced to $10 million from the original figure of twice that amount, but at least a treaty had been approved.

The *New York Daily Tribune* offered the opinion that dropping the provision concerning Mexican financial claims was worth about $2 million. Thus they summarized, "This leaves eight millions to be paid for converting territory now free into slave territory…".[27]

The *Tribune's* rival New York newspaper, the *Daily Times*, called the final vote of passage "a very respectable majority surely for an instrument so confidently declared to be dead, used up, and so nefarious in its negotiation, object and aims."[28] The paper also pointed out, "Those here who best know Santa Anna's sentiments, express the belief that the treaty as amended by the Senate, will be far more satisfactory to him than the original instrument, because it gives us so much less territory."

President Pierce, however, was very unhappy with the revised agreement since it still contained reference to an isthmus company, and he decided not to immediately ratify it. He even considered canceling the treaty entirely in favor of new negotiations. Instead, at the urging of Senator Rusk and others, by special messenger he sent the document back to Mexico with the understanding that he would agree to it if Santa Anna did.

The *Charleston Daily Courier* said of the administration's position: "As the treaty is a very good one for the United States, it is surprising that President Pierce should object to it. For Mexico, it is not so good a treaty, but still it is thought that Santa Anna will, by his necessities, be compelled to take it."[29]

Congressional opponents of the agreement, though, were still attempting to defeat the measure. They unsuccessfully pushed to have the Senate's secret debate over the treaty made public, hoping the damning personal attacks made against Santa Anna behind closed doors would infuriate him enough to reject the revised settlement. These politicians, the *Detroit Free Press* wrote, "are moving Heaven and Earth to secure the publication of the correspondence and debates on the treaty immediately. The object is transparent...It certainly would be a vulgar and most undignified proceeding to publish these virulent assaults upon Santa Anna, to be sent out to Mexico at the same time with a treaty...".[30]

Shortly after the revised agreement was sent south, James Gadsden also returned to Mexico, greatly disappointed with the document which bore his name. In a letter to Secretary of State Marcy, he emphatically described his objections, including the loss of what he considered a natural border between the two countries. Although the reduction in the size of territory acquired did not particularly concern him, Gadsden characterized the loss of what he perceived as a physical barrier between the nations as, "A great derangement has been committed in the boundary as altered by the Senate."[31]

Gadsden's biggest complaint about the changes made in the Senate, though, concerned the role of the United States in dealing with its southern neighbor. "The substituted treaty however is most exposed to objections as reopening many of the national issues which the compact which it supersedes had settled, and in its want of equality and reciprocity in most of the provisions which are the only reliable bonds of respect for international agreements,"[32] he wrote in politically obscure language referring to Mexican concerns with Indian raids and American filibustering expeditions into its territory along with the isthmus issue. Then he continued, "The weaker party imposed on, or forced without consultation to acquiesce in conditions offensive and humiliating, will not recognize the obligations to observe or regard them when change of circumstances would authorize and justify repudiation."

Based on that viewpoint, Gadsden thought the revised treaty would actually harm the relationship between the United States and Mexico. He concluded of the document: "I feel it due on this occasion to myself, and to the character of the Government I represent, to record my dissent to the exclusion and changes made by that Honorable Body [U.S. Senate] in the provisions of a treaty under adverse and opposing influences which are well designed to impair the relations which it is the policy and interest of the United States to preserve with her nearest neighbor."[33]

Despite those misgivings, on June 6th, 1854, Gadsden formally submitted the new treaty to Mexican Foreign Relations Minister Bonilla. He added, moreover, that any attempt by Mexico to further modify the agreement would be rejected since the United States Senate would never approve the changes. Thus, he requested Bonilla to respond as quickly as possible.

Privately, regardless of the *New York Daily Times* earlier prediction that they would support the revised text since it meant the loss of less land, the Mexicans were outraged by the changes made to the treaty. Gadsden told Marcy that both Santa Anna and Bonilla "expressed their unqualified dissent to an instrument which was deficient in all the higher binding requisites of international agreements, which was not reciprocal but onerous and offensive to the weaker party in all its provisions, which did not adjust the issues between the two Republics so as to promise harmony of relations in the future, which would reopen many of a most threatening character…".[34]

The most objectionable provision to the Mexicans, Gadsden wrote, was the one in the amended treaty which indicated U.S. military assistance would be provided to the isthmus company if problems should arise. To that and other complaints, he didn't have a reply. "While it was difficult to rebut, on my part, all these acknowledged and perplexing truths," Gadsden wrote the Secretary of State, "I felt deprived of both the will or ability to urge any consideration in favor" of the agreement.[35] In the end, the American who had negotiated the original treaty was personally hoping the Mexicans might reject the revised document.

That, though, didn't happen. To remain in power, Santa Anna needed money as quickly as possible. A revolt against his government had already begun, and a new war with the United States could occur if the treaty were rejected. The Mexican president, therefore, had no real choice. He had to accept the agreement and did so in a message sent to President Pierce on June 20th.

The anti-slave forces in the United States along with those who opposed a southern transcontinental rail line, however, had one last chance to defeat the treaty. On June 21st, the House of Representatives received a message from President Pierce requesting the allocation of funds needed to fulfill the terms of the agreement. Congressmen hoping to scuttle the deal took this final opportunity to try and do so.

Thomas Hart Benton of Missouri, the leading advocate for a St. Louis to San Francisco railroad route, had stepped down from his Senate seat to take one in the House, and led the opposition in a debate on the 28th. Focusing on the Pierce administration's correspondence concerning the treaty, Benton indicated these incriminating documents, including the instructions given to Ward and what he had done with them, had been supplied to the Senate and kept secret by them. They were not provided to the House, however, under a long-standing separation of powers doctrine.

Benton moved to insert a clause in the required funding measure which read: "No part of the sum herein appropriated shall be drawn from the Treasury until the President shall first have communicated to this House [of Representatives] all the correspondence, instructions, etc., connected with the negotiation of the treaty."[36] His motives for this motion were obvious. He hoped the time needed to deliver these documents would be long enough, the legality of his action uncertain enough, and the contents of the secret messages upsetting enough, that the tide toward ratification could be reversed.

A Representative from Mississippi pointed out that the correspondence Benton sought had nothing to do with the document actually adopted by the Senate. "The treaty against which you have all argued, the President's treaty, has been repudiated and rejected; the treaty the House is called upon to consider, is a treaty made by ourselves, made by our Senate."[37]

A member of the House from Ohio, though, remarked, "It is said in the newspapers throughout the country, that some of the correspondence in reference to this treaty is utterly derogatory, and disgraceful to the United States."[38] He called for another round of negotiations to be conducted in a fair and honorable fashion.

The *Chicago Daily Tribune* considered this lively public debate the most interesting of the entire legislative session.[39] In the end, Benton's amendment was defeated and the House adopted the required appropriation by a vote of 103 to 62.

President Pierce ratified the treaty on June 29th, 1854, and the next day proclaimed it to be the law of the land. On July 1st, a check for $7 million was presented in Washington, D.C. to a representative of the Mexican government, with $3 million more to come later.

The Gadsden Treaty between the U.S. and Mexico was thus finally concluded. Even though scorned by its namesake, opposed by the Presidents of both countries, and loudly criticized for costing too much for too little barren land, the deal was done. The United States would have the territory it needed to build a southern transcontinental rail line.

CHAPTER EIGHT

"The most feasible if not the only practicable route for a railway to the Pacific"

After the ratification of the treaty which carried his name, but not his endorsement, James Gadsden remained in Mexico as American Minister. Among those living with him was his teenage nephew Philip, whose long letters home provide a glimpse of their lives, the household, and the nation in 1854 and 1855.

Gadsden was described by his nephew as a man who, though occasionally ill, would daily take long morning walks whenever he could with his two Newfoundland dogs or go on horseback rides into the countryside around Mexico City. He sometimes wrote poetry but also "had a six shooter buckled to his waist under his coat, it being best to be prepared for any emergency."[1] The greatest misfortune in his life, Gadsden told Philip, was being educated outside his home state of South Carolina.

On July 4th, 1854, the teenager noted: "Most of the morning both English and American gentlemen called, the latter to pay their respects. They were invited to drink in celebration of the day."[2] Later in the year, however, despite everyone in the city being ordered to do so by Santa Anna's government, the American Minister refused to illuminate his home in honor of the Feast Day of the Virgin of Guadalupe because he would not celebrate an "idol".

The house the Gadsden family occupied was a brick and stone structure with a large gate that was locked with iron bolts and chains every night at nine. The residence contained several bedrooms, a sitting room, and a chandeliered parlor which was "handsomely furnished, the carpet and curtains brought from Charleston, [and] also a fine pianoforte."[3] The home additionally had two small rooms which the senior Gadsden and his secretary used as offices for official diplomatic business.

Running water was piped from the street into tanks located around the house, and Philip thought the water of Mexico City "beautifully clear and good to drink," but that opinion didn't convince the young man to bathe very often. As he wrote his mother late in the year: "I am now going to take a warm bath, a thing very necessary in this climate. I take one every week, but ought to take it twice."[4]

His uncle gave the teenager several jobs, including serving as his bookkeeper, being responsible for buying groceries for the household, and copying written material by hand. Nevertheless, Philip had ample time to explore his surroundings and he discovered a country with many beggars and thieves and a capital city where "the suburbs are filthy and the houses low and built of sun burnt bricks, but the principal streets are well paved and lined with handsome stone buildings."[5]

Since he was in charge of obtaining food items, Philip Gadsden took special note of the fruits and vegetables which were available in the markets. He also commented on the local cuisine, exclaiming: "In one dish would be different meats, fruits, vegetables, and above all green peppers of different kinds cooked together. Hot enough to make ones palate jump out of his mouth."[6]

Festivals and pageants were a major part of life in Mexico City at the time, along with public executions of criminals. Early in his stay Philip mentioned that three men were being garroted for robbery and a month later another execution of two men who had robbed a church took place. The queasy teenager wrote of the spectacle: "On the square were a great number of horse and foot soldiers [and] also hundreds of people, both male and female. The Mexicans, judging from what I saw this morning, are fond of witnessing such scenes."[7]

On a more pleasant note, the teenager was able to witness several national and religious celebrations and it was the shrine dedicated to the Virgin at Guadalupe outside Mexico City which perhaps made the greatest impression on the young man. After first visiting it in August he noted: "The church was very handsome, especially the interior which had much silver about it and [was] lit with handsome chandeliers. We heard fine music. There were three priests dressed very handsomely and two boys who attended on them, perhaps their sons."[8]

The young Episcopalian could be excused his ignorance of Catholic practices and altar boys, once having concluded of the faith, "The Roman Church is the true Church, but the Church in error."[9] He had also written from Mexico, "The Church in this country is immensely wealthy, the salary of the Archbishop alone is 130,000 dollars."[10]

On the feast day of the Virgin of Guadalupe in December of 1854, Philip returned to the shrine and he bought his mother a holy card depicting the nation's patron saint. "A copy of her picture is hung in every dwelling in Mexico," he wrote, "and prayers are offered up to her as if she was a God."[11]

The previous summer, Philip had accompanied his uncle James to Guadalupe for a bishop's consecration ceremony in which the nation's President was participating. After the event was over the young man observed: "Mr. Santa Anna rode home in a very fine coach. In front and behind it were officers on horseback dressed very handsomely, and behind these officers were a great number of lancers."[12]

Throughout his letters of 1854 and 1855, Philip Gadsden openly expressed his views on the Mexican dictator, often in very unflattering terms which may have reflected his uncle's perception of the man. In a message sent to Jefferson Davis just after the treaty had been approved, the American Minister offered his own opinion of Santa Anna. "If he can command a revenue he may have a brief triumph," Gadsden wrote. "But the ignorance of himself and cabinet in not yielding to the spirit and progress of the age…will prove the downfall of centrality and tyrannical exactions."[13] Based on that view, he predicted of the Mexican President's future: "So you may rest satisfied of one fact, that the political elements are convulsed, and an explosion will upset centralization and restore the federation, and with success expose Santa Anna to another successful retreat into exile…".

Gadsden's nephew Philip elaborated on some of the causes of this pending political storm. In July of 1854 he wrote, "Santa Anna has made a decree which is, 'if anyone speaks against the government he shall be imprisoned two months, and anyone who hears another speak against the government and does not inform against him shall be fined 200 dollars'."[14]

By the end of the year Philip was saying: "Today has been appointed by Santa Anna for the election to see whether the people wish him to be president or not. It is a mere farce, and will only lead to give him more power. The military were out and I have no doubt but that all who vote will do so for him."[15] In another letter, Philip indicated his forecast had been incorrect. One man, he said, had actually voted against Santa Anna, but the next day he and his family were ordered to leave Mexico City.[16]

In June of 1855, the young man was expressing his hope for political change in very strong terms, along with his personal dislike for the dictator and his policies. "I am in a country that has been off and on for the last thirty years convulsed by civil wars," he wrote, "and soon within the gates of this beautiful capital is expected to be seen another revolution. My sincere wish is that it may be a revolution in every sense of the word."[17]

That was a hopeful prediction in those turbulent times. On August 8th of 1855, Santa Anna was forced from office once again, and some historians maintain his approval of the Gadsden Treaty was one of the causes of his regime's demise.[18] After the humiliation of the Mexican-American War and the Treaty of

Guadalupe Hidalgo, the further loss of national pride resulting from the new agreement with the United States reduced Santa Anna's popularity while simultaneously strengthening the position of his opponents. In addition, almost all of the money secured through the treaty had been spent within a few months of its receipt, including a payment of $700,000 to Santa Anna himself. Thus, it was only a matter of time before the dictator would be driven from power.

Nevertheless, just before he once more went into exile, the Mexican leader had amazingly made one last attempt to obtain additional funds from the United States. In hopes of raising some quick cash, he offered to sell even more territory to his country's northern neighbor. James Gadsden, however, wasn't interested in dealing with Santa Anna and his associates, whom he despised, and who were soon to be replaced anyway. He wrote Secretary of State Marcy, "I cannot reconcile it to my judgment to negotiate with such a temporary oligarchy of plunderers."[19]

While the Gadsden Treaty may have been contributing to a change of leadership in Mexico, it also helped to intensify the demand of American southerners for the first transcontinental railroad to run along the 32nd parallel route. At a "Southern Commercial Convention" held in New Orleans in January of 1855, the delegates considered a number of resolutions in support of this line. One speaker labeled the project to be built westward from slave-holding states, "not only important to those States, but indispensable to their welfare and prosperity, and even to their continued existence as equal and independent members of the [federal] confederacy."[20]

The delegates, however, were informed that time was not on their side in securing the transcontinental rail line. The free states of Minnesota, Oregon, and others were eventually to be added to the union, and once that happened, the political balance in Washington would be tipped in favor of the North. "Then you will see a railroad built to the Pacific Ocean by the votes of these men," a speaker predicted, "who have no constitutional scruples to stand in the way. Then you will see the government of the United States assisting in this great national work, and building the road, with national means, from a point north of St. Louis."[21] To counter that possibility, those at the convention were urged to consider that southerners, and Southern states, construct the 32nd parallel railroad themselves.

That sort of sectional interference with the project was, of course, what the transcontinental railroad surveys ordered earlier by Secretary of War Jefferson Davis had been intended to avoid. By the end of 1854 all the reports had been compiled and the findings showed some of the potential routes to be possible. Because of its topography, though, Whitney's far northern line was considered by many to be too expensive to build. The same conclusion was quickly reached about Thomas Hart Benton's favorite, the St. Louis to San Francisco route via the

38th parallel. A possible option which started farther north of there, from near Council Bluffs, Iowa, was found to be favorable, however. So too were both the 35th and 32nd degree alternatives.[22]

In hopes of locating an even better route through the newly acquired territory of the Gadsden Purchase, Lt. John G. Parke had returned to the area in the spring of 1855. He looked for a path which would follow the Gila River all the way east from the Colorado to beyond the San Pedro River, then turn south to the previously established line.[23] He found this to be possible if the small perennial stream "Rio Arivaypa," were traced from the Gila back to the traditional railroad right-of-way along Philip St. George Cooke's desert cutoff. Parke mapped this potential concept and, along with other minor modifications to earlier findings, labeled it his "Proposed Railroad Route".[24]

If this line were to be adopted, however, it would result in the tracks not going anywhere near the village of Tucson. Despite that, this revised 32nd parallel possibility was described by William Emory as one which "affords water in abundance, and traverses valleys capable of continuous settlement."[25]

On the other hand, a different survey effort had discovered a serious problem with the western end of the southern railroad route. It was intended to reach the west coast at San Diego, but a practical path through the mountains east of that community couldn't be located. The result was that the line from the Colorado River would have to swing farther north to get to the Pacific Ocean, thus lengthening its distance considerably. The affect of this change could mean this route's short mileage to the coast, which had always been one of its major advantages, might be diminished.

That was just one factor, however, which would be taken into consideration by Jefferson Davis when the results of all the transcontinental railroad surveys were analyzed. To help him complete this task, Davis had originally selected Major Emory. This appointment, though, was immediately criticized by Thomas Hart Benton. The elected official from Missouri objected to Emory's previous support of the southern route, his family ties with the owner of the Texas Western Railroad Company, and his investment in shares of the proposed town of New San Diego.[26]

Davis was also a personal friend of Emory, and it was toward the Secretary of War that most opponents of the 32nd parallel route focused their antagonisms. Some people saw the components of a conspiracy headed by Davis to ensure that the tracks would be laid to benefit the South. The appointment of South Carolina railroad man Gadsden to negotiate a treaty with Mexico, the contents of the agreement, and the procedures proposed to analyze the national railroad survey results all cast doubt on Davis's objectivity in reviewing the various cross-country alternatives.

The Library of Congress

JEFFERSON DAVIS

In addition to the economic benefits the transcontinental project could provide to his part of the country, Davis had another reason for backing the southern route. He wondered why slavery, or "associated labor" as he referred to it, had not taken hold in California. Concluding it was due to a lack of easy access westward from the South, he wrote: "If we had a good railroad and other roads making it convenient to go through Texas into New Mexico, and through New Mexico into southern California, our people with their servants, their horses and their cows would gradually pass westward over fertile lands into mining districts, and in the latter, especially, the advantage of their associated labor would impress itself upon others about them and the prejudice which now shuts us out of that country would yield to the persuasion of personal interest."[27]

In spite of the perception by many that Secretary of War Davis could not be impartial in his consideration of the national railroad surveys, he proceeded to have them analyzed anyway. Emory, however, was removed from overseeing that effort. Davis received the conclusions of this review in February of 1855, and it determined that all the routes but one had merit. The lone exception, not surprisingly, was the option Benton supported west from St. Louis.

After considering this comparative analysis, the Secretary relied on several factors in making his final recommendation. These issues included such things as the total estimated cost of implementing each alternative route, the ready availability of needed materials, development potential of the surrounding territory, and the weather. He downgraded the far northern route because he felt snow could adversely impact it while also pointing to the engineering difficulties which would be experienced along the line proposed to be built west from Council Bluffs, Iowa. An exorbitant cost estimate, probably too high by some accounts, reduced the prospects for the 35th parallel line.

Thus it was the 32nd degree route which emerged as Davis's clear favorite. He minimized problems with a lack of lumber and water along the way, as well as the difficulty in reaching San Diego. He also overlooked the potential for political compromise between North and South which may have been possible with the more centrally located 35th degree option. In the end his conclusion was simply that "the route of the thirty-second parallel is, of those surveyed, 'the most practicable and economical route for a railroad from the Mississippi River to the Pacific Ocean'."[28]

That recommendation was, of course, praised by the supporters of the southern proposal. Those favoring other routes and wanting the railroad for their own part of the country weren't swayed, however, and the handling of the surveys by Davis did nothing to change their minds. Instead of settling the railroad route controversy, his recommendation only helped intensify it. The Secretary's apparent bias in favor of the South, combined with the intransigence of almost everyone involved with the issue, meant the national deadlock over the route of a transcontinental railroad would continue into a second decade.

While this attempt at a rational approach to federal decision-making proved fruitless, another survey effort did have results. After being relieved of his duties as assistant to Secretary of War Davis, Major Emory was appointed to oversee the delineation of the new boundary line between the United States and Mexico as defined by the Gadsden Treaty. This project was successfully completed by the end of 1855, and the Major was proud that it cost only $104,000, much less than the total amount spent for Bartlett's wanderings across the same territory a few years earlier.

Emory's lengthy report on this work was published in 1857 and provides another view of the newest part of the United States. In a chapter entitled, "Sketch of Territory Acquired by Treaty of December 30, 1853," he describes the special topographical features at the southern end of the Rocky Mountain chain which made this land so important for railroad building. "The mountains which transverse this territory run mostly in the same general direction...," he wrote, "so that a traveler passing from the Rio [Grande] to the Pima villages may, by deflecting slightly from a straight line, pass most of the way over a mesa, the different planes of which vary but slightly in elevation, and are usually from 3,000 to 4,000 feet above the sea."[29]

Based on this characteristic of the region's desert terrain, Emory concluded, "It is that peculiarity which gives this territory a leading interest as affording a practicable passage for a national railway to the Pacific...".[30] Referring to the recently completed national railroad surveys and their analysis, Emory agreed with the conclusion of Secretary Davis about the preferred line. He also thought the Gadsden Treaty had "secured what the surveys made under the orders of the War Department demonstrate to be the most feasible if not the only practicable route for a railway to the Pacific."[31]

At the time of the 1854 property transfer from Mexico, only a handful of communities existed within the purchased territory. These the Major listed as: "The Mesilla Valley settlement, containing about fifteen hundred inhabitants of the mixed Spanish and Indian races, all engaged in the pursuit of agriculture. At Tucson there is a settlement consisting of about seventy families, engaged in the same way. South of Tucson there is a small settlement at San Xavier of semi-civilized Indians, called [Tohono O'odham]; and further on, at Tumacacori, a small settlement of Germans."[32]

As he had done previously in 1846, Emory again gave special attention to the Indians living along the Gila River. He wrote of them: "The most considerable and interesting settlement in the new territory is composed of a confederacy of semi-civilized Indians, the Pimas and Coco Maricopas. Their population is variously estimated at from five to ten thousand."[33]

A more detailed description than Emory's of the actual 1855 boundary surveying experience was provided by Lieutenant Nathaniel Michler in his report on
the portion of the work he oversaw. He was responsible for the line from where it
angled northwest at the 111th degree of longitude all the way to the Colorado
River.

Upon arriving at the Colorado in late December of 1854, the Lieutenant
noted that boat traffic on the river from the Gulf of California was expected to
supply goods to those further upstream. That possibility, he said, had brought
potential investors to the land near the junction of the Colorado and Gila rivers.
"A city on paper, bearing the name of 'Colorado City,' has already been surveyed,"
he wrote, "the streets and blocks marked out, and many of them sold. It is situated on the left bank, opposite Fort Yuma."[34]

East from this riverfront property, which would later become the village of
Yuma, the land along the new border quickly became a vast empty wasteland
located under a usually clear and hot desert sky. Because of delays, much of the
survey work would be performed in the spring and summer heat during 1855,
and that left a lasting impression. "Imagination cannot picture a more dreary,
sterile country..." Michler commented. "The burnt lime-like appearance of the
soil is ever before you; the very stones look like the scoria of a furnace; there is no
grass, and but a sickly vegetation, more unpleasant to the sight than the barren
earth itself...".[35]

Although not immediately apparent, the territory did have its share of residents, even if the summertime temperature reached 120 degrees. Michler
observed the lizards, snakes, and Gila monsters of the locale and concluded,
"When you lie down on your blankets, stretched on the ground, you know not
what strange bedfellow you may have when you awake in the morning."[36]

Portions of the new border were very difficult to delineate because of the
rough terrain, but at least the weather cooperated and summer rains fell which
supplied the survey crew with water and provided moisture for the vegetation. In
the midst of this enormous desert, Michler commented on the rumored mineral
wealth in the area labeled "ajo" earlier by Peter Brady while he was a member of
A.B. Gray's reconnaissance party for the Texas Western Railroad Company.
Michler wrote that the region was "represented to be rich in copper, gold and
silver," but he thought the lack of water combined with the long distance to any
transportation system would make mining ventures in the region both futile and
unprofitable.

East of the spot called "ajo", the Lieutenant remarked on the settlements at
Tubac and Tumacacori which were located near the Santa Cruz River some distance south of Tucson. "Tubac is a deserted village," he wrote. "The wild Apache
lords it over this region, and the timid husbandman dare not return to his home.

The mission at Tumacacori, another fine structure of the mother church, stands, too, in the midst of rich fields; but fear prevents its habitation, save by two or three Germans, who have wandered from their distant fatherland to this out of the way country."[37]

Despite the danger, some American miners and speculators had also begun to make their way into the new United States territory. Among them was Charles Poston, who initially came to the region shortly before final ratification of the Gadsden Treaty and was later one of those involved with founding "Colorado City" along the river.

Poston considered the land purchase concluded under the treaty to be disappointing because it did not provide the U.S. with a port on the Gulf of California. He mistakenly wrote years later, "A larger territory could have been secured as easily, but the American Minister had only one idea, and that was to secure 'a pass' for a Southern Pacific Railroad from the Mississippi River to the Pacific Ocean."[38] In more rhythmical language, as part of a book-length poem entitled "Apache-Land," Poston would pen whimsically of the new territory, the treaty, and the Mexican dictator who had lost half his left leg in battle:

> We bought this land from Santa Anna
> When he sold out under the hammer.
> The old, one-legged Peter Funk!
> Ten millions must have made him drunk.
> The treaty made with old Gadsden
> Was all very well, as things went then.[39]

Among the characteristics which attracted Poston to the region was, "That the country north of Sonora, called in the Spanish history "Arizunea" (rocky country) was full of minerals...".[40] The mineral wealth of the area was also of interest to Major Emory. While he acknowledged that after the ratification of the Gadsden Treaty prospectors had flooded into the territory in search of riches, he agreed with Lt. Michler that there were several reasons why these resources could not be quickly exploited. One was the scarcity of water, another the lack of transportation facilities, and the third was the threat from hostile Indians.

Not all the natives were enemies of the outsiders, though, as Lt. Michler wrote of the Tohono O'odham people living near Tucson. "This tribe is comparatively well off in worldly goods," he said, "they plant and grow corn and wheat, and possess cattle, and many fine horses...They appear to be a good, quiet, and inoffensive tribe."[41]

In his own report of the survey work, Major Emory recalled an encounter with the Pima and Maricopa Indians who lived near the Gila River. Wanting to know how the transfer in jurisdiction from Mexico to the United States would impact them, they sent a delegation of officials over one hundred miles south to confer with the boundary surveyor while he was inspecting the new international border.

Also affected by the change in the border, but residing at the eastern end of the new U.S. territory, the former Mexican citizens of the village of Mesilla accepted the revision without incident. The Stars and Stripes were raised over the town in November of 1854, but it wouldn't be until 1856 that United States soldiers were sent to the newly acquired territory around Tucson, sometimes referred to as "Gadsdonia" by its American residents. The new troops replaced the Mexican military which was in the process of leaving. Before the arrival of U.S. soldiers, a San Francisco newspaper correspondent who was visiting Tucson and was frustrated by the long delay in sending men to protect the area, posed the question: "Why in the world is the Government about to leave the settlement here to the mercy of the most barbarous savages—the most villainous set of human beings? How could they suffer our Southern emigrants to be murdered and plundered without making an attempt to chastise the perpetrators of these crimes…"?[42]

When the American soldiers eventually did arrive, instead of being stationed at Tucson, for a short time they were located south of there near the new Mexican border. In June of 1857, the troops relocated to Fort Buchanan which was built several miles north of the international line. The officer in charge thought it more important to protect the miners and ranchers residing near the border than the residents of Tucson. Of the impact of his decision on this latter group, he said, "The only ones there to suffer from choosing a site elsewhere were the whiskey peddlers and those who hoped to profit from the dissipation of the soldiers."[43]

Prior to that time, Mexican troops had departed Tucson for the last time and urged the local population of a few hundred "to accompany them on their exit, as it would be hazardous to remain among the gringos."[44] Instead, most of the people chose to stay in the village and become residents of the United States.

After the Mexican soldiers left, about one dozen Anglo citizens of the community decided to formally raise the American flag on a pole made of mesquite wood. Thus, in March of 1856, this portion of the Gadsden Purchase unofficially became part of the United States. Within a short period, these people would also begin calling for their own territorial status separate from New Mexico, under whose jurisdiction they then fell.

A few months later, James Gadsden would be recalled from his post as United States Minister. He had made enemies with both the new Mexican government as well as among American speculators in Mexico, and they were finally able to persuade the Pierce administration to remove him. He left his position in

October of 1856, having achieved an agreement between the United States and Mexico which accomplished one major objective: the peaceful acquisition of the route necessary to build a southern transcontinental railroad line.

That agreement had also brought into the United States a mostly desolate desert territory. The land was rich in minerals and agricultural possibilities, but subject to savage battles between some native Indians and incoming settlers. It would be these resources and conflicts, and not the railroad, which would at first characterize the region.

On the other hand, the treaty had done nothing for the Mexican people, except perhaps to be one of the causes of Santa Anna's final downfall. Conversely, the money paid by the United States to the Mexican leader had enabled him to stay in power for a few more months.

In the end, the Gadsden Treaty failed to achieve most of its initial goals. Following the bitterness caused by the Mexican-American War, the agreement had been intended to smooth the relationship between the two countries, but the reality was that because of changes made by the United States Senate, the treaty had, to a large degree, done just the opposite.

Chapter Nine

"The most magnificent project ever conceived"

From Mexico, James Gadsden returned to South Carolina, where in 1858 he was visited on his rice plantation, known as Pimlico, by a correspondent for the *Illustrated London News*. The purpose of the interview was to allow Gadsden to demonstrate how kind and benevolent he and other southerners were to their slaves. As the English writer put it concerning a practice he termed nauseating and hateful: "The slaveowners actually think they have done something in the vindication of slavery when they have proved, as they easily can, that they do not scourge, disfigure, maim, starve, or kill their negroes, but that, on the contrary, they feed them well, clothe them well, provide them with good medical attendance for the ills of the flesh, and spiritual consolations for the doubts and distresses of the soul."[1]

The former American Minister's estate was twenty-seven miles from Charleston and Gadsden had between 200 and 300 slaves on the property, most of whom worked in the rice paddies while children up to age fourteen spent the day in the slaves' housing village. On Sunday all the black people could attend a religious service, but it was "performed by a missionary allowed to have access to the slaves upon condition of not preaching freedom to them…".[2]

Gadsden had a mansion at Pimlico but lived there only occasionally since he preferred a cooler and less humid climate. While at the plantation, according to the article, he and his guests would dine on fish, game, and turtle. For refreshments they had their choice of Indian ale, claret, or other beverages.

As Gadsden showed the newspaper writer around his property, they met an elderly slave, and his master told him the Englishman had come to take him back to Africa. The black man protested vehemently and was relieved to learn it was only a joke.

At the end of his article the author said of the tour, "On this plantation I have no doubt from what I saw that the slaves are kindly treated…But I do not wish to depict this one as a sample of all, but confine myself to a simple narrative of what I saw."[3] Despite his experience with Gadsden, the Englishman concluded: "Slavery has many aspects, and upon some future occasion I may be enabled to lay before your readers some other facts, less patent, which may throw light upon its operation not only upon the fortunes and character of the white men who hold them in bondage, but upon the future destinies of the United States of America."

That future destiny was, of course, the catastrophic Civil War, which James Gadsden would not live to see. On the day after Christmas, 1858, he died at the age of 70. In a short obituary, the *New York Times* wrote: "General Gadsden's name is chiefly associated with the Treaty executed in 1854, between Mexico and the United States. That instrument is generally known as the 'Gadsden Treaty'."[4]

Gadsden had worked much of his life to provide the foundation for a southern transcontinental railroad in order to help the economy of his state in particular and of the South in general. If the tracks were laid through Texas and the New Mexico territory all the way to the California coast, they would also enable slavery to be more easily exported to the western United States. Gadsden understood the national importance of the project and had been instrumental in obtaining the land physically required to implement it. However, the political logjam that existed in the nation and in the Congress over which of the various cross-country routes to select would continue even though the Gadsden Purchase had opened up an apparently short and inexpensive option which avoided mountains in getting to the Pacific Ocean.

The South Carolina railway man had hoped the southern alternative would be selected, but he certainly wasn't alone in advocating for a transcontinental line to be built. A few years before Gadsden's death, a new crusader emerged upon the railroad scene, pushing a specific central path across the nation which he considered the most beneficial. Not since Asa Whitney had such an ardent advocate of one route appeared, but civil engineer Theodore Judah was a man who was committed to his beliefs about the cross-country railroad. Calling it "the most magnificent project ever conceived," this New Yorker had moved to California in 1854 and thought the transcontinental tracks would be a means "to peace and future prosperity. An iron bond for the perpetuation of the Union and independence which we now enjoy."[5]

Judah attributed the national deadlock over which route to select in part to the concept of using public revenues to finance the project. He rejected that notion outright and called instead for private capital to pay for construction of the line after an adequate survey of the proposed route had been completed. Believing that earlier reconnaissance work had been insufficient, he insisted that an effort headed by a competent engineer was needed, one which would precisely measure the route with a chain and also determine its elevation changes.

Outlining his proposal to Congress in an 1857 report entitled, "A Practical Plan for Building the Pacific Railroad," Judah pushed for implementing his type of detailed survey to find out how much it would actually cost to lay tracks from St. Louis to San Francisco. With this data, and a map showing the topographical profile of the line, he thought private investors would have the information needed to judge the economic feasibility of the project. This was the only reasonable course, Judah believed, since the public considered government involvement with the effort suspect. "They have little confidence in their ability to carry it out economically," he wrote of the country's view of Washington politicians, "or to protect themselves and the treasury from the rapacious clutches of the hungry speculators who would swarm round them like vultures round a dead carcass."[6]

Problems with snow and hostile Indians could arise along his proposed line, Judah acknowledged, but the former was not a new obstacle and the latter would "soon find that the wild horse of the prairie is no match for the iron horse of civilization."[7] In the end he concluded, construction of this railroad would enable passengers and freight to get from St. Louis to San Francisco in three days time, an average of almost 28 m.p.h. for the 2,000 mile journey.

Judah's frustration with the political bickering over the final selection of a cross-country route was understandable. After the completion of the Gadsden Purchase in 1854, President Pierce lost interest in the transcontinental project. Despite that, Secretary of War Jefferson Davis tried to keep the issue alive by arguing in favor of the military necessity of the railroad to protect the nation west of the Mississippi River but Congress still could not agree on any route to endorse.

Support for a transcontinental railroad project turned out to be a minor issue in the Presidential race of 1856. The Republican Party favored building the "most central and practicable route" to the Pacific, while the platform of Democratic nominee James Buchanan did not specify a location for the tracks. After he won the election over John C. Frémont, however, Buchanan indicated a preference for the 32nd parallel route through the territory of the Gadsden Purchase.[8]

This Presidential support for the southern option was further enhanced by the 1858 initiation of a federally subsidized overland mail route from St. Louis and Memphis to California. Selected by the Postmaster General, two trails from the east merged at Little Rock, Arkansas, and then went on to El Paso, Fort Yuma, Los Angeles and San Francisco. Operated by John Butterfield, the stage line took up to twenty-five days to reach its destination and the stops along the way which were established to supply essentials to the mail-carrying carriages would soon become tiny outposts of America in the remote western territory.

Despite the topographical and climatic advantages of this southern border route for transporting the mail, Congress continued to argue over which of the options to select for a transcontinental railroad. Northern interests pushed for a central line to San Francisco, pointing out the need for goods to reach the settlements which were being founded by Mormons in Utah. After the discovery of silver in Nevada in the late 1850s, they also stressed the requirements of miners rushing there. Southerners, however, thought if the central line were adopted, they would be taxed to pay for a project which would not aid them in any way. Some attempt was made to gain votes for two transcontinental routes, but this and all other railroad-related efforts ultimately failed.

Disregarding the long-standing political stalemate, Jefferson Davis did not give up on his goal of implementing a southern cross-country railroad. After serving as Secretary of War under Pierce, he returned to the Senate to represent Mississippi. In January of 1859, he proposed that the federal government solicit proposals for constructing a railroad to the Pacific Ocean.[9] While not designating either a specific route or terminal points for the project, Davis was confident that the 32nd parallel option would be chosen under his legislation. By restricting the amount of subsidy to $10 million, his proposition would favor the cheapest transcontinental alternative, which he and many others assumed to be the southern route.

Davis's proposal to get the project moving, along with all other Congressional ideas for implementing a transcontinental railroad, went nowhere. Northern Republicans controlled the House of Representatives and, fearing an expansion of slavery, they were not going to support a southern line, or even two cross-country routes. The Democratic-dominated Senate, meanwhile, was not inclined to solely endorse a central path. Thus, the logjam continued.

By this time, the never-ending series of unsuccessful legislative proposals to provide federal assistance to build a railroad from the Mississippi River to the Pacific Ocean had stretched on for almost fifteen years. It led one publication to write in exasperation of the men in Congress and their consideration of the issue, "They consequently delude themselves and their constituents with the most nonsensical propositions, which do very well for the time, because their absurdity cannot immediately be demonstrated."[10]

In California, however, steps were being taken to actually do some work as part of a grand scheme to connect the country together by rail. After establishing himself around Sacramento as a reliable railroad engineer who could implement projects, Theodore Judah located a route through the Sierra Nevada range which would allow tracks to be installed. Judah insisted the seemingly impenetrable mountains which rose up like a solid 7,000-foot high wall east of the state capital could be breached by a railroad.

Judah, however, was an engineer, not a businessman, and he needed financial backing for the construction project which could only begin after a detailed survey of his proposed 115-mile mountainous route had been completed. In order to raise the tens of thousands of dollars required to pay for that effort, Judah approached the money men of San Francisco, but was rebuffed. To describe his proposal, he also called a meeting in Sacramento, which was attended by only a small group of local merchants. From these, eventually four risk-taking entrepreneurs would emerge to provide support for Judah's idea: Charles Crocker, Mark Hopkins, Collis Huntington, and Leland Stanford.

Crocker was a native of New York state who went west in 1850 at the age of twenty-eight. He had dropped out of school when twelve years old to sell newspapers, a business the youngster ran successfully. He then worked in an iron-forge, where in his own words he had been "very saving and economical," before leading a small group of others to California. After laboring a short time as a miner, this large, burly man opened a store with one of his brothers and eventually moved to Sacramento to begin a dry-goods business. When this store burned down in 1852, he rebuilt and by 1860 was out of debt and prospering.[11]

Mark Hopkins was nine years older than Crocker and also originally from New York state. He was a thin, soft-spoken man who moved to California in 1849 to become a miner, but ended up in the hardware business selling merchandise to miners. Hopkins had an accountant's mind, was expert at keeping figures straight, and was thoughtful in his decision-making.

His partner in the Sacramento store in 1860 was 39-year old Collis Huntington from Connecticut. This heavy-set man had sailed for California the same year Hopkins went overland to the coast, and along the way Huntington got stuck in Panama for three months. While there, he more than tripled his net worth by buying and reselling merchandise. A driven businessman, Huntington spent one miserable morning working in the gold fields of California before turning to the retail trade as an occupation.

Three years younger than Huntington, New Yorker Leland Stanford arrived in California in 1852 after working as a lawyer in Wisconsin. At first a merchant in a small mining town, by 1855 he had moved to Sacramento to run a grocery store opened by his brothers. Stanford, a slow, long-winded man, ran unsuccessfully for state treasurer in 1857 and two years later failed in his bid to become governor of California. His personal wealth by that time, however, was substantial since he had done very well as an investor in a local mine.

The Library of Congress

COLLIS HUNTINGTON

It was these four businessmen who in 1860 initially decided to back Judah's survey of a proposed railroad route through the steep mountains northeast of Sacramento. They would incorporate as the Central Pacific Railroad Company of California the following year, and Crocker later remembered of the four, "We none of us knew anything about railroad building, but at the same time were enterprising men, and anxious to have a road built, and have it come to Sacramento, having our property and interests there."[12]

Besides each being a successful retailer, their political affiliation also bound the four men together. All were Republicans in a Democratic state, and in addition to Stanford, both Hopkins and Crocker had participated in local politics. The two had served together on the Sacramento City Council in 1855 where they shared a similar philosophy, and later Crocker would run successfully for the state legislature. Years afterward he recalled of his campaign for that office: "When we were canvassing the County, I made some very radical speeches, and some in localities where the people were mostly in sympathy with the South. I made straight-out anti-slavery speeches…".[13]

It was slavery and secession, not the proposal to build a transcontinental railroad, on which the 1860 Presidential election hinged. Nevertheless, the issue of the cross-country project was mentioned by the candidates. The two Democratic nominees both supported the general idea without endorsing a specific route, while the Republican platform adopted in Chicago, a convention Leland Stanford attended as a delegate from California, stated: "That a railroad to the Pacific Ocean is imperatively demanded by the interests of the whole country; that the federal government ought to render immediate and efficient aid in its construction…".[14]

Abraham Lincoln's victory in November was followed by one final attempt to settle the railroad issue in Congress before the new President took office and the country split itself apart. On December 18th, 1860, in a futile, last-minute effort at decision-making, the House of Representatives cast its earlier disagreements aside and adopted a bill which called for both central and southern roads to be built. Concurrently, though, James Gadsden's home state of South Carolina was seceding. By the time the proposed railroad measure was considered by the Senate, five more southern states had dropped out of the union, and thus the last hope for a railroad compromise was lost. The dreams of southerners for the first transcontinental line to connect their region with California had finally been defeated by their own departure from the nation.

The Civil War divided not only the country, but also the loyalties of those who had been involved with the many issues leading up to the ratification of the Gadsden Treaty. After negotiating the 1848 Treaty of Guadalupe Hidalgo, Nicholas Trist left government service. He held jobs in New York and Philadelphia before becoming a clerk for the Philadelphia, Wilmington, and Baltimore Railroad Company and was employed by them for twenty years at an annual salary of around $1,200. Even though he had southern sympathies, and his son lived in Georgia, Trist voted for Lincoln in 1860. Fourteen years later he would die at the age of seventy-three.

After returning to the United States from his wanderings along the Mexican border, John Russell Bartlett settled in Providence, Rhode Island and served for fifteen years as Secretary of State. He authored several books on the state's history, as well as compiling other works. He died in 1886, a prominent member of his community.

The locally famous meteorites Bartlett had seen in Tucson would also go east. In the early 1860s, they were separately sent to San Francisco, with the larger one soon going on to the Smithsonian in Washington, D.C. Many years later, the other meteorite would join it there.[15]

Surveyor William Emory remained a U.S. army officer during the Civil War despite his support for the southern railroad route and his friendship with Jefferson Davis. In 1876, he retired with a rank of brigadier-general after 45 years of military service and died eleven years later.

Both Philip St. George Cooke, the leader of the Mormon Battalion, and John Parke, who oversaw the national railroad survey of the 32nd parallel route east of the Colorado River, also served in the Union Army. Parke was involved in numerous battles during the war and eventually became a major-general. He retired in 1889 and passed away in 1900.

Cooke was appointed a brigadier-general in 1861 and for awhile was superintendent of recruiting for the U.S. Army. He left the military in 1873 and lived another twenty-two years. Henry Standage, who was part of the Mormon contingent under Cooke's command, had settled in Utah by 1847 and fifty-two years later died in Mesa, Arizona, at the age of 81.

Andrew B. Gray remained true to his adopted state of Texas and became a captain in the confederate army. Before the war, he resided in Tucson and was employed as a surveyor for mining properties and for establishing the boundaries of an Indian reservation along the Gila River. Once fighting between the states broke out, he left the west to join the southern Army of the Mississippi. In early 1862 he was assigned to determine if the confederate military works along the Mississippi River on the eastern border of Arkansas could be strengthened. While undertaking this study, he was killed when the boiler aboard his river steamer exploded.[16]

Peter Brady, who accompanied Gray on his surveying mission for the Texas Western Railroad Company, also moved to Tucson in the 1850s, but he would remain there. He was sheriff for awhile, a member of the Territorial legislature, and before dying in 1902, was involved with developing a copper mine in the area called "ajo" along with a silver mine northwest of Tucson.

As a resident of the Gadsden Purchase region during the Civil War, Brady would have been aware of the federal government's move to finally implement the transcontinental railroad project. It obviously would not be built along the southern route, but instead from Council Bluffs, Iowa, to Sacramento, California. It wasn't exactly the central path Thomas Hart Benton of Missouri had fought so long for, but it certainly was not the line that Jefferson Davis, by then President of the Confederate States of America, had envisioned.

With the outbreak of fighting, the cross-country railroad effort took on new importance. It was a way to show the nation, and especially those in the south, that the northern states could implement the idea without them. It would be a matter of pride and self-assurance to prove that it could and would finally be accomplished.

The secession of the southern states provided a unique legislative opportunity to break the long-standing logjam regarding which route to select. As one Pennsylvania legislator put it in 1862 about the need for immediate Congressional action: "When in process of time [southern representatives should return] we shall find them, with the same arrogant, insolent dictation which we have cringed to for twenty years, forbidding the construction of any road that does not run along the southern border. The result will be no road, or, by necessary compromise, three roads the whole way. This would be too heavy to bear."[17]

The construction job wouldn't be easy, though. To conquer the high snow-capped mountains, deep canyons, and raging rivers that stood in the way was an imposing task which would require immense engineering skill, but Theodore Judah knew it could be done. By late 1862, his survey through the Sierra Nevada was completed. The track-laying effort which followed needed plenty of man-power during wartime, so thousands of Chinese laborers would be used for the western work, and hundreds of them died due to accidents. The project would also need money, a lot of money.

Judah had preached that private investors should entirely pay for the road, but that was just wishful thinking. To get the California line moving eastward toward the mountain peaks it would have to cross, state and local governments eventually chipped in some monetary support.

To supply federal financial aid, on July 1st, 1862, Lincoln signed the Pacific Railroad Act, which pushed the transcontinental project forward by mandating it be finished no later than 1876. The bill provided that a strip of land 400-feet wide adjacent to the tracks would be given to the private companies building the line, along with ten square miles of public property for every mile of completed work. The firms would also receive government-guaranteed bonds to help pay for the project, along with a direct federal subsidy. This grant would be $16,000 per mile in flat land, $32,000 in foothill areas, and $48,000 a mile in the mountains, and the total of this monetary assistance was not to exceed $50 million.

These provisions, however, proved to be insufficient for the financial backers of the construction effort and a new railroad bill was adopted by Congress in

1864. It doubled the land grant, speeded up the process by which the government subsidy would be paid, and made other concessions in order to insure the project was feasible.

Two companies would build the line until they met somewhere in the middle. The Union Pacific headed west from Council Bluffs, Iowa, and the Central Pacific eastward from California. In January of 1863, Leland Stanford, by then Governor of the state, along with Charles Crocker and Mark Hopkins, participated in a groundbreaking ceremony in Sacramento to initiate their portion of the route. Crocker, who would oversee construction of the massive western undertaking, boldly promised those attending, "It is going right on, gentlemen, I assure you."[18]

The monumental project was finally finished on May 10th of 1869, when the tracks met at Promontory in Utah. Theodore Judah would not be at the ceremony held that day to mark the completion of his dream. He had died six years earlier at age thirty-seven of yellow fever, having been infected with the disease while sailing from California to New York via Panama.

After the driving of a gold spike in Utah, which for the first time linked the country together by rails, Leland Stanford criticized the government subsidy program for the project as too cumbersome.[19] Most of the others in attendance, however, were jubilant, for what Judah had called "a great and grand national measure" was successfully finished. It had been almost twenty-five years since Asa Whitney originally proposed the concept, but finally the transcontinental railroad project was completed.

Implementation of the first cross-country line, however, didn't extinguished the hopes of those residing within the area of the Gadsden Purchase for their own railroad. As early as 1857, residents of the newest part of the United States were saying, "The Southern Pacific Railroad, which will be built because it is necessary to the country, will find its way easily through [the proposed new territory of] Arizona."[20]

This region of the country was enthusiastically described as very rich in minerals and having a climate which was "so mild and healthy...that emigration is practicable at all seasons. Snow never lies on the soil, and frost is almost unknown."[21] The population of "Arizona" in 1857 was estimated to be eight thousand and increasing, while of Tucson it was boastfully written: "It is fast becoming a thriving American town, and will before long be a place of more importance than ever before."[22]

Another settlement was developing along the Colorado River at a location which would eventually be known as Yuma. "This point is destined to be one of great commercial and pecuniary importance," one commentator wrote.[23] "Situated at the present head of navigation, at the point where the overland mail route crosses the Colorado, and where the Southern Pacific Railroad must bridge the stream, it is a necessary stopping place for all travel across the country."

After ratification of the Gadsden Treaty, Americans though had not flocked to the region in large numbers, in part because of Apache raids and also because the U.S. government had yet to establish civil order. Early settler Charles Poston characterized the situation as one of anarchy, but also wrote, "There have not been many conflicts and murders, because every man goes armed to the teeth, and a difficulty is always fatal on one side or the other."[24]

To remedy that situation while also subduing hostile Indians, the newly-arrived American residents of the Gadsden Purchase wanted the southern transcontinental railroad built and more United States troops sent to the area. They additionally demanded to have the region split off from the Territory of New Mexico. In a 1857 petition to Congress, more than five hundred individuals asked for the new "Territory of Arizona" to be created in order that its people could govern themselves.

These men partially got their wish in 1863 when Arizona was designated as a Territory by an act of Congress. Rather than dividing the Gadsden Purchase from New Mexico with an east-west running boundary line along the Gila River as had earlier been requested, the bill split the two down a north-south line instead. This was apparently done in part to prevent confederate supporters living south of the Gila from dominating territorial politics.

After creation of the new territory, the push to build the southern transcontinental railroad intensified. In his 1864 message to the first legislature of Arizona, Governor John Goodwin stated: "For many years, even before it was acquired by the United States, attention was directed to this territory as the most feasible route for a railroad to the Pacific. The severity of the seasons, and the great obstacles presented by mountain chains seriously impede the progress of the road now building, and must greatly enhance the cost of constructing and running it," he said of the first transcontinental line then being implemented.[25]

The governor wanted to promote an alternative to the central cross-country line which would avoid many of its problems. "These difficulties have forcibly suggested the practicability of a route through New Mexico and Arizona," he said. "It has indeed all the advantages to make it the highway between the oceans."[26]

These sentiments were elaborated upon further during the following year in a letter to the *New York Tribune* from Richard McCormick, then secretary and future governor and delegate to Congress of the new territory. He outlined the mineral wealth of the area, declaring that Pima County, which included Tucson, had "silver veins [which] are among the richest upon the continent," and that its copper mines "are surprisingly rich, yielding in some instances as high as 90 percent of pure copper."[27]

It was, however, a time-consuming overland journey to reach the region for those wanting to explore for those minerals. McCormick said emigrants coming to Arizona by wagon from Missouri would need ninety days to reach Tucson. He thought though, "The inevitable continental railroad can follow no parallels more favorable for its economical construction and successful working than the 32nd...".[28]

The people of New Mexico were not to be outdone in their enthusiasm for a railroad to be built through the area of the Gadsden Purchase. In 1868 their delegate to Congress, Charles Clever, pointed out the vast mineral rewards which were held in the land ready to be exploited. He also offered yet another reason for building a railroad to the territory, writing, "The red man must give way before the iron-horse, as the army of Assyria perished when breathed upon by the angel of death...".[29]

The construction of a railroad across southern New Mexico was inevitable, Clever thought. "Whatever other roads may be built," he said, recognizing the ongoing implementation of the first transcontinental line through snowy northern mountains, "the laws of climate will make that which should run through New Mexico the most agreeable to the traveler and the most certain to meet the demands of trade."[30]

Regardless of the hopes of politicians and residents of New Mexico and Arizona in the 1860s, railroad tracks were not to arrive in their territories for a decade or more. After the 1869 completion of the first transcontinental line through northern Utah, it would be several more years before work could begin on the second such undertaking.

CHAPTER TEN

"Not to quit 'till they feel the point of the bayonet in their rear"

The goal of increasing the population within the Gadsden Purchase while shipping its mineral wealth out of the region depended upon the provision of convenient and economical transportation. Without a railroad, the southern parts of Arizona and New Mexico would remain isolated from the remainder of the country. Going overland with freight to and from the end of the train tracks near the Mississippi River took several months, and for passengers the journey may have been quicker, but was extremely tortuous.

One graphic account of a mail-carrying stage coach trip from Missouri to Arizona is provided by Raphael Pumpelly in his 1870 book, *Across America and Asia: Notes of a Five Year Journey Around the World and of Residence in Arizona, Japan and China*. In 1860, he headed west to become chief engineer at the Santa Rita silver mine south of Tucson and provided a detailed description of the arduous experience of getting there.

"Having secured the right to a back seat in the overland coach as far as Tucson," Pumpelly noted dryly, "I looked forward, with comparatively little dread, to sixteen days and nights of continuous travel."[1] The seating arrangement of the vehicle, however, would quickly change that opinion. "The coach was fitted with three seats, and these were occupied by nine passengers. As the occupants of the front and middle seats faced each other, it was necessary for these six people to interlock their knees; and there being room inside for only ten of the twelve legs, each side of the coach was graced by a foot, now dangling near the wheel, now trying in vain to find a place of support."

Those weren't the only hardships facing the travelers. As the author remembered, "An unusually heavy mail in the boot, by weighting down the rear, kept those of us who were on the front seat constantly bent forward, thus, by taking away all support from our backs, rendering rest at all times out of the question."[2]

After several days of continuous movement Pumpelly recalled: "The fatigue of uninterrupted traveling by day and night in a crowded coach, and in the most uncomfortable positions, was beginning to tell seriously upon all the passengers, and was producing a condition bordering on insanity…In some persons, this temporary mania developed itself to such a degree that their own safety and that of their fellow-travelers made it necessary to leave them at the nearest station, where sleep usually restored them before the arrival of the next stage on the following week."[3] That didn't happen in every case because, "Instances have occurred of travelers jumping in this condition from the coach, and wandering off to a death of starvation upon the desert."

Eventually, though, Pumpelly arrived at his destination, where he found a place to sleep before being, "awakened by the report of a pistol, and of starting up to find myself in a crowded room, where a score or more of people were quarreling at a gaming table. I had reached Tucson, and had thrown myself on the floor of the first room I could enter. A sound sleep of twelve hours had fully restored me, both in mind and body."[4]

After recuperating in the saloon from his sleep-depriving and nerve-wracking trip of more than two weeks duration, the author became acquainted with his new home. He was impressed by the weather, terrain, and plants of the area, commenting: "Climatic influences have given a marked and peculiar character to the vegetation of this part of the continent. Toward the coast of the Gulf of California the plains are barren and arid deserts, where the traveler may ride hundreds of miles without seeing other plants than dry and thorny cacti. Granite mountains bordering these deserts are even more awful in their barrenness; neither tree nor cactus, nor even a handful of earth, can be seen on their sides…".[5]

Further east toward Tucson, however, Pumpelly noted that palo verde and mesquite trees grew, as well as the giant saguaro. He was especially impressed by this cactus, comparing it to the architecture of the ancients. "So strongly do these cacti resemble Grecian columns," he thought, "that one is almost tempted to look for fallen Corinthian capitals and ruined temples."[6]

Regarding the land south of the Gila River which contained the saguaro and other desert vegetation he commented: "The abundant growth of grass, and the mildness of the winters, render central Arizona a country well adapted to grazing. But away from the Gila River, excepting at a few scattered points, there is no land suitable for cultivation, owing to the absence of water for irrigation."[7]

A somewhat similar view of the Gadsden Purchase was taken by U.S. Army General William Tecumseh Sherman. While in the area he was told that only water and society were needed to improve it. "That," Sherman replied simply, "is all hell lacks."[8]

Unlike most residents of the region, Pumpelly was somewhat sympathetic to the plight of the Apache Indians and regretted their treatment by the newly arriving American population. "If it is said that the Indians are treacherous and cruel," he wrote, "scalping and torturing their prisoners, it may be answered that there is no treachery and no cruelty left unemployed by the whites. Poisoning with strychnine, the willful dissemination of small-pox, and the possession of bridles, braided from the hair of scalped victims and decorated with teeth knocked from the jaws of living women—these are heroic facts among many of our frontiersmen."[9]

The author continued to hold this outlook on the Apaches even after they had murdered his compatriot, and boss, at the Santa Rita silver mine. The man was, according to Pumpelly, "A true friend of the Indians, [but] he fell by them a victim to vengeance, for the treachery of the white men."[10]

While working at the mine south of Tucson, Pumpelly became acquainted with Charles Poston, the Kentuckian who had earlier come to the area. The two journeyed together to the spot on the Colorado River where travelers and freight traditionally crossed. It was there that Poston had some years before helped to establish the community which would later become known as Yuma.

It was to extract its mineral resources that had brought both Poston and Pumpelly to Arizona, but for mining to be successful, the latter believed transportation infrastructure needed to dramatically improve. Pumpelly noted that the necessary mining machinery had to be sent overland to Tucson by wagon from Indianola in Texas, a distance of 1,087 miles, or from Fort Yuma, which was 250 miles away, or almost 400 miles from Guaymas, Mexico on the Gulf of California. While that bulky, heavy equipment could be transported to those destinations by ship from San Francisco, the east coast of the United States, or even Europe, the final hundreds of miles by freight wagons made the cross-country journey time-consuming, expensive, and dangerous. That situation could not sustain the mining industry in the territory, Pumpelly thought, and he concluded, "A shorter and safer route than any of these will be necessary, and when furnished with a good wagon road, or ultimately with a railway, the first essential to the development of industry of any kind will have been attained."[11]

When Governor Richard McCormick addressed Arizona's fifth territorial legislative assembly in 1868, he also pointed out the extreme difficulties in reaching the region as one argument why a railroad was so urgently needed. In addition, there was an even more pressing necessity he said. "The building of a railroad across the Territory is one of the most important steps toward the subjugation of the Apache that can be taken," McCormick told the legislators, "and for this reason and for many others that will occur to you, I suggest that you pray

Congress to render such assistance to the company or companies proposing to build such road as will insure an early completion of the work."[12]

It wasn't only Arizona politicians who were pushing for Congressional support to build a second transcontinental railroad. The press in both the territory and on the east coast of the United States was also urging action on laying more tracks. "Arizona without this Railroad is worse than worthless to us," commented the *New York Tribune* in 1870, "she is a bill of expense to our Government; and a temptation to the loss of their scalps to our adventurous citizens: with the Railroad, it will prove a vast treasure-house, the seat of novel industry, enterprise, thrift, and National wealth."[13]

To accomplish that objective, in 1869 a bill had been introduced in Congress which would provide support for the construction of the 32nd parallel railway, and by March of 1871 it had become law. The Texas Pacific Railroad Company was chartered to build a line from the eastern border of Texas to El Paso, and then on to San Diego.[14] In exchange for crossing the Gadsden Purchase, the company would receive twenty sections of federal property for each mile of track laid in New Mexico and Arizona and ten in California. Bonds to pay for the work were also authorized and construction was to begin at both termini of the route. By 1873, fifty miles at each end of the road were to be completed and the entire project finished no later than 1881.

Despite the financial incentives, however, the effort floundered. Only 23 miles of track had been laid within two years of the law's passage, all at the eastern end of the project. To stimulate more interest, in 1872 Congress amended its earlier legislation to provide greater flexibility in the use of bonds and it changed the name of the company to the Texas and Pacific. It also extended the completion date by another twelve months while reducing to ten miles the amount of rails required to be laid eastward from San Diego in the first two years, with twenty-five miles annually mandated after that.[15]

Even with those concessions, work still did not progress noticeably, and nothing was done in San Diego. Congress then further revised the legislation in both 1873 and 1874 to try and encourage construction. While some tracks were laid in eastern Texas, little else was happening and difficult economic times nationally led company officials to seek direct government financial support for the effort in the form of guaranteed interest on construction bonds. Federal payments per mile of track laid had been granted to the first transcontinental railroad, and the Texas and Pacific Company wanted a somewhat similar incentive for the second.

Tom Scott was then president of both the financially weak Texas and Pacific and the immensely powerful Pennsylvania Railroad, the largest freight carrier in the world. Some people though Scott had visions of connecting the two lines, thus forming a transcontinental route which would include the southwest and northeast sections of the country. A few southerners resented that idea since it would not provide their states with a cross-country route. Many others from the South, though, supported the Texas and Pacific because Scott pledged its rails would run to Memphis, New Orleans, and Vicksburg.[16]

Combining this promise with an aggressive public relations campaign, Scott secured the support of most southern leaders, including its Congressional representatives. Despite that, his Texas and Pacific Company could not afford to proceed west from central Texas without direct federal financial aid, but many in Washington opposed the idea because of earlier bad experiences with the first transcontinental project. In addition, the potential drain on the national treasury was of great concern.

While Scott was seeking help in Congress for his southern railroad, change in the new territory of Arizona had slowly begun to occur. The telegraph was extended inside its borders, and social conditions were improving. Life, however, was still very rough, and the population of the territory in 1870 was less than 10,000 people, over 3,200 of whom lived in Tucson. Two years later, with her infant daughter in her arms, Josephine Brawley Hughes made the back-breaking, 420-mile trip from San Diego to join her husband in Tucson. It was a non-stop, four-day stagecoach adventure, and when Josephine arrived, she was the third white American woman in the community.[17]

Mrs. Hughes found that all the homes in Tucson were constructed of adobe, since it was an ideal building material for the climate. The sun-dried mud bricks were easily produced in the desert while lumber was a very rare and expensive commodity because of the difficulty with transportation. Each room in her house had a fireplace, and to light the rooms she initially burned rags set in a pan of grease, but soon sent east for a candle mold. Hughes also had to make her own soap, and to decorate the dwelling she used colored paper cut into intricate patterns.

Carpeting for the house consisted of long strips of material which were sewn together before being placed over a mat of straw and paper laid on boards which covered the dirt floor. As for furniture, after a few years the Hughes household sent to San Francisco for new pieces upholstered in blue. "The bill of lading was dated March 23, 1875, and accounted for '9 packages measuring 247 ft. at $1.00 per foot—total $247'," according to one report of the freight cost.[18] "Its routing was indicated—'San Francisco—for Colorado River—to any Colorado Navigation Company's vessels at the mouth of the Colorado—to be delivered in good order and condition at Ft. Yuma.' It was taken from Yuma to Tucson by wagon train."

A railroad, of course, would greatly speed the delivery of such merchandise, while also making the freight charges of $1.00 per foot considerably less expensive.

More importantly, access to the ore produced in the rich mining areas of the new territory might turn a handsome profit for the owners of a railroad company. It was not surprising then, that by the time the Texas and Pacific Company was approaching Congress to ask for direct monetary aid for their proposal, four men in California were also looking at laying tracks across Arizona and New Mexico to connect the Gulf of Mexico coast with Los Angeles.

Charles Crocker, Mark Hopkins, Collis Huntington and Leland Stanford had been considering the idea for some time since they controlled only the western portion of the nation's first transcontinental line, the other end being operated by the Union Pacific Company. Why shouldn't they have a road of their very own from southern California to the Mississippi River? Of course they had no legal authority from Congress to build tracks through the two territories east of the Colorado River because the Texas and Pacific Railroad Company had it. Ignoring that small detail, the four were still thinking about the project, as Huntington told Hopkins in 1875. "If we had any rights to build in Arizona it would help us lay track," he said, "in fact I do not know just how to handle this matter before Congress. We can hardly say we are going on to build through Arizona when we have no rights there to do so."[19] That fact, though, didn't stop the four men from considering the possibility.

Even before completion of the first transcontinental railroad, in 1868 they had purchased the Southern Pacific Company of California with the intention of tying San Francisco to Los Angeles by rail. At the same time they were buying other railroads in the state and began consolidating the tracks throughout California under their control. The personal wealth they amassed was enormous, and by the 1870s each was worth tens of millions of dollars. In addition, their political influence in Sacramento and Washington was substantial. As their power grew, public resentment toward them also increased. They set freight rates which were considered too high by their customers, while also being perceived as having many politicians in their hip pockets. On the other hand, they built and operated railroads and, after acquiring the Southern Pacific Company, within a few years they were having tracks laid south from San Francisco which would arrive in Los Angeles in September of 1876.

Prior to the completion of that effort, the company was already looking to build eastward from Los Angeles. Survey crews were inspecting possible routes in California to reach the Colorado River and also investigating a pair of points at which to cross into Arizona. One of these was at Yuma, the other about 45 miles farther north. This latter line might then be extended to the tiny community of Phoenix on the Salt River before turning south to the settlements at Florence and Tucson. From there it could head to El Paso.[20] If the river were bridged at Yuma, the tracks would follow the south bank of the Gila River eastward.

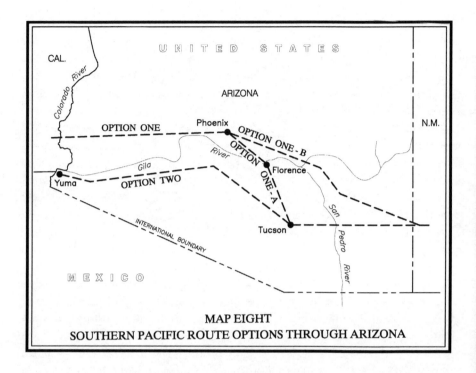

MAP EIGHT
SOUTHERN PACIFIC ROUTE OPTIONS THROUGH ARIZONA

Before this field work had been finished, Collis Huntington was already thinking about the financial return which a southern transcontinental line could provide, while also plotting to get Congressional permission to lay tracks through the Gadsden Purchase. In New York City, where he had moved in order to raise capital and buy equipment and materials for the Southern Pacific Company and his numerous other business interests along with being able to personally lobby Congress on a frequent basis, Huntington had decided by December of 1875, "I shall do what I can to get the Texas Pacific Act amended so as to allow the S.P. to build east of the Colorado River, but I much doubt being able to do anything fast."[21] At the same time, in his scribbly, hardly legible handwriting, he was asking his longtime business partner Mark Hopkins: "Would you think it advisable for the S.P. to agree to build to El Paso? Please give your views on this at once."[22]

From San Francisco, where the others within the firm had located their offices, Hopkins replied that the company would be in the strongest position to make that decision, as well as politically with members of Congress, once it had reached the Colorado River.[23] Huntington concurred and directed the work eastward from Los Angeles toward the river be completed as quickly as possible.

While Southern Pacific officials were contemplating laying tracks through Arizona and New Mexico, the firm that had federal legal authority to do just that was maneuvering to stop them. Tom Scott was in Washington trying to prevent the giant California railroad conglomerate from building over his line.

Scott had support from several sides. Not only did most southerners in Congress back him, but others opposed Huntington and his associates because of the concentrated power they were accumulating. The four men already controlled the Central Pacific portion of the first transcontinental railway, along with the Southern Pacific routes in California. Allowing this latter line to stretch east across Arizona and New Mexico would result in large sections of the nation's only two cross-country railroads being in the hands of the same four men. That, some members of Congress believed, could not be tolerated.

Huntington, however, had his own ideas, and his own set of Congressmen to counter Scott. One of his proposals was to lay the tracks through Arizona and New Mexico and, at the same time, legislatively obtain the land grant subsidy previously awarded to his Texas and Pacific rival.[24] An act was introduced in Congress to allow that to happen, with the stipulation that at least 20 miles be built annually,[25] but it was not adopted. Despite the setback, Huntington concluded, "The South wants a [rail]road and I think the North is disposed to let it have one."[26] He also believed, "If we can push our own road into Arizona for, say, 100 miles, Scott can never get the government to give him aid to build a parallel road."[27]

The winter of 1876 provided a graphic example of why the southern route would have advantages over the original transcontinental railroad built across northern Utah and Nevada. On February 1st, A.N. Towne, general superintendent of the Central Pacific Railroad Company, telegraphed Huntington that on the main line, "A plow and fourteen (14) engines buried in snow yesterday but released this morning...Passenger train delayed some twenty-four hours. Not over seventy freight cars moved over during the last two weeks. Nothing will be left undone to keep the road open."[28]

Later that month, S.P.'s survey party was reporting its initial results from the Arizona territory. Two routes to cross it seemed feasible, and they had little difference in distance. One possible line, which was somewhat similar to that recommended by Lt. John C. Parke over twenty years before, ran along the Gila River's north bank to Phoenix, then cut southeast through the San Simon valley toward El Paso, thus totally bypassing Tucson. The other proposed path went along the south side of the Gila before heading to Tucson and New Mexico, but whichever route was chosen, the conclusion was that there was "a good, cheap and easy line to build to El Paso."[29]

By early May of 1876, the entire Southern Pacific railroad survey of Arizona had been completed, and it was determined the Colorado River crossing at Yuma had distinct advantages over the other option farther north. These included easier grades, lighter work, and the availability of some water. Thus, Southern Pacific's chief engineer, George Gray, concluded: "The crossing at Fort Yuma is from all accounts about the best on the river."[30]

The following month Huntington noted that, far to the east, the Texas and Pacific Company "are at work building road again."[31] To counter this possible threat to his plans to cross Arizona and New Mexico with track, he commented in a letter to Charles Crocker, "I do wish we could build to the Colorado River this fall, and then build a little on this [the eastern] side."

To try and accomplish that, having employed a cutoff north of Los Angeles, Southern Pacific grading and track-laying by hundreds of Chinese laborers and others had reached within 119 miles of Yuma by May of 1876. Construction was then halted for the hot desert summer months and only began again the following January. After it resumed the work didn't progress very rapidly, however, in part because of a shortage of rails caused by slow production by east coast steel works. Despite that, Huntington had already been negotiating a contract to build a bridge across the Colorado River at Yuma and had even talked to Tom Scott about a settlement which would allow it to legally happen.[32]

Scott, however, was determined to prevent Southern Pacific from bridging the river since he knew it might signify his company had lost the competition for the southern route. To show it meant business, a Texas and Pacific crew had been in Yuma during October of 1876 to do some preliminary grading work for their own bridge. While crossing the Colorado was only one small part of a very long line of tracks through the Gadsden Purchase, the bridge at Yuma was critical to whichever company wanted to control the 32nd parallel route. Like a military operation which seeks to take the high ground in order to control everything around it, construction and operation of the bridge would result in one company having the upper hand on completing the entire southern transcontinental railroad.

On his own, Huntington had tentatively determined that it would be the Southern Pacific Company which would build the bridge and lay the track through the territories of Arizona and New Mexico. To insure the federal government didn't prevent them from doing just that, he considered inviting twenty-five southern Congressmen to tour the proposed line in order to show them how the tracks could be built by S.P. without a direct federal subsidy. Of course the company would cover all expenses for the politicians, and the cost of the excursion could be up to $10,000, but Huntington concluded, "It would be money well expended."[33]

While political maneuvering between Scott and Huntington was going on in Washington, D.C., the people of Arizona were starting to get excited about the prospects of rail service. In Tucson, the *Weekly Citizen* reported that 100,000 ties had been delivered to Oakland, bound for S.P.'s southern California route toward the Colorado River. Once the river was reached and crossed, possibly as early as January of 1877, Arizonans would finally be connected to the outside world, or as the newspaper whimsically put it: "Having been long isolated and our hopes so often dampened on railway matters, it does sound more like romance than reality to write as we now do, but reality it is nevertheless. There is so much of comfort in contemplating a railway connection at Yuma, that we can easily defer speculation upon its construction eastward from there."[34]

Anticipation of the road going beyond Yuma was heightened, however, when an official with Southern Pacific boldly announced in September of 1876: "If we get permission to extend our line east of the Colorado, and the assistance which we need from Congress, we shall be at El Paso, in Texas, in three years. I say 'three years,' but I believe we can do it in much less time than that."[35] Based on that prediction, the people of the territory were told their mines, which were presently almost worthless because of high freight costs for the ore, would quickly become valuable. It was also said that the days of terrible travel by stage coach would be replaced by rail cars fit for royalty.

By October of 1876, the battle over the yet-to-be-built bridge was headed for a show down. Even though the Texas and Pacific Company didn't have rails within 1,200 miles of the Yuma crossing, and the Southern Pacific track laying was stopped over one hundred miles away in the California desert, the decision was apparently about to be made. Not only had his company done some initial grading for a bridge, but a representative of Scott appealed directly to the Yuma Village Council for the needed right-of-way and permission to begin actual work toward building a structure. Their S. P. competitors learned of this request, however, and sent telegrams in opposition.[36] Thus, when it met on October 24th, the Yuma Council adopted a motion which read in part, "That they do not at this time consider it expedient to grant any franchise or privilege to any [rail]road."[37] Instead, it was decided the members would only deal with the company which actually reached Yuma with rails.

The Council was then quickly given another opportunity to decide the bridge issue. On November 20th, Los Angeles area railroad man General Phineas Banning came before them representing the Southern Pacific Company. He outlined the advantages which could be realized by Yuma if the village provided S.P. with certain concessions. In response, the Council granted 100 acres of unoccupied land to the company, along with a right-of-way through the community. In exchange, Southern Pacific agreed to have its tracks in Yuma, Arizona

Territory, by July 1st of 1878.[38] Thus, the battle for the Colorado River bridge appeared to be settled before either the Texas and Pacific or the Southern Pacific companies were anywhere near the crossing site.

The fight between the two railroad firms to lay tracks through the Gadsden Purchase, though, would continue. The Texas and Pacific had a Congressional charter to cross New Mexico and Arizona; Southern Pacific did not. While a compromise between Scott and Huntington had earlier been discussed, the deal fell through, and the two men resumed their bitter feud by lobbying in the halls of Congress. Scott's men in the west were also apparently preparing to begin construction eastward from San Diego toward the Colorado River, but nothing resulted from those plans.

Given all that had happened, at the end of an especially important year in the history of the 32nd parallel route, Yuma's *Arizona Sentinel* weekly newspaper summarized the railroad events of 1876 by concluding that the Southern Pacific Company would shortly be laying tracks through the community. "Yuma will have a railroad very soon, if not sooner," they wrote. "Let all croakers dry up. The iron horse will soon snort so that all can hear."[39]

Over twenty-two years had elapsed since ratification of the Gadsden Treaty, though, so it wasn't surprising that railroad matters after January 1st didn't go exactly as anticipated. Track-laying in the California desert was proceeding slower than expected, and at the same time Southern Pacific officials continued to be concerned about their lack of legal authority to actually build into Arizona. Because of Scott's opposition and influence, they knew Congress wouldn't grant them the necessary permission, so instead they looked to the territory for assistance. As Huntington wrote Hopkins in late January of 1877: "I much doubt whether we can get any legislation this [Congressional] session in allowing us to come east with the S.P. through Arizona. So you will have to do the best you can with the Territorial Legislature."[40]

The cooperation of the legislature was extremely important because S.P. lawyers had apparently found a way around the Texas and Pacific federal charter. Under the provisions of an act adopted by Congress in 1875, any railroad company incorporated in a territory and which filed its projected plans and organizational papers with the U.S. Secretary of the Interior would be eligible for substantial benefits. These included a 200-foot wide right-of-way where the tracks ran across federal land, sufficient government property for needed depots and other railroad buildings, and permission to use natural materials found along the way to develop the roadbed.[41]

Both chambers of Congress had extensive debates on the provisions of this bill before approving it, and in the House of Representatives one member commented of the remote regions where these railroads were likely to be built: "The lands where these lines are to run are as worthless without these railroads as if they were in the center of Africa or in the midst of the desert of Sahara. The building of these roads is the only thing which can or will give them any value."[42]

The issue of one railroad company wanting to build over the same route as another which already had a federal charter for the right-of-way apparently did not come up in the Congressional deliberation of the law. Thus, after passage of the 1875 act, Southern Pacific could claim some legal authority to the 32nd parallel line if it could simply incorporate separate companies in Arizona and New Mexico and file a copy of their organizational papers along with its proposed route with the U.S. Secretary of the Interior.

The foundation for meeting those relatively simple Congressional requirements to build through Arizona was laid by S.P. supporters in early 1877. In his message opening that year's legislative session, Territorial Governor Anson P.K. Safford predicted S.P. tracks would be in Yuma by March 1st and then added: "The effect this will have upon the development of our resources and the stimulation of trade will be magical. Capital will flow into the country without stint, cheap communication and transit will afford facilities for developing with profit our immense mining interests, the stockraisers, with abundant ranges where the snow never falls, will find ready sale for their beef and mutton to supply the markets of New York or San Francisco, and the Territory...will awake from lethargy to life and prosperity."[43]

Safford called on the legislature to offer any and all assistance to insure the tracks were built through the territory as quickly as possible. A few days later, on January 5, 1877, Representative Estevan Ochoa of Tucson introduced a bill entitled, "An Act to secure the construction and operation of certain railroad and telegraph lines, and to provide for other matters relating thereto."

Called "one of the most enterprising merchants [in Arizona], as he is admitted to be one of the coolest and bravest men in all the southwestern country,"[44] the 45-year old legislator was a partner in the Tucson freighting company of Tully and Ochoa. Their large fleet of wagons rolled across the desert region, hauling supplies throughout the area. Ochoa obviously knew that competition for the freighting business from a railroad might be the financial ruin of his firm, but he introduced legislation to encourage the track-laying anyway.

The Arizona House of Representatives took up the measure, but its outlook initially appeared dim according to a Tucson newspaper, and it was reportedly defeated three times.[45] Despite that, the bill survived, thanks in part to Ochoa, along with the lobbying efforts of General Banning on behalf of Southern Pacific. According to folklore, another reason for the act's escape from demise was intervention by Huntington. The story is told that to insure passage of the bill he sent

Governor Safford $25,000 to distribute as needed among legislators. All but $5,000 of that amount was returned, though, along with a message that the S.P. man had vastly overestimated the worth of an Arizona law-maker.[46]

To secure the necessary political support, Ochoa's proposed legislation also soon contained authorization for two rail lines through Arizona, one along the 32nd parallel route, the other cutting across the center of the territory. After some additional modifications were made, the bill was approved and signed into law by Governor Safford on February 7th. A few days prior to that, Huntington had received a telegram from his west coast business partners telling him, "Southern Pacific Railroad Bill passed both houses of the Arizona Legislature on terms satisfactory to us."[47]

The act did more than grant S.P. the right to build two rail lines across the territory. It set a maximum rate for passengers at 10 cents per mile, and 15 cents for a ton of freight. It also allocated any land owned by the territorial government, but needed for railway construction, to the company.[48] To promote safety, the bill required every Southern Pacific locomotive in Arizona to have a bell, which weighed at least 20 pounds, to be rung over one-quarter mile before any public crossing of the tracks. The bill additionally exempted all property in the territory owned by Southern Pacific from taxation until the second transcontinental route was completed, or 1881, whichever came first.

While it was the federal government that owned most of the land in Arizona and which had given the Texas and Pacific Company a charter to build across the territory, passage of this act by the legislature was a major step toward insuring that Southern Pacific could meet the requirements of the 1875 Congressional legislation and thus have some legal authority to build along the 32nd parallel route. Track-laying in California west of the Colorado River may have been going slower than hoped, but S.P. was taking giant steps toward guaranteeing that it, and it alone, would control the second cross-country line.

Even before final passage of the Arizona legislation, early pioneer Charles Poston had written Collis Huntington. Long-absent from the territory, Poston was returning to Arizona and asked for funds in order to advertise the "Arizona Migration Company". One of the intents of this business, according to Poston, was that, "a MODEL CITY may be built on the line of the proposed railway near the center of Arizona which will, ere long, become the capital of a great and opulent State."[49]

To realize that goal, by early 1877 work on track-laying in the California desert was again moving forward, and Charles Crocker wired Huntington that the railroad by May 1st would reach Fort Yuma on the west bank of the Colorado River.[50] As he and his San Francisco associates considered extending the line even farther east, however, that proposal made them very nervous, in part because the

United States had been in an economic recession for several years. While recognizing the mineral wealth of Arizona, Crocker wrote that he and Hopkins agreed, "Unless we can get money at a reasonable rate of interest on time, say until two years, it would not be safe for us to go beyond the Colorado River."[51] As for the opinion of the fourth member of the group, Crocker commented: "I cannot get anything positive out of Governor Stanford as to his views of building on beyond Yuma. He says it will depend on finances, how much we owe, and who we owe it to, and I despair of his informing himself on those questions."[52] Given that indecision among the three men, Crocker concluded firmly regarding an eastern extension into the Gadsden Purchase, "I assure you, the feeling here is, that we should hold up."

In New York, Huntington had a different perspective about quickly pushing further inland from Yuma, in part because of the glowing reports he had received about the mineral wealth of the territory from General Superintendent Towne. Huntington also believed it would be essential to lay tracks into Arizona in order to prevent the Texas and Pacific Company from eventually building its own line. Plus, he thought Congress was interested in seeing the project completed rapidly. "There is a disposition at the North to do some clever things for the South," he wrote Crocker in late March, "and one of those things is to give them a southern railroad to the Pacific."[53]

Stressing again the importance of laying tracks beyond Yuma in 1877, Huntington told Crocker in April, "I can well understand why you all hesitate about pushing the road east into Arizona with the present financial outlook, but it is one of the things that we can afford to take some risk in."[54] At the same time, he recognized his partners' reluctance and thus concluded in his hard-to-read handwriting, "As to building east of the Colorado, I am willing to take the risk and go on if all the rest of you are, and if you think it better to stop at the river, I am satisfied."

While the four had disagreements about track-laying into Arizona, bridging the river was not in doubt. Crocker had a preliminary cost estimate of $40,000 for the work, and he had also obtained permission to approach the bridge site over the property of Fort Yuma in California. "I have procured the right to cross the Military Reservation from the War Department," he wrote Huntington in late April after visiting the fort, "and the Commandant at Yuma informed me he had received his orders to permit us to go on and do about as we please."[55]

Three weeks later, a detailed cost estimate for the wooden bridge had lowered the total price to $28,000.[56] Its seven piers would run about $9,400, the draw structure, since the bridge would have to swing open to allow river traffic to proceed on the Colorado, another $7,800, and Crocker believed construction could be completed within three months.

He, however, continued to worry privately about the financial risks involved with extending the tracks any farther into Arizona along with the company's legal authority to do so. Despite having the Territorial Legislature's permission to build in Arizona, Crocker wasn't confident it was legally sufficient. At the same time, though, he thought Southern Pacific's public position in Washington concerning Scott's Texas and Pacific proposition should be forceful. "Here we are at the Colorado River with our hundred and twenty-five miles of steel on hand ready to lay down," he wrote Huntington in early May, "anxious to lay, and are only restrained from doing so by lack of authority from Congress. I think that is the most effective policy to meet Scott with."[57]

Huntington agreed, and added another factor to that equation: in order to build across Arizona and New Mexico, Southern Pacific would only require legal authority from Congress for the right-of-way, not the type of monetary incentives Scott was demanding from the federal government. He felt that business from the mines should be sufficient to justify the risk of extending the line. By May of 1877, however, Huntington too had concluded for the time being the company was in no financial position to actually continue laying more tracks after reaching Yuma.[58]

While Southern Pacific officials internally may have made the decision to at least temporarily halt work at the river, the press of the Arizona territory was anticipating just the opposite. From Tucson, the *Arizona Weekly Citizen* proclaimed long before the tracks reached the Colorado: "It has been published that the Southern Pacific would be built, this year, about 150 miles east of Yuma. The announcement has not had many believers, and late advices from California indicate that it will be done."[59]

By the end of May of 1877, Southern Pacific had selected the 100 acres of property it desired in the Arizona community of Yuma, and the Village Council deeded it to them. This vacant land would be used for freight and passenger depots along with maintenance yards, and much of it was near the Colorado River in the heart of the mostly undeveloped town.[60]

Also on the Arizona side of the river, on May 31st Chinese laborers had begun grading the approaches to the bridge site, while across the Colorado the *Sentinel* reported work was winding down on the United States military reservation. Three hundred and fifty Chinese laborers had been let go since their job was almost completed. In their camps they left behind some materials which Yuma residents were sorting through, but the local newspaper asked derisively: "Poor scavengers! What of value do they hope a Chinaman would leave behind?"[61]

While grading work was progressing quickly on the approaches to the bridge site, Crocker reported to Huntington that Mark Hopkins's health was deteriorating rapidly and asked his New York partner to come to California as soon as possible.

"We are all very much alarmed," Crocker wrote of Hopkins. "He cannot do any business, his head becomes confused as soon as he attempts to confine his thoughts to any difficult or important matter, figures particularly bewilder him."[62]

From New York, Huntington expressed concern about his longtime friend's condition, especially because of Hopkins's habit, as he said, of "always seem[ing] to know just what is the best thing to do in all cases."[63] In early July, Huntington made his annual summer trip west, by which time Hopkins's health had improved enough for him to invite his partner to visit his mountain retreat. Together they could forget business and perhaps consider "fishing, riding over the mountain trails, climbing the higher peaks, rolling rocks from the mountain tops, lounging in the shade of the trees, listening to the breeze in the piney forest and thinking pleasant thoughts. Why not come up?" Hopkins asked his partner.[64] Why not indeed? Huntington quickly accepted.

Along the Colorado River, construction on the bridge site continued, and one newspaper concluded it was time for Congress to finally settle the question of who would lay tracks across the territory. "Arizona needs above all things a railway through her whole length," the *Arizona Weekly Citizen* wrote, "…[and] we repeat our hope that whatever action Congress intends to take affecting the 32nd parallel railroad, will be decisively taken [by] the next Congress, or that the rival companies will compromise and give us the road."[65]

That hopeful scenario was not to occur. As Southern Pacific pushed construction on the bridge forward, its Texas and Pacific rivals aggressively tried to prevent it from finishing the project. Scott's company demanded any further work that was needed to approach the river across the Fort Yuma military reservation in California be halted by the federal government. In late August, Crocker sent a telegram to Huntington that officials of the Texas and Pacific were complaining to the War Department.[66] Almost a year earlier, preliminary permission had been given to the T&P to do some work on the military property, but that approval had been revoked a month later. The Southern Pacific, however, was being allowed to continue across the reservation, and their Texas and Pacific competitors wanted to know why S.P. was being treated differently.[67]

Crocker recommended to his New York partner that he should encourage the War Department in Washington to allow both bridges to be built, especially because it was highly unlikely their competitor's could actually do anything. "You had better see the Secretary of War before he acts upon this matter and get him to permit Texas and Pacific but not stop us," Crocker wired Huntington. "Our bridge will be completed in three weeks if not stopped."[68]

Before Huntington had time to respond, both the Southern Pacific and the Texas and Pacific were given written permission by the War Department to cross the military reservation of Fort Yuma. This approval, though, came with a major condition: the companies would have to obtain from Congress at its next session a legal right-of-way over the land, or "must move its tracks from the Reservation and abandon the road."[69]

While their bridge was within a few weeks of completion and laying the tracks was about all that still remained to be done on the military reservation, Southern Pacific officials faced a real dilemma. Since approval from Congress was very unlikely given the number of legislative friends the Texas and Pacific Company had, the S.P. could keep working and face wasting the money which would be spent on finishing the project, or they might halt work and wait to see what happened.

By early September, the question of what to do became even more confusing after the War Department changed its mind again and ordered all railroad work on the Fort Yuma military reservation to stop. In response, Crocker directed construction on the almost-finished bridge to continue at every place except specifically on the federal government's property. A few days later, however, he was having second thoughts about what to do. The War Department had once again reversed itself and reinstated its earlier position that any work done would either have to be approved by Congress at its next session or be removed from the military reservation. Based on that latest switch, Crocker asked his partner in New York for suggestions on how to proceed. "I want your advice as to whether we shall stop when we get the draw bridge completed so that navigation will not be impeded," he wrote Huntington, "or whether we shall go on and lay track and finish up. Of course, you will see that we are liable to be ordered off the Reservation unless we get the right-of-way from Congress. Please telegraph me whether, in your opinion, we can go on regardless of the specifications as to namely preventing waste to our work."[70]

By the 20th of September, the issue had still not been resolved, and Huntington was urged by his associates in California: "You must see Secretary of War and have him authorize completion of bridge or our loss will be large. Full force is there and bridge can be completed in five or six days sufficient for trains to pass."[71]

On the east coast, Huntington had been working to get political approval for construction to continue. He had spoken to the Secretary of War, and it was his understanding President Hayes had given orders the work be allowed to be finished.[72]

Even with all the political indecision and change of direction, however, by the 25th of September Crocker sent his east coast partner a letter stating: "So far as going on and finishing the bridge is concerned, we have given orders to our men they're not to quit 'till they feel the point of the bayonet in their rear, and I guess the bayonets have all gone away."[73] That wasn't really much of a threat to the railroad employees since there were only three or four soldiers at the military post in California and S.P. had a large contingent of workmen on the site. Just in case there was any confusion about proceeding though, Crocker wrote: "The Commandant at Fort Yuma likes whiskey pretty well, and I told [the work foreman] to give him plenty of that article and convince him that it is absolutely necessary to build that bridge in order to prevent waste and damage to our property, and I think he will do it!"

The advance of the tracks was good news throughout Arizona. In Tucson it was proclaimed in the *Arizona Weekly Star* that when the Southern Pacific, and possibly other roads looking at building into the territory, actually did so, "Arizona will have become thoroughly awakened from her slumber of centuries of silence and isolation; and with firm and strident tread, march forward in the path of progress and development."[74]

Just before the end of September, the *Star* quoted an announcement from the *New York Herald* that trains were running to Fort Yuma and "one hundred and sixty miles are under contract in Arizona, to be finished by the 1st of January. This will bring the western end of the great Southern Transcontinental line to about the longitude of Tucson, and within four hundred and forty miles of El Paso. It is asserted that the Southern Pacific Company of California mean to push the western end as fast as they can get contractors to work...".[75]

That totally unfounded prediction certainly would have been news to Huntington, Crocker, and their associates. A final decision about what exactly the company was going to do once it reached Yuma in the Arizona Territory had yet to be made. When and whether they would proceed farther into the land of the Gadsden Purchase continued to be under consideration, but at least on September 30th, 1877, Crocker could telegraph New York: "Bridge across Colorado complete and train carrying United States mails, passengers and express crossed over to Arizona side of river this morning. People of Yuma highly elated over the event."[76]

CHAPTER ELEVEN

"The fact is that there are not ties and rails enough stored
within fifty miles of Yuma to build one mile of new track"

The September 30th, 1877 jubilation in Yuma and throughout the Arizona territory over completion of the railroad bridge across the Colorado River was very
short-lived. The next day, Charles Crocker from San Francisco telegraphed Collis
Huntington in New York, "The United States authorities there [in Yuma] are
hostile and unless directed otherwise from Washington will probably order trains
discontinued."[1] Believing Southern Pacific had violated earlier directives about
crossing the military reservation in California, local army officials three days later
commanded the draw bridge be turned to prevent train traffic, and the decision
was to be backed by thirteen reinforcements sent to Fort Yuma.

Despite the Army's mandate, the bridge continued to be useable for awhile,
but it was feared it could be swung open at any time. That is exactly what
happened on October 5th, when the fort's commander ordered the bridge be
turned. "If [a] train attempts to go over the bridge," Crocker wired Huntington,
"it will be stopped by force, and in future trains will not be allowed to go upon
[military] reservation [of Fort Yuma]."[2]

The people of Yuma, Arizona, naturally, were outraged by this move, since it
cut them off completely from train service and required a return to the use of
ferries to cross the Colorado River. In response, the local Village Council immediately adopted a resolution which characterized the action as "a positive detri-
ment to our people" and a "condition [which] creates great uncertainty, loss of
time and other evils, which in the changing character of business, proves [to] be
oppressive if continued."[3] The Council called on the President of the United
States and the Secretary of War to reverse the order.

The Library of Congress

THE COLORADO RIVER BRIDGE

Not only were trains prohibited from using the bridge, but another impact of the action was that any potential track-laying beyond the Village of Yuma ground to a halt. "But for the lack of rails," the *Arizona Sentinel* reported, "the track could ere this have been laid far beyond the town limits, as the road bed is all ready. While the soldiers keep the draw bridge open, no more material can be brought over [the river] and the work stops."[4] The newspaper noted, however, that a quick resolution of the problem was possible.

In Washington, the cabinet met twice on the issue and Huntington went to the White House to see Rutherford B. Hayes. He needed to explain to the President why and how the bridge had been completed despite earlier orders that the work be terminated. "He was a little cross at first," Huntington wrote of Hayes, "said we had defied the government, but I soon got him out of that belief. I said to him that we were very much in earnest about building the S.P."[5]

Huntington proceeded to tell Hayes a story about the bridge building, which may or may not have been true. The railroad crew had been directed to work day and night to finish the project, he said, but a soldier from Fort Yuma told them they should stop, so the Southern Pacific men adjourned to eat supper, as did the military man. When he went to sleep, however, they returned to finish laying tracks across the bridge "so as to be sure and have it so trains could cross before they received any order to quit."[6]

At the conclusion of his anecdote, Huntington reported: "The President laughed heartily at that and said he guessed we meant business. He then said, 'What do you propose to do if we let you drive over the bridge?' I said push the road right on through Arizona. He said, 'Will you do that? If you will, that will suit me first rate'."[7]

Because of his successful lobbying effort, Huntington could write, "I think I have the bridge question settled for the present." To insure that was in fact the conclusion to this sticky situation, he casually informed his colleagues in California, "Now I think you had better spend a little money building east from Yuma."[8]

The bridge question had been settled indeed, at least temporarily. On October 9th the War Department, at the directive of the President of the United States, notified Southern Pacific officials they could use the structure. The company, however, would still need to eventually obtain Congressional approval to cross the military reservation's land. His associates congratulated Huntington on his work in Washington, and Crocker added, "I join with you in thinking that this administration would have a pretty hard time to keep back the only live company now engaged in building a Southern Pacific railroad."[9]

In Arizona the news was, of course, welcomed. The *Weekly Citizen*, which had moved from Tucson to Florence by this time, reiterated Huntington's pledge to push the tracks eastward almost immediately. The newspaper also characterized as "demagogues and blackmailers," the Texas and Pacific Company for their financial aid requests to Congress.[10]

Huntington's persuading President Hayes to let Southern Pacific cross the military reservation and open the bridge with the intention of building quickly through Arizona must have come as a great shock to Tom Scott and those backing the Texas and Pacific effort. It was Scott's influence with southern members of

Congress, after all, which had helped swing the controversial election of 1876 in Hayes's favor. Despite that, by the end of 1877 the President had not only sided with the S.P. about entering Arizona, but he had also raised serious questions concerning the request for federal subsidies by Scott's railroad company.[11]

But undeterred after the Yuma skirmish between the War Department and Southern Pacific had been fought and finished, Scott tried a different tactic to slow down the competition. He and his supporters began looking into the railroad act adopted earlier in 1877 by the territorial legislature. Their goal, Crocker thought, was to protest S.P.'s right to build in Arizona. At the same time, Scott was discussing a possible reduction in his monetary request to Congress for each mile of track laid by the Texas and Pacific.[12]

Huntington, however, was telling people in Washington his company hoped to soon continue laying tracks east from the Colorado River without a subsidy and planned on being to the Gulf of Mexico within three years. Meanwhile, the press in the territory was reporting that enough land to store 500,000 railroad ties was needed in Yuma by Southern Pacific and that 200 miles of rail was on hand in San Francisco, ready to be sent south.[13]

Where the line would pass through Arizona once it reached the center of the territory, though, had not yet been firmly established. The route "is definitely located as far east as Maricopa Wells," a company spokesman announced in October of 1877 about the Gila River stage stop 156 railroad miles from Yuma, "but from that point eastward there are two or three lines under consideration, and he [Huntington] cannot say at this time whether the road will pass through Florence or not."[14] That uncertainty, according to Tucson's *Weekly Star* newspaper, showed that "anxiety as to what portion of Arizona is to be honored with the track of the Southern Pacific Railroad is still unabated, and no one can yet breathe free on the subject."[15]

While the people of the territory were wondering where the tracks would go beyond Maricopa Wells, top officials within the railroad company were debating whether to actually build east of Yuma at all. Despite what Huntington had told the President, the press, and the public, the opinion of most of those in San Francisco was: "We do not want to build any more road east of the Colorado River on the 32nd Parallel for some time. We want rest."[16]

General Superintendent Towne, however, kept writing Huntington of the rich mining prospects of Arizona and the potentially lucrative business which transporting the ore could bring to the Southern Pacific Company. "Still we are only on the extreme western limit of that great and rich territory," Towne emphasized in a letter from November of 1877, "to reach and control the wealth of which is a strong inducement for Californians and their capital. I have no doubt you will agree with me that the road should be extended across the only desert left, to wit, that between Yuma and Maricopa Wells."[17] Towne very optimistically estimated the total project could be built for less than $300,000, given the company's track-laying supplies on hand in San Francisco.

One of the reasons for the very cheap cost of extending the rails into Arizona was the easy availability of the natural items needed for preparing the roadbed. "The material for embankments," S.P. Chief Engineer George Gray wrote Huntington, "is gravel, sand, and loam, readily obtained from the sides of the line without haul, and can be put in by scrapers and shovels."[18] Given the mostly level terrain, the lack of need for much lumber to build supports for the tracks, the small amount of cutting and filling which would be required, and the easy access to materials, Gray concluded the distance between Yuma and Maricopa Wells could be graded and made ready for rails at a cost of no more than $250,000.

Publicly, however, Huntington was saying the company could build the whole project for a total price of $10,000 a mile. That was still a tiny fraction of the more than $110,000 a mile their portion of the first transcontinental railroad had cost the four men to complete almost a decade earlier. That figure, of course, had been influenced by the scarcities resulting from the Civil War, the high price of rails and locomotives, and the extremely difficult mountainous terrain which had to be conquered. The easy grades through the Gadsden Purchase, though, would obviously also have a significant effect on the price differential.

Despite these tremendously attractive prices, Charles Crocker and his associates in California did not want to keep going east from Yuma, at least for some time. "I assure you I do not want to build any more railroads for three or four years to come," he wrote Huntington before Christmas of 1877.[19] "It seems to me as though the first thing we must do is to get out of debt and get near the shore. I shall oppose any further expenditures until we get our debt very much reduced."

Superintendent Towne, though, was relentless in his support for quick action to keep building toward Maricopa Wells. After meeting with some men interested in investing in mines south of Tucson, he told Huntington, "There is a strong Arizona fever; and I believe if the road was cut 150 or 200 miles further, with what advertising we could do judiciously, it would bring a great many eastern people to that territory with money to develop the mining and agriculture resources."[20]

This and other letters sent to Huntington describing the mineral wealth of Arizona in sparkling terms certainly had an impact. Weighing even more on his mind, though, was the potential threat in Congress that the Texas and Pacific Company posed to Southern Pacific's plans to link Los Angeles and the Gulf of

Mexico coast by rail. "It is very important that you do some work on the S.P. east of Yuma," he informed Crocker early in 1878, "and I hope you will send a firm down there to work while Congress is in session."[21]

The decision had been made, at least by Huntington, to begin building into Arizona from Yuma. As he had previously stated, he thought the partners could afford to take the financial risk, and was counting on the development of the Arizona mining industry to supply the company with a lot of freight and ore to transport. Crocker, on the other hand, was pessimistic about the potential for shipping business from the territory and didn't want to take the chance the project could fail economically.

Huntington, however, instructed that a public announcement of the track extension be scheduled for the middle of January of 1878.[22] Then a sudden financial panic struck San Francisco and banks were calling on the railroad company to pay its debts, with $300,000 being sought from Leland Stanford personally. While they were able to meet their monetary obligations, the Southern Pacific officials in California became even more opposed to laying any more rails east of the Colorado River.

Thus, while the President of the United States had been promised the company would keep building as quickly as it could, and the people of the territory had been led to believe work would commence early in 1878, absolutely nothing happened. Based on this, Yuma's *Sentinel* newspaper concluded that everything Southern Pacific had offered Arizona was simply a mirage.[23]

The newspaper had previously been a major cheerleader for the company, but the delay in laying more tracks turned them into ardent skeptics. "The fact is that there are not ties and rails enough stored within fifty miles of Yuma to build one mile of new track," the weekly publication reported sarcastically in a late January edition.[24] In California there wasn't a collection of materials either, they said. Thus, the paper summarized that Yuma was "likely to remain as the terminus of the Southern Pacific Railroad for years to come, if not forever."

Ignoring the criticism, and because he still perceived a threat from the Texas and Pacific Company, Huntington urged the expenditure of at least a little money to begin laying tracks in the Arizona desert. He was looking at things differently than his California partners because of the increasing possibility the T&P might finally obtain federal subsidies to extend their line westward from Texas. To oppose that outcome, at the end of January of 1878, Huntington testified in Washington before the Congressional Committee on the Pacific Railroads. He explained why Southern Pacific built the Colorado River bridge and expressed disdain for his rival's lobbying efforts to obtain taxpayer's money. "Does it not occur to you," he asked members of the Committee, "that if the same time, effort and means which has been employed so unsparingly in manufacturing this popular opinion had been devoted to building road, the track would have been half way to the Rio Grande by this time…".[25]

Huntington stressed that Southern Pacific wouldn't require financial support from the federal government, but just needed the authority to lay tracks across its land. "We should not be asked to wait at the Colorado River indefinitely for an embarrassed and mismanaged connecting company to build 1,250 miles to give us connection," Huntington pointedly said of the Texas and Pacific, "when we are ready to construct right along and willing to provide the outlet to the East for ourselves without cost to the Government."[26] That appeal for legislative permission to cross the two territories was, of course, contested by his opponents and failed to win approval.

For his part, Tom Scott was alleging that if the Southern Pacific Company received the desired Congressional charter, they wouldn't continue eastward but would simply stay in Yuma. This could not only prevent any other railroad from coming into the two territories, he said, but would also insure that cross-country business remained on the northern transcontinental route, a project in which Huntington and his three associates, of course, held a large financial interest.

In Yuma, the *Sentinel* picked up on that viewpoint, called future track-laying pronouncements from the S.P. "humbug", and concluded of the company: "It is now plain that the only intention has been to drive off competitors from the 32nd parallel and to prevent Arizona from having any railroad at all, except that now terminating at Yuma. This would stifle the Territory."[27]

The *Citizen*, however, still put its trust in the California company. They thought it "unjust to oppose the Southern Pacific for not advancing its road east of Yuma, and unfair to say it does not intend to build it when its strongest efforts to get legal power to build it are stoutly opposed and as yet withheld by Congress."[28] Then the Florence-based newspaper demanded, "Give the Southern Pacific the lawful right to build over its surveyed route in Arizona."

The *Sentinel* wasn't buying that argument. While it admitted preferring the S.P. over Scott's company, the newspaper concluded in typically picturesque language, "If Arizona wishes to succumb to the fascinations of the Southern Pacific, as a toad does to the charms of a snake, and to allow itself to be taken by the heels at Yuma and gradually to be sucked into the creature's digestive organs, then the *Citizen* may be reflecting public opinion."[29]

In addition to being held up to this type of public ridicule, combined with his private worries about Southern Pacific's financial strength, Charles Crocker had also become immensely concerned with the legality of Huntington's plans to build further into Arizona. The federal act of 1875 along with the Arizona territorial legislation of 1877, Crocker obviously believed, were insufficient to accomplish the goal. Instead, he wanted a specific Congressional charter for the

S.P. to cross Arizona and New Mexico, just like the one the Texas and Pacific Company had earlier obtained. "We are none of us here in favor of spending any money east of Yuma," he wrote his New York associate in the middle of February of 1878, "at least until we have a charter to build under, and so far as I am concerned, I don't think I want any more railroads in that dry sandy country. We are, however, all united in our opposition to building any road there until we have a charter."[30]

Huntington, though, still held that rails needed to be laid into Arizona as quickly as possible, and offered some financing options to his San Francisco partners to accomplish that objective. At the same time, in order to beat the Texas and Pacific challenge, and despite his partners' concerns, Huntington was relying on his contingency plan to construct the road through the Gadsden Purchase whether Congress gave the company the authority to do so or not. In early March of 1878, he wrote Crocker suggesting the formation of the Southern Pacific Railroad Company of Arizona. This subsidiary would then contract to lay the tracks east from Yuma under the provisions of the 1875 federal law along with the rights granted by the territorial legislature.[31]

Charles Crocker and his California associates were uniformly unimpressed with this idea. After presenting it to them, Crocker wrote that he told the others that if they wanted to organize the Arizona company and build the line: "I had no objections, but as for my part, I did not intend to build any more roads in the desert...I do not believe that so much railroad is good for any man, especially in Arizona and New Mexico."[32] His west coast partners agreed with that position, and to emphasize the point Crocker concluded: "It strikes me that the only thing for us to do now is to pay our debts before we talk of building any more railroads; anyhow, so far as I am concerned, count me out."

In an earlier letter, Crocker had provided the economic basis for his opposition to extending the tracks. "I don't believe that the road being built two hundred miles east of Yuma would make up the interest on its bonds," he wrote Huntington.[33] After reviewing the disappointing receipts of the existing S.P. line in California, he added, "I ask you, how long can we continue to build roads upon such a showing as this? A few years of such financing would suffice to bust the Bank of England...".

Despite those strongly held business opinions of his partner, Huntington made a startling recommendation in order to gather more southern Congressional support for an S.P. charter to extend their line eastward. He suggested that a former confederate general, someone like Joseph E. Johnston or Pierre Beauregard, be elected as vice-president of the company. Once again, Huntington was demonstrating his "win at all cost" approach in the fight with Tom Scott, who clearly had the backing of many southerners in Congress.

Crocker, however, a man who prior to the Civil War had run for elective office on an anti-slavery platform, was extremely scornful of the proposal. He tersely commented that the view of the idea from California was, "We do not want any of that kind of blood in the management of the present Southern Pacific railroad."[34]

While Huntington and Crocker waged an aggressive letter-writing battle over building the line away from Yuma, 64-year old Mark Hopkins traveled by train to that community for his health. He had been ill for months, but had recovered somewhat and it was thought the dry desert climate might help him further. On March 29, 1878, though, Huntington received a telegram from San Francisco which read simply: "Mark Hopkins died at Yuma this morning."[35]

Crocker said in California, "Mr. Hopkins's death has struck a chill upon all our feelings out here."[36] Then he added, "The death of Mr. Hopkins is going to act unfavorably on our finances and we are weaker instead of being stronger than before."

For his part, the usually stoic Huntington wrote tenderly of his business partner of many years: "My old friend Mr. Hopkins has gone over the river. His death has made me very sad. I was very fond of Mr. Hopkins."[37] In another letter he grieved: "Mr. Hopkins has gone. I liked him so much, and his death has hurt me more than I can tell. If I had not so much to do for the living, I would stop for a time and think only of the dead."[38]

A few days after Hopkins's death, Swiss native Francis Berton along with a friend boarded a train in San Francisco bound for Yuma, intent on exploring some of the Arizona territory. They took with them, naturally, "Shot guns, rifles, and revolvers, obligatory equipment for every traveler who sets out for the unknown."[39]

After a twenty-two hour train trip to Los Angeles, the men spent some time there and then departed for Yuma on April 8th. Arriving the next day, Berton wrote about the only railway station in Arizona, "A score of Indian men and women and a few whites are waiting for us on the platform."[40] Of the native-American men he noted: "Their costume, bizarre enough, consists of a belt with a strip of calico attached before and behind, passing between their legs. Some have on old shirts of wool or calico, but none are wearing trousers." As for the women in those proper Victorian times, they wore "a kind of short skirt of gaudy material, which does not reach below the knees. Their legs are bare, as are also the torso and breast; their skin is dark chocolate-color."

Upon checking into a hotel room "which is not furnished with great luxury but which is clean," Berton and his companion explored Yuma. About this community the author wrote: "The population of Yuma City is about 1,800. Most are Mexicans, one-fifth are Americans. The streets are wide but not paved. It rarely rains and the heat is excessive in summer, both night and day. The temperature rises to 125 degrees Fahrenheit in the shade, and the entire population sleeps on the roofs. The houses are all of one story; the roofs, made of reeds or straw covered with earth, are almost flat."[41]

The two men had come to take a steamer on the Colorado River north from Yuma. To pass the time before it departed, they visited the territory's prison which had been established in town only two years before. They also saw a local game being played by the natives. "Two Indians, each equipped with a long pole, throw a six-inch iron ring so that it rolls ahead of them; they run after it and, when it is about to stop, throw their two poles forward, one on each side of the ring: the owner of the pole on which the ring stops and rests wins a point, and he who succeeds in passing his pole through the ring wins the game."[42]

After returning to Yuma from their river voyage, the men experienced a sandstorm which lasted all day. Sandstorms and other realities of desert life were reasons why people on the west coast had warned Berton not to make the trip. "At Los Angeles everyone had tried to dissuade us from our voyage, saying that Arizona was a horrible country where we should not find anything pleasant. We therefore had needed a good supply of tenacity and perseverance to keep on. I am far from regretting it, for everything I see interests me, and on the head of comfort and well-being we could be much worse off."[43]

Berton might have thought differently if he had traveled to the region before the arrival of the railroad. Prior to the tracks reaching Arizona, the easiest way to get to Yuma had been by ocean steamer from San Francisco down the Pacific coast and then up the Gulf of California to the mouth of the Colorado River. From there passengers and freight were loaded on to flat bottom steamboats for the trip farther up river, a journey according to Berton of almost 200 miles in the very curvy channel which passed mostly through Mexican territory.

The impact the arrival of the tracks had on the American community twenty miles north of the international border was enormous, and exemplified by the price of produce. "Before the construction of the railroad," Berton wrote, "communication between Yuma and California was difficult and costly. Vegetables could not be had at any price. [A local woman] told me that, having read in a newspaper that cabbages had been induced to grow at Tucson and that they could be had for one dollar each, she had written to Tucson to get one. The cabbage came by stage and cost seven dollars to ship. She gave a party in honor of the Cabbage and all the notables of Yuma had a share of it. This happened in 1875."[44]

Once the railroad arrived in town, the cost of most goods dropped dramatically. A front page ad in the *Sentinel* announced that a local merchant was "constantly and regularly receiving fresh California products," including vegetables and produce, and that they were all "offered at prices which defy competition".[45]

Thus, while it hadn't extended its line further into the territory, the S.P. had brought change to Yuma for both travelers and freight transportation. Even before Berton departed the Arizona territory in a comfortable sleeping car, which only let in a little sand, he had concluded, "This town is, for the time being, the terminus of the Southern Pacific Railroad, but the rails will be extended to Texas, across Arizona and New Mexico."[46]

Crocker also visited Yuma a few weeks after Hopkins's death, by which time the *Sentinel* was softening its rhetoric toward the Southern Pacific. While complaining about the high freight rates charged by the company, the newspaper did admit that S.P. had invested heavily in the village by erecting several substantial buildings. It additionally debunked as "silly" a rumor that the rails to the community were to be pulled up and re-laid over 130 miles to the north at a Colorado crossing along the 35th parallel.[47]

About the same time, the *Weekly Citizen* in Florence was reporting, "We have recent reliable assurances that the Southern Pacific Railroad will commence extending their road eastward from Yuma as soon as Congress adjourns, whether they get the desired legislation or not."[48] Huntington had apparently either convinced his partners to change their minds or had simply overridden their concerns in his quest to beat the Texas and Pacific challenge. Whichever the case, the *Citizen* concluded, "We confidently expect that a year hence the iron horse will be within forty miles of Florence, and we are much mistaken in our probabilities if the next three years does not witness the completion of a Southern Transcontinental Railroad."

On May 27th of 1878, Huntington informed Leland Stanford that he had ordered 10,000 tons of rails for delivery beginning in October, and he repeated his assertion that, "I believe we shall all think best to build some road east of Yuma this year."[49] There was no response from his colleagues in California. Thus, the issue had finally been settled: the Southern Pacific would extend its line from Yuma into the Gadsden Purchase sometime before the end of the year.

How exactly S.P. was going to legally justify laying its tracks east of Yuma was still problematic, however. When Huntington sought Congressional authority to build, he was blocked by Scott. He thus fell back on the idea of having the Southern Pacific Railroad Company of Arizona be incorporated and have it contract for the work under the authority granted by the territorial legislature in 1877. Incorporating a separate company was necessary to conform to the requirements of the 1875 Congressional act which Huntington was relying on to give S.P. the legal right to lay its rails across the territory. Meeting this standard would also supply the company with most of the right-of-way they would need for their tracks as well as land for depots and other buildings along with the natural building materials necessary to construct the roadbed in the desert.

Meanwhile, Scott persisted in trying to get Congress to deny S.P. the right to even cross the military reservation at Fort Yuma. President Hayes may have temporarily intervened, but the decision to require legislative authorization to utilize the land still stood. Scott worked to insure that Southern Pacific didn't get that approval, and he succeeded. Despite that, the bridge remained open and trains to and from California continued to use it.

By the summer of 1878, Scott was employing yet another tactic to derail the efforts of his competitors. He had Charles Poston, who was by then Registrar of the United States land office in Florence, Arizona, advertise at $2.50 per acre the sale of property in the territory granted to the Texas and Pacific Company under its charter from Congress. The *Citizen* labeled this move "cheeky", and it was pointed out this land didn't even legally belong to the railroad company since it hadn't conformed to the track-laying requirements of the federal legislation which established it. Poston then clarified the program to indicate he was merely offering an option on the property, with payment due "upon the perfection of their [Texas and Pacific Company] title".[50]

This whole scheme was very suspicious to some in Arizona. They thought Scott and Poston were trying to entice people to acquire an interest in the property for reasons other than land ownership. If it could be demonstrated to Congress how much harm would be done to these potential buyers if the Texas and Pacific didn't build the tracks through Arizona, this reasoning went, the company's attempt to obtain a subsidy might be enhanced in Washington.[51]

Scott's efforts to sidetrack the Southern Pacific, however, weren't working. The *Citizen* published a column in July which predicted that with the arrival of lower temperatures in the fall, the track-laying would begin, and that would mean great things for the territory. "With the building of this road," they wrote, "will come a hegira [flight] of miners and settlers, to fill our mountains and valleys with a busy throng eagerly seeking the golden fleece and bringing wealth, prosperity and peace with them, and therefore, the iron horse can not too soon force his way upon us."[52]

Thus, by September of 1878, potential competition from the Texas and Pacific Company had been put aside, at least for the short-term. But at the same time a possible new rival for Southern Pacific had appeared on the scene. Surveyors for the Atchison, Topeka and Santa Fe Railroad were looking at optional routes across the Arizona territory. While their tracks were only to northern New Mexico on the way to Albuquerque, the company was eventually planning to move west. That line, according to press reports, could potentially meet the Southern Pacific at Tucson, or even Maricopa Wells.

In New York City, though, Collis Huntington had different ideas. If the S.P. and the Santa Fe were to be linked, according to Huntington, that point should be El Paso in Texas.[53] At the same time he repeated his plea to his California compatriots: lay tracks east of Yuma as soon as possible in order to keep thwarting Scott's hopes in Washington.

To accomplish that goal, by late August Southern Pacific's proposed route between Yuma and Maricopa Wells was being marked and mapped in the field by engineers and surveyors. As a correspondent for the *San Francisco Bulletin* who had traveled in the area reported: "All along the road we have had the surveyor's pegs for our companions as an earnest of the future. To this point [Maricopa Wells] the location is said to be completed, and it is even whispered that work may commence in September. Never did country worse want a railroad...With the track to this point, all freight would be delivered twenty days in advance of the present schedule time, and the teamsters' chances for heaven would rise 100 percent."[54]

Creation of the subsidiary, the Southern Pacific Railroad Company of Arizona, was also moving forward. Official papers had been filed, capital stock of $20 million authorized,[55] and the first board of directors meeting held in Yuma in early October. Five officials, two from the parent company and three from the territory, including former Governor A.P.K. Safford, were named to the board. This group quickly authorized a contract for building the road through Arizona and approved the specific route from Yuma to Maricopa Wells.[56]

That meeting, along with the arrival of some track-laying materials, convinced the previously skeptical *Arizona Sentinel* that Southern Pacific finally meant business. Probably a more important reason for its change of attitude, however, was that the editor of the newspaper had been named to the board of directors of S.P.'s territorial company. Thus, as rail cars carrying thousands of redwood ties began arriving in Yuma, while more were expected on a daily basis, the once critical and cynical *Sentinel* concluded, "Every indication now points to a speedy construction of the railroad which is to do so much for Arizona."[57]

But due to the sudden death in California of another leading company official, Huntington was asked by an associate in October, "Will you not wish to postpone active work beyond Yuma for a few months at least, and should not shipments of ties and other material be stopped?"[58]

That possibility apparently never crossed Huntington's mind. By the first of November he had purchased and shipped enough steel rails to reach almost to Maricopa Wells, but at the same time had to inquire of Leland Stanford, "Who is to attend to that business of building the road east of Yuma?"[59] The reply was telegraphed from San Francisco on November 2nd: "J.H. Strobridge goes to the front tonight to take charge of the work with instructions to push it with the greatest force consistent with economy."[60]

Another easterner who had gone west in the gold rush of 1849, James H. Strobridge had been the chief of construction on the Central Pacific's monumental conquest of the peaks of the Sierra Nevada range and the completion of the first transcontinental line. On this new project through the Gadsden Purchase, though, there would be no railroad tunnels to drill through solid rock, no mountain cliffs to navigate along, nor deep canyons to bridge. Instead, the mostly flat terrain would allow the work to move forward rapidly. In general, after graders prepared the roadbed on a line indicated by survey pegs, the track-laying crew would follow. They would put steel rails on redwood ties, then nail them in place with spikes, and bolt the rails together using fishplates.

Huntington asked the fifty-one year old Strobridge, who was to be paid $10,000 a year for his work, to telegraph him every day as to how much track had been laid. He would get that information into the newspapers, he said, and "it will help us in Washington more than anything else."[61] His goal, Huntington told Crocker, was to have the rails laid to Maricopa Wells by April "on account of our fight with [the Texas and Pacific]".[62]

The cost of the work to be done was of concern to Huntington, who wanted it completed as inexpensively as possible. Writing of the project he said: "There are several reasons why it should be built cheaply. It will have but little business to do for a long time so it should be built for the least possible amount of money. If we expect to get a fair return for our money then we can ill spare the money at this time so the amount for that reason should be the smallest possible sum."[63]

The penny-pinching Crocker concurred, and by the fall of 1878 he had returned from a trip to Europe to oversee construction for the company, just as he had done on the original cross-country line over a decade earlier. After completion of that historic transcontinental project, Crocker remembered: "I was always on the watch that a dollar came as near buying a dollar and five cents worth of material as possible. I was particular on that."[64]

While the two partners agreed the track-laying through the Gadsden Purchase needed to be done cheaply, the enormous financial and other benefits to be derived from the extension of the railroad was the focus of attention in the territory. "Fares and freights will be greatly reduced and time in greater proportion," the *Arizona Weekly Citizen* offered. "Instead of seventy-two hours [by stage coach from Maricopa Wells] to Yuma, the passengers will go in fifteen, and instead of freights being twenty to fifty days, they will be one or two. Perishable but very useful articles, especially of food, which now cannot be brought here, will then be plentiful and cheap...Dangers and hardships of travel will about cease, and generally protection to life and property be much nearer perfect."[65]

By the first of November, the *Sentinel* in Yuma was reporting the arrival there "of 55,500 redwood ties, and of 1,024 steel rails; besides the usual compliment of fishplates, bolt and spikes…The average car loads have comprised each, 44 rails, 6 kegs spikes, 88 fishplates, and 3 boxes of bolts, weighing 23,000 pounds."[66]

As huge quantities of construction material rolled into Yuma, Southern Pacific officials were also acquiring the private property they needed to build eastward. The first 45 miles inland from the Colorado River was finally secured by November, and from there to Maricopa Wells the line crossed only government-owned land.

While track-laying work was about to commence in Arizona, Leland Stanford was talking with representatives of the Atchison, Topeka and Santa Fe Railroad and telling them the best place for the two lines to eventually meet would be El Paso.[67] In New York, Huntington also met with Santa Fe officials to discuss a future junction point of the two roads. "They say they will go down the Rio Grande and connect with us when we strike that river," he wrote Crocker, but then added suspiciously, "all of which may be true or may not."[68]

Even as this potential competitor was being dealt with somewhat cordially by the partners of the Southern Pacific, the *Sentinel* noted that a total of 135,000 ties had arrived in Yuma and 10,000 more tons of steel rails were on there way from California. Then on Saturday, November 23rd the newspaper wrote: "Last Saturday came nine cars for handling rails during construction, watercarts and wagons, and a number of laborers and mechanics. On Sunday came four car loads of supplies and 22 horses. On Monday, 23 horses, a car load of provisions, two car loads of turntable material, one car load of water tank material, and a lot of employees and Chinamen."[69] The list of arriving men and materials got even longer as: "On Tuesday came a water wagon for supply of outlying camps, 25 carts, 25 scrapers, a car load of tools, insulators and brackets, 67 horses, a lot of employees and two car loads of Chinamen. On Wednesday came 249 Chinamen in six cars, and three car loads of rails. On Thursday came eight cars with over 300 Chinamen, and yesterday 91 more came in. All through the week have come ties, rails, telegraph material, and lumber and timber for trestle-work and culverts."

All of these laborers and construction items would quickly be put to work in extending the tracks away from the Colorado River. After a delay of almost fourteen months, the reality of resuming railroad building in Arizona was finally being accomplished. "Grading is going on very fast," the *Sentinel* also reported on November 23rd. "Track-laying began in earnest on Monday [the 18th] and has already advanced the front four miles beyond Yuma."[70]

With the initiation of track-laying by the Southern Pacific Railroad Company into the Arizona territory, the outcome of the long challenge from their Texas and Pacific rivals seemed to have been permanently settled. It appeared that at last, more than twenty-four years after the ratification of the Gadsden Treaty, the nation's southern states were finally going to get a transcontinental railroad built along the 32nd parallel, even if by a California company operated by staunch anti-slave Republicans. Despite that, as one Georgian put it: "The question with the South is simple but grave. Will she have a road through Texas to the Pacific, whose connections are on southern soil? If yes, then the only hope of one for many years is in the Southern Pacific."[71]

CHAPTER TWELVE

"The Southern Pacific Railroad is the wedge that opens Arizona to development"

"The work on the [Southern Pacific] road is now being rapidly pushed eastward from Yuma; the roadway is alive and busy for many miles with the road builders," proudly proclaimed the *Arizona Weekly Citizen* at the end of November, 1878.[1] "The air is full of music of the pick and shovel far up the valley of the Gila; the atmosphere is misty with the dust that hundreds of workmen are raising as they clear the way for the track. The great road builders have come at last…".

The newspaper, which had relocated to Tucson by this time, optimistically outlined the advantages which the tracks were to bring to the territory. These included stopping Apache raids while insuring increased population growth. Travel would also be faster and Arizona products could thus be shipped to coastal markets more easily at the same time that much needed items would be readily imported. The transformation the railroad was to accomplish, the *Citizen* concluded, would mean "the Arizona of today is very soon to be changed into a new Arizona."[2]

In San Francisco, Leland Stanford also foresaw great things for the future of the line in terms of profits for the company. "When the S.P. has its connection through to the Gulf of Mexico," he wrote Collis Huntington, "it is to be a very important and valuable road. I think it will take a great part of our wheat crop that goes to Europe that way, and it will bring large quantities of anthracite coal to this coast."[3]

Thus, in late November of 1878 when a small army of men under the direction of James H. Strobridge set off into the Arizona desert with military-like precision, there were very high hopes for the railroad project. Strobridge thought they could install the tracks to Maricopa Wells within four months, and his tight organization of the grading and track-laying teams would result in a steady stream of daily reports to Huntington that one mile, or even one mile and one-half, of rails had been laid.

In a series of articles, the *Arizona Sentinel* reported on the work being done as the construction moved forward. The route for the rails had been staked by a survey crew well in advance, and as the newspaper noted, these markers replaced those put in the ground but never used by the Texas and Pacific Company almost a decade before. In addition, the S.P. tracks were often laid very close to the dirt road on which mule-drawn wagons still operated hauling freight across the territory.

The long-awaited railroad effort employed a total of 1,300 workers, eleven hundred of whom were Chinese. There were also 200 wagons and carts involved, along with 300 animals, mostly horses and mules. This conglomeration of men and beasts was stretched out along a line many miles in length running eastward through the Arizona desert.

Some ten miles or more ahead of the actual track-laying crew were brush cutters and burners, who raised plumes of smoke into the intensely blue fall sky with their work. Following them were laborers to build temporary culverts over numerous desert washes. Then came several teams of graders, each with approximately 100 Chinese men to a group.

Most of the grading work across the level terrain of southern Arizona would be done simply with animal-powered scrapers and hand-held shovels, but just east of Yuma some rock blasting using powder was required to skirt a low, rocky peak. Plus, according to the *Sentinel*: "There are a number of extensive fills to be made through this hilly section of three or four miles. Chinamen are crowded on these; and work with a monotonous industry that reminds one of the ant. These men appear to be neither happy nor miserable, just stolid and indifferent. It is plain that they move dirt much more slowly than white men but as they have no pipes to fill and no political reforms to discuss, they manage to get in a fair day's work before night falls."[4]

The Chinese laborers would spend those cool nights in tents grouped together in a string of large desert camps. In these movable settlements the Chinese ate their own meals, since wages for them did not include the provision of food.

After the earth had been graded to establish a roadbed for the tracks, the construction train would push forward to accommodate the actual installation of rails. While track-laying progressed, telegraph poles were also being raised next to the roadbed and wire strung in a simultaneous operation. Once an insulator had been put in place on a pole lying on the ground, a hole was dug, and the pole put in it. The whole process, said the *Sentinel*, took about three minutes, and twenty poles per mile were being erected.[5]

Simultaneously, ahead of the construction train came dozens of men, almost all of whom were white, involved with the process of putting the ties and rails in place. Once wood and steel had been moved on small horse-drawn cars from mass storage piles on the ground: "Men alight and rapidly bear the ties along on their shoulders, dropping them across the roadbed between ropes stretched on stakes, and as nearly as convenient at regular intervals. A man with a pick pulls and turns them into proper position. Other men follow and with tongs drag a pair of rails end-wise from the car and lay them into temporary position across the ties; on these the cars advance until their load is discharged, when the loaders jump on, and the horses draw them back, at a trot, for more material."[6]

Once the ties were put in place on the ground and the rails initially laid, a man would properly space the tracks using a measuring bar. To fasten the steel together: "Two Chinamen at once join abutting ends with fishplates, inserting bolts, and loosely placing nuts. These two are the only Chinamen now employed in track laying; they are professional 'strappers' as their peculiar occupation is called, and have been in the company's service, at the same business, for about ten years; they are considered experts."[7]

Following this preliminary work, the *Sentinel* said, "come two men with wrenches and hammers who tighten nuts and bolts; they are accompanied by a man with bar and measuring bar who keeps just ahead and pries the rails into unvarying distance apart." Once it was assured the tracks were separated by the correct distance, on each wooden tie spikes were laid which were then driven two-thirds of the way in on every third tie. This was followed by temporarily spiking the other ties, and then the nails were driven all the way in by workers "attended by a man who shoves a lever under the end of the tie, and steadies it to receive the blow."[8]

With the ties now secured to the roadbed, a crew of men followed to finalize the track-laying process. They "straighten out little bends in the track, level up little depressions and cut down little elevations from under the ties." After this work was completed, "The track is still far from finished, but it allows the construction train to be moved along nearer to the scene of operations."[9]

The *Sentinel* described the construction train as having twenty-four cars, most with a different purpose. The first cars were those that carried the materials essential for track-laying and in back of them came a "complete blacksmith and wheelwright shop on wheels," staffed by three men.[10] These were followed by a carload of odds and ends, then came a crude sleeping car, which had forty-two bunks in three tiers and another sleeper with forty-eight bunks. Both of these cars housed the manual laborers working on the track-laying, their superiors having somewhat better accommodations.

Behind the sleeping cars was a communal dining car with long tables followed by a kitchen supervised by an experienced railroad cook aided by six Chinese assistants. The food they prepared, however, was fed only to the approximately 200 white workers. "Nice bread, choice butter, fair sugar, syrup, pickles and condiments accompany every meal," the *Sentinel* reported.[11] "Dishes of roast beef with plenty of potatoes and onions, palatable stew, beans 'a la mode Boston,' and apple pies were scattered over the tables, interspersed with dishes of codfish (it being Friday)...". The menu, the newspaper decided, meant the two basic fundamentals of cooking for the working man had been satisfied: "Plenty of grease to make grub stick to ribs; plenty of salt to prevent stomachs souring and to keep tempers sweet."

In back of the kitchen was Strobridge's car with "its two front sections are fitted up as offices, with stove, and instruments kept in constant connection with the main telegraph line; behind the offices is a nice little bedroom and behind that is a good bathroom."[12]

The remainder of the construction train consisted of another sleeper, but this one for "foremen, engineers, and 'bosses'", then a commissary car followed by a car full of tools. Next came a specially-built huge vehicle which was used as a rolling convenience store, after which was a car containing powder for blasting, and then cars of hay and grain for the animals. These were followed by water tanks, and near its end the construction train had cars loaded with ties and rails, with sixteen of these required to provide enough material to lay one mile of track. At the end of all this was the locomotive "which advances the construction train when necessary, and acts as its messenger to and from the base of supplies."[13]

Following the massive effort to grade the roadbed and lay tracks on it came a pivoting pile driver mounted on a flatbed car. This machine was supplied with power from a "donkey engine" [vertical boiler connected to capstan or winch] that would be used to construct "permanent trestles over gullies which are now bridged by temporary crib work of ties."[14]

While the work was progressing away from Yuma, back in the community an enormous amount of construction material was accumulating and numerous railroad buildings were being erected. Heading for the front one day, a writer for the *Sentinel* said he went by "piles of rails, spikes and telegraph material; past round-house, cattle-corral, tool-houses, repair shops, coal bins, water tanks, ice-house and other buildings; past huge stacks of railroad ties (nearly 150,000 of them) and past great piles of baled hay...".[15]

As all of the track-laying supplies were making their way to the construction front in Arizona, on the east coast Huntington was diligently trying to insure sufficient rails kept being steadily shipped west, while also securing bids for even more. The lack of needed steel, however, would result in recurring interruptions for the company over the next several months and years.

The Chinese graders and laborers who prepared the roadbed for the rails were reluctantly paid about $1 per day. According to Leland Stanford, "We were compelled to give the Chinese $26.00 per month, or else wait indefinitely, with an uncertain result. I concluded that it was better to pay that price and have the work go forward, than to wait and get the men, even a month later, perhaps at $23.00 which we had previously offered."[16]

That cost, of course, did not include food, but even so, Charles Crocker's son wrote Huntington that he considered the amount extravagant. "I feel that $26.00 per month is entirely too much, though there can be no doubt it had to be done," he said.[17]

What his father thought of this salary is not recorded. It had been Charles Crocker, after all, who in 1865 had convinced James Strobridge to experiment with using Chinese laborers for grading and other jobs on the first transcontinental line. With workers in short supply because of the Civil War, combined with many men's thirst for quick riches in the California gold fields, Crocker proposed giving the Oriental immigrants a chance.

"I will not boss Chinese!" responded Strobridge, reflecting the common perception that the Asians were too little, too weak, and too effeminate to do the tough and dangerous manual labor required. "I will not be responsible for work done on the road by Chinese labor," he insisted. "From what I've seen of them, they're not fit laborers anyway. I don't think they can build a railroad."[18] In reply, his boss simply asked the angry Irishman, "But who said laborers have to be white to build railroads?"[19]

To settle the dispute, an experiment was conducted with fifty of the Asian men working for a month on the project. At its conclusion, Strobridge was convinced. The Chinese worked well together as teams, didn't often slow down the backbreaking labor, and remained very healthy. In addition, the non-drinking construction foreman appreciated that the Chinese abstained from drinking liquor, were honest and clean, and didn't fight among themselves or with others. In general, they were wonderful employees.

The Chinese did have some vices, of course, just like all the others working on that first transcontinental line. They gambled, enjoyed the company of prostitutes, and smoked opium in their free time. Compared to the white men employed on the project, though, and despite being physically much smaller, the Chinese often out-performed them.

At the end of that epic effort to tie the country together with a ribbon of steel, Charles Crocker praised the Chinese role in completing the job. "Wherever we put them, we found them good. And they worked themselves into our favor to such an extent, we found if we were in a hurry for a job of work, it was better to put Chinese on it at once."[20] Leland Stanford, originally an ardent opponent of Chinese labor added, "As a class they are quiet, peaceable, patient, industrious, and economical."[21]

Part of the reason for the Chinese ability to get a lot of work done was the organizational structure they brought to the job. Grouped into gangs of twenty, the Chinese would elect one as their leader while another served as cook. All wages were paid to the leader, and after the cost of food and other essentials were deducted, the balance was given monthly to the men.

Unlike the grease and salt, meat and potatoes diet of the whites who were working to lay tracks through Arizona, the Chinese probably ate more balanced and healthier meals. They bought fish from the Indians in Yuma and on the earlier transcontinental construction project it was reported, "The Chinese menu included dried oysters, abalone and cuttlefish, dried bamboo sprouts and mushrooms, five kinds of vegetables, pork, poultry, vermicelli, rice, salted cabbage, dried seaweed, sweet-rice, crackers, sugar, four kinds of dried fruit, Chinese bacon, peanut oil and tea."[22]

This final item was an important distinction between the white and Chinese laborers. While the former drank coffee, whiskey, or well water poured from communal pails, the boiled water in their tea helped protect the latter from numerous diseases.

The Chinese were also personally cleaner than their white counterparts. They bathed regularly, while the other laborers did not. Their tea-drinking habits combined with their cleanliness meant the Chinese were healthier, and one of their advantages as employees was that they were seldom sick.

Despite all these positive attributes, however, newspapers routinely belittled the Chinese while politicians called for prohibiting any more of them from entering the country and labor organizations blamed them for everything from taking jobs from white Americans to helping sink the nation into an economic downturn. This abysmal treatment was observed first-hand by Robert Louis Stevenson in 1879 as he rode across America over the first transcontinental rail line.

In the chapter "Despised Races" from his book *The Amateur Emigrant*, the Scottish author commented: "Of all stupid ill-feelings, the sentiment of my fellow-Caucasians towards our companions in the Chinese car was the most stupid and the worst. They seemed never to have looked at them, listened to them, or thought of them, but hated them *a priori*...They declared them hideous vermin, and affected a kind of choking in the throat when they beheld them."[23]

The Chinese working for the Southern Pacific Company weren't the first of their nationality in Arizona, but almost. Twenty of their countrymen were listed in the 1870 territorial census. The railroad project, however, would bring so many more that by 1880 the census showed over sixteen hundred Chinese, most of them railroad workers.[24]

In the desert east of Yuma, the initial grading work by the Chinese laborers proceeded slowly because of the rocky, hilly terrain. Strobridge telegraphed Crocker in early December that he or Stanford should come down to the front to inspect two optional lines for the road through this area, the first laid out by the surveyors, the other recommended by himself. "It must be decided very soon," Strobridge said, then requested, "Don't send anybody, but come one of you."[25]

In response, Crocker made a quick trip to Arizona and reported to Huntington: "I found Strobridge in full blast. He is full of energy—as much so as I ever saw him, and I assure you the work under his charge is going forward splendidly and economically…It seemed like old times to meet 'Stro' out there, and hear him order things around."[26]

While at the construction site in Arizona, Crocker directed the roadbed be kept low to the ground. He thought this could offer greater protection from washouts during heavy desert thunderstorms than a higher mound would provide. As for changing the proposed line of the road, Crocker backed Strobridge's decision and concluded, "I think more of his judgment in such matters than I do of the engineers."[27] In the end, though, it was the latter's path which was followed because it was the best route.[28]

Once past the natural obstacle which had slowed the work down, the rate of grading and track-laying increased substantially. "Heavy work over, will now go fast," was wired Huntington at this time.[29] For his part, after his visit to the front, Crocker told Huntington, "From this time on, you will hear pretty lively reports of progress."[30]

In addition to this good news for the company, ahead of the graders and track-layers was level ground all the way to well beyond Tucson; thus, installing a mile or more of rails each day was not beyond expectation. The final course of the line had not been specifically determined past Maricopa, but whatever the decision on that route, the topographical advantages of the Gadsden Purchase for building a railroad were about to be realized by the men working on the Southern Pacific line.

As they moved forward toward the first major destination east of Yuma, the workers passed a point which none of them probably knew about. The *Sentinel* did, however, and commented, "The railroad graders will work pretty near to the old Oroville ruins. They may be lucky enough to find two yeast-powder cans full of gold dust, which were left there in 1872 by old Gardner. He buried the gold near the old house while he was drunk, and could never find it again after he got sober."[31]

After passing that spot, by the end of 1878 the rails were approaching a point about thirty miles east of the Colorado River, a station which would be called "Adonde". The Spanish place name, according to Towne, meant, "where, to what place, whither". To publicize its passenger train schedule from Yuma to this new station, Arizona's first railroad timetable would be prepared by Southern Pacific.

In Tucson, the *Arizona Star* noted the trip by train from Yuma to Adonde would take two hours and cost three dollars. It also wrote that the new station already had "a temporary platform for delivery of freight, barber shop, two saloons, one hotel, telegraph office with lady operator, Chinese wash house, railroad office and one butcher shop."[32] The newspaper didn't mention, though, that the hotel was "portable", presumably being a rail car fitted out with rooms. The *Star* did say that a 50,000-gallon water tank for the steam engines had been erected at Adonde.

Charles Crocker was impressed by the quality as well as the speed of the construction work to this point. "If they [members of Congress] have got an idea that we are not building a good road down there," he wrote Huntington in January of 1879, "you can say to them that we can run over the road [at] 50 miles an hour with perfect safety."[33] In the same letter he also expressed great concern for the health of Leland Stanford, writing that their partner "has been sick for the last two weeks and over."

A New York newspaper had just published a short notice which said that the 54-year old Stanford "is dangerously ill from a combined attack of congestion of the lungs and brain."[34] A few days later, however, Crocker wrote that Stanford was recovering, and General Superintendent Towne blamed the whole episode on a young physician who had misdiagnosed the illness.

That conclusion proved to be premature. A month later Stanford was still ill in bed, and by February 25th Crocker was writing, "I am sorry to say that Mr. Stanford is worse again."[35] The cause was thought to be noxious gas from a privy vault in his ranch house and Crocker wrote, "The Doctors say that it will require at least a year to eradicate this poison from his system."

While acknowledging that the physicians thought Stanford would ultimately recover, Crocker insisted their partner's condition should convince Huntington to go slowly, very slowly, about extending the rails beyond Maricopa. In January, when it looked like Stanford would quickly regain his health, Crocker had written his associate: "I assure you Mr. Huntington that I really think we ought to get out of debt before we build any more road. We are all of us getting old, and I feel like putting my house in order before I die."[36] In a March 14th letter, after Stanford's physical condition had deteriorated again, he wrote, "For the first time since Gov. Stanford's illness, I feel somewhat alarmed...the fact is that the Gov. is constantly getting worse."[37] Noting that Stanford could only keep milk in his stomach and had a temperature of over 101 degrees, Crocker said: "It becomes necessary for us to look the thing square in the face. Whether or not the probable loss of Governor Stanford should have any effect on our work in Arizona is a matter for consideration."

In response to Crocker's alarm, Huntington replied calmly: "I am very sorry to hear of Stanford's continued illness and notice what you write of continuing work on the S.P. and while I cannot but share in your anxiety as to the matter of which you write, I am still inclined to think we will be stronger come what may to continue work on the S.P. than not to do so."[38]

In early April, Stanford himself dictated a letter of his own to his east coast partner and concluded it with a frail, wobbly signature. He was recovering, he wrote, having discarded the medicine his doctors had prescribed for him. That, he said, cleared up his stomach problems, and then he added hopefully, "I think that I am fairly on the road to complete health."[39]

Well before Stanford's recovery, the tracks in the Arizona desert had been extended even farther. In late January, Crocker had exclaimed, "Everything is going on at the front remarkably well. Strobridge has not lost any of his old vigor."[40] A few days later, Towne wired New York, "Company will open up to business a new station called Texas Hill sixty-four and a quarter miles east of Yuma on Saturday the first [of February]."[41]

Before that station was established, the portable hotel had been moved to Texas Hill and testing was going on in the area to locate good water. A source had been found only fifty feet below the surface, but it was too salty for use by the steam engines and Crocker commented: "One great difficulty we have in Arizona is the water. Even the water from the Gila is bad, and foams when engines are working to their best capacity, and the well water so far as we have bored has all been salt."[42] To overcome the problem, he was looking for someone to drill deep wells to a depth of 1,500 to 2,000 feet. "We must have water for that road," he wrote, but in the meantime the company was having "to haul everything now in water cars for engines, stations, and the construction forces." To partially address the issue, it was eventually decided to pump water from the Gila River through almost four miles of pipe to the Texas Hill station.

Even with the water problems, Crocker had visited Arizona again and reported: "Everything moves like clock-work. But all the steel that was on hand and [scheduled] to arrive, up to tonight, will be laid out today or tomorrow when things will go slow until steel comes faster. The graders are several miles in advance of the track, and as all their water has to be hauled to them, they will have to suspend work until steel commences coming again."[43]

While the company was facing water and rail shortages, tragedy struck in Yuma. As the sun was setting on the afternoon of January 27th, a young boy climbed aboard a slow moving freight car, but ran off after being spotted by company employees. He returned, however, and his severed body was later found on the tracks, having been run over by a train. According to the *Sentinel*, this was the "First Railroad Mishap in Arizona". "The train men have repeatedly warned parents and have done all they could to keep boys off and to prevent their climbing onto cars in motion," the newspaper emphasized, "but the little fellows have been like flies; driven off from one car they lit on another. Since the accident, we notice that boys give the cars a wide berth."[44]

Despite this tragic mishap, Crocker was more than satisfied with the progress being made on the line. He had arranged to pay for the construction across Arizona through the issuance of bonds in three series, and he wrote of the work: "I do not think we have ever built a railroad before as cheaply as this is being built, and it is a good road at the same time. I came back over it from the front, at the rate of 30 miles an hour, and it rode as smoothly as the New York Central."[45]

The slow delivery of rails, however, was continuing to cause difficulties. While Huntington was pleased with the progress of construction and doing what he could in New York to insure that a steady supply of steel kept being shipped west, Crocker thought the work party in Arizona would have to be reduced if deliveries didn't pick up. That, he said, could cut the effort back to one-half mile per day. Then he added in warning of the approaching summer heat: "It will be a great pity if we have to disband our forces before completing the road to Maricopa Wells."[46]

In the meantime, though, the work kept moving steadily forward, with the graders remaining many miles ahead of the track-layers because of the delayed delivery of rails. Despite that, by March 1st the construction train had reached more than 85 miles beyond the Colorado River to the new station at Stanwix, named after the nearby stage coach stop. The *Sentinel* told its readers in Yuma that a level, sandy site was chosen for the location "in order to afford greater facilities for reaching the famous Agua Caliente (Hot Spring) to which it is expected there will be much travel. These Springs are said to have no superior for the cure of rheumatic affections."[47]

Several weeks before Stanwix was reached by rails, Southern Pacific officials had to contend with an effort by some members of the territorial legislature to revoke their authorization to cross Arizona. Governor John C. Frémont wrote Crocker he didn't know where this opposition was coming from,[48] but the attempt was defeated in the House by a vote of 12 to 6.

"This action on the part of the legislature is commendable," offered the *Arizona Star*, "and is not only in accord with law, but with good faith."[49] The newspaper thought it incumbent for the territory to "encourage everything which this enlightened age is bringing forth, from the sewing machine to 'Edison's electric light'."

The move to repeal S.P.'s right to lay tracks through Arizona may have been the Texas and Pacific Company's last gasp to try to scuttle the project. Huntington was told that a few politicians in Washington, D.C. who backed Tom Scott's railroad, "have been declaring that you have asserted that you would build the Southern Pacific R.R. to El Paso law, or no law, and that Congress wouldn't dare stop you...".[50] Southern Pacific officials reiterated, however, that they were laying the tracks under the provisions of the federal legislation passed in 1875, which granted "right-of-way through the public lands of the United States...to any railroad company duly organized under the laws of any State or Territory".[51] Because it had secured permission from the Arizona legislature and incorporated a subsidiary company in the territory, S.P. officials believed they could legally proceed with the work.

Questioning that conclusion, a Senator from South Carolina, who was a supporter of Scott's proposal, inquired of the Secretary of the Interior about the legal status of the project.[52] Huntington had already filed maps of the route with the Interior Department, along with a copy of the Arizona railroad company's incorporation papers, and from Florence, Arizona, Charles Poston forwarded to Washington additional plans for the line. Poston noted, however, that the S.P. route was within the land grant provided by the federal government several years before to the Texas and Pacific Company.[53]

Despite Scott's last chance effort to stop Southern Pacific's work, by this time most members of Congress couldn't back a railroad company that continued to want a federal subsidy to build a line along the same route where privately financed tracks were already being laid. For his part, Huntington was finally expressing confidence that the challenge had been met and was even thinking of negotiating a transfer of the Texas and Pacific federal land grant to the S.P.[54] After all, acquiring the twenty sections of government land promised for every mile of track laid through the Arizona and New Mexico territories might help financially.

Facing these realities, Tom Scott sailed for Europe in hopes of regaining his declining health, and the railroad battle for the Gadsden Purchase ended quietly for the time being. In March of 1879, the *Sentinel* published a short obituary which read, "Our dispatches from Washington inform us that the workers for the Texas Pacific Railroad, after six years of constant labor, have at length abandoned all further hopes of success."[55]

With its long time adversary apparently finally defeated, Southern Pacific's construction effort through Arizona kept moving methodically forward. The approach of spring, however, meant much warmer temperatures weren't far away, and Crocker was contemplating just how much longer the work could continue.

In the middle of February he acknowledged that only enough ties had been ordered to reach Maricopa, and wondered whether to move past that point in the heat of summer. He asked Huntington's opinion while adding, "I think likely the men could stand it to work then."[56]

By early March Crocker also wrote: "The weather in Arizona now is simply superb, and no better conditions could exist for building road cheaply and well than now do, if we had the rails. They are laying them as fast as they come to hand, a little over a mile a day. The grading is now some 20 or 25 miles in advance of the track completed."[57] Based on that, he wanted to "continue building if the weather does not get so warm as to drive them [the workers] out." At the same time, though, some of the Chinese graders were laid off because of the uncertainty over exactly how far the track-laying would progress.

During the first week of April, Crocker had decided to keep laying track beyond Maricopa, but didn't know how long the men could withstand the desert heat. "The other day Strobridge wrote me that he expected that most of his track layers would quit after the next pay-day," he wrote Huntington, "as the weather had got to be very hot. The day he wrote, the thermometer stood [at] <u>100</u> in the coolest place he could put it in his car, and of course the men will not work in such hot weather if they can help it…Still we will go on as long as we can, and do it anywise profitably."[58]

While company officials were contemplating shutting down work for the summer, the *Sentinel* in Yuma was reporting otherwise. "There are many things of more or less importance which indicate that continuous construction is in contemplation, if not already determined upon," the newspaper mistakenly wrote.[59] As for the heat, the paper pointed out that farm labor was done in the San Joaquin Valley of California during the summer months and then stated humorously, "THE THERMOMETER DOES NOT GO AS HIGH here as it does there."

As the debate over warm weather construction by the workers continued within the company, by April 1st the tracks had reached a place three miles from the existing stage coach stop of Gila Bend. Located near a huge turn in the river, this new terminal point wouldn't attract much of a population for quite some time, with only about forty people living at the coach stop according to the 1880 census.[60]

Shortly after the railroad station at Gila Bend opened, large amounts of freight began arriving there. These deliveries included ten iron safes, having a combined weight of almost 9,000 pounds. Massive quantities of fruits and produce were also sent, and as the *Sentinel* noted about one of the changes occurring in Arizona commerce, "Formerly we used to receive oranges from Sonora [Mexico], now we find that fruit and even eggs are shipped with profit from Los Angeles to Arizona by the Southern Pacific Railroad."[61]

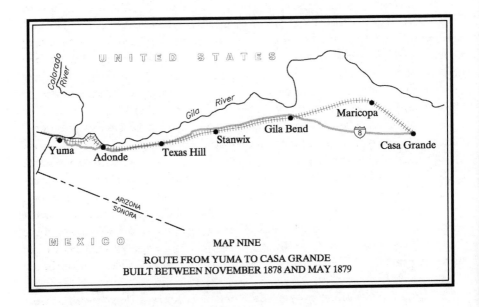

MAP NINE
ROUTE FROM YUMA TO CASA GRANDE
BUILT BETWEEN NOVEMBER 1878 AND MAY 1879

From its newest station at Gila Bend, the company could run daily trains west to Yuma, while stage coaches and wagons were available to carry passengers and freight in other directions. This was the same routine which was followed at every new terminal point: as the tracks were extended forward, stage and freight routes would retreat to accommodate the evolving realities of travel and transportation of goods in the Arizona territory.

Despite the new competition, existing freight company owners for awhile at least weren't complaining. Their business actually increased after the arrival of the railroad because of the rapidly growing demand for goods in newly developing mining and farming districts which were accessible only by wagon.

Even though this new freighting business was brisk for a time, the prosperity of each "end-of-track" station was short-lived. As the rails moved forward, a community like Gila Bend would spring up, but within a month or so a new town would have been established farther down the road. When that happened most of the portable businesses which had opened in one place would simply pick up and move, leaving the abandoned spot as not much more than a deserted outpost for railroad operations.

While it was still the last station on the line, however, regular stage coach service was provided from Gila Bend. It cost $17.00 for the 14-hour, 83-mile ride north to the small community of Phoenix, whereas the 173-mile trip south to Tucson lasted twenty-nine hours at a price of $30.00. For those going east to Florence, the 98-mile journey required 16 hours and $20.00 up front.[62]

Florence was described by one traveler as having "a population of 500; four stores, a good school-house, Catholic church, two hotels and restaurants, one brewery, a smelting furnace, three flouring mills in or near town, and some fine residences."[63] The place was also known, this visitor noted, for its streets lined by shade trees.

To learn more about this community, and the rest of southern Arizona, Huntington had his field surveyors and engineers report to him periodically on the topographical characteristics of the territory as well as its economic prospects. One of these men wrote that Florence "has nothing to keep it up save the surrounding farming lands on the Gila River, and the trade caused by the passage of teams to and from," a nearby mine.[64] If that venture proved profitable, the report concluded, branch tracks could easily be run to the mine from the main line.

Whatever the outlook of that one particular mine, the newspapers of the region continued to proclaim the great future in store for Arizona. In April, the *Citizen* reprinted a story from the *Chicago Tribune* which announced, "One year ago no mines of this region were heard of outside the Territory; within that time the fame of the marvelous richness of Tombstone and other districts has penetrated to every city of the Nation, mills and other reduction works are predicted on every hand, and the American population of Southern Arizona has more than doubled…".[65]

That wasn't the first acknowledgment given of the potential richness of the Tombstone silver mines and the impact they could have on the territory. Some time before, one man had told General Superintendent Towne that he expected ten thousand people to be living in Tombstone within fifteen months, and other boosters extolled the district's rich mineral wealth.[66]

While promotion of the territory's future possibilities was growing across the nation, the track-laying continued on toward Maricopa. The tiny stage stop there was thought to have a very bright and important future since it would be the point where wagons and coaches going to the Salt River Valley farming communities around Phoenix and the mining districts further north near Prescott would intersect the tracks as they turned south. According to the *Sentinel*: "Maricopa has a very fair chance of becoming the capitol of Arizona…Its accessibility from all quarters is certainly no mean advantage…Excellent water has been found there, by wells of moderate depth."[67]

In addition to those factors, the agricultural soil in the bottom lands of the Gila and Salt rivers was considered excellent for farming. "This soil, with irrigation," one S.P. official wrote, "produces abundant crops of corn, wheat, barley, beans, and sugar cane."[68] Another company representative concluded of the land between Maricopa and Phoenix: "Settlements are rapidly advancing up the [Salt] River, and the soil wherever water can be applied produces abundantly...The fertility of the soil is almost incredible and seems limited only by available water."[69] It was reported that forty thousand acres of land in the vicinity were already under cultivation and a lot more was available for farming.

Much of the existing farming, of course, was being conducted by Pima and Maricopa Indians, just as they had been doing for centuries. Over 4,000 of them lived on a nearby reservation and according to one visitor: "They have from time immemorial been quite successful agriculturists, and now raise considerable quantities of wheat, pumpkins, melons, etc. In 1876 they sold nearly two million pounds of wheat at about three cents per pound. They prepare their wheat for market in a manner that would be creditable to the best eastern farmers."[70] The arrival of the railroad, therefore, would help not only the territory's new residents, but also some of its original settlers.

On April 28th, 1879, Huntington was notified that the rails had finally reached Maricopa, 156 miles east of Yuma. Within weeks, a community would develop which was described as a "bustling town of more than 500 people, with post office, express office, stores, hotels, saloons, and new buildings going up on every side."[71] There were reportedly two lumber yards and the S.P. company itself was planning to build a large depot and hotel along with a 4,100 square foot warehouse to accommodate the booming freighting business which was occurring.

To encourage even more growth in the new community, Southern Pacific officials arranged for a special train to leave San Francisco on May 10th. A round-trip ticket cost $40.00, which included a sleeping berth, and the entire journey took five days. "An important feature of the excursion," according to an S.P. publicity pamphlet, "will be the sale at public auction of a large number of town lots" in Maricopa.[72]

Over two hundred made the trip, and the auction began almost immediately upon their arrival. They had come by train to a land which one San Francisco newspaper writer romantically described as: "There is hardly a sunrise, sunset, or midnight in this country that is not replete with either beauty or impressiveness."[73] After some brief confusion about which county Maricopa was actually located in, fifty-one total lots were sold by the railroad company at prices ranging from $25 to $1,000, for a total investment of over ten thousand dollars.[74]

The once pessimistic Crocker was impressed by those results as well as with the future prospects of the whole territory. "We had a sale of town lots at

Maricopa at auction," he wrote Huntington enthusiastically, "and sold a little over $10,000 worth, the <u>first pop</u>, so you will see that things are brightening up down that way. There is great talk of new mines being discovered all around throughout the territory adjacent to the railroad. How much truth there is in it I am unable to say, but certain it is that public attention is being directed to Arizona now, since our road has progressed so rapidly, and we can expect still greater results."[75]

The speculators who bought land at Maricopa may have been spurred on partially by baseless press reports that the track-laying was going to continue throughout the summer. "No more talk is being made about hot weather," the *Sentinel* announced in late April of 1879, "...it can be safely predicted that the track will be within fifty miles of Tucson by the Fourth of July—or sooner."[76]

In Tucson, the *Citizen* reported that summer work would be pushed forward rapidly, while the *Star* went even further and predicted the tracks would reach town by the 4th of July. Once that happened, the newspaper offered, "The first sound of the locomotive's whistle will be the notice of a new life for our city and its vicinity; and we look forward to the time when the last spike is driven that connects Tucson with the outside world by a band of iron with a degree of pleasure that we cannot describe."[77]

Although Arizona's major newspapers were confidentially predicting track-laying would continue throughout the summer, Charles Crocker had just returned from another trip to the front and concluded differently. He wired New York in the middle of May, "Have directed construction to stop at a point twenty-six miles east of Maricopa Wells until November as ties are not coming fast enough to keep work going and we need some steel for repairs."[78]

A few days later he explained his decision in a letter to Huntington. "My idea of stopping the road was based on the fact that the reserve of ties on hand was pretty much exhausted," he wrote, then said that new deliveries "were so irregular that we could not expect to continue the construction except at intervals."[79] In addition to that problem, he added, "The weather was getting so hot that the men could not work much longer to good advantage."

As soon as the Chinese graders had reached the stopping point southeast of Maricopa, they were disbanded. As the *L.A. Commercial* somewhat gleefully observed of this desolate desert site: "Not a Chinaman is to be seen—well, hardly any. But the scattered heaps of old clothes and abandoned provisions with the croaking of ravens and snarling of coyotes mark their last camp very distinctly."[80]

Most of the Chinese men laid off from the railroad work returned to California, but some ventured to Phoenix or Tucson. Those who went north joined five of their countrymen who were already operating a laundry in Phoenix. By the time the census was taken in the following year of 1880, 109 Chinese were living there, and their business activities included three restaurants, as well as presumably some small grocery stores.[81]

At that time, Phoenix's total population was less than 2,500, or about one-third the number living in Tucson. The community built near the Salt River had been described a few years earlier as: "Well laid out, with a fine growth of shade trees along its principal streets, rendering it pleasant, attractive, and beautiful…A court-house, jail, school-house, hotel, restaurant, and several good stores, pleasant residences, etc., make up the town. The population is about one half each, white and Mexicans."[82]

Other Chinese railroad workers moved to Tucson, and the census of 1880 identified 159 of them as living in Arizona's largest community. Legend has it that some of the first to arrive were the Wongs, who left the S.P. work gang at Gila Bend and established a restaurant in the center of Tucson. According to one account of this business, "A laundry basket was used instead of a cash register and meals were seventy-five cents each."[83]

North of Tucson, by May 19th the rails had been laid from Maricopa to the new terminus. It was named "Casa Grande" after the famous Indian ruins several miles farther east. Just like all the other stations along the way from Yuma, within a few days numerous portable and temporary structures had instantly appeared. It was also reported that some stores, along with the railroad and stage offices "are on wheels, ready to move on as soon as opportunity presents."[84]

The rails extended one mile beyond the new station, and road building materials rolled into town to be piled up for future use. Once the tracks reached Casa Grande, however, work on the Southern Pacific Railroad stopped. The *Sentinel* expressed surprise, but acknowledged that the graders and track-layers "have been constantly working at high pressure speed since November last, under the disadvantages of warm days, cold nights, scarcity of water and inhaling the dust of 182 miles now accomplished."[85]

The newspaper summarized of the track-laying project so far, "It is a wonderful feat that Col. Strobridge may well be proud to add to his many triumphs."[86] Continuing, the *Sentinel* wrote, "It is difficult to appreciate the effect this undertaking is having and will continue to have, upon the development of Arizona… The Southern Pacific Railroad is the wedge that opens Arizona to development by steam and electricity."

Shortly after the suspension of work, and close to the 25th anniversary of the ratification of the Gadsden Treaty, a southern-Arizona couple took the round trip by rail from Casa Grande to Yuma. They left their Tucson home at one in the afternoon and after a sixteen-hour stage coach ride reached the new station at Casa Grande early the next morning. The westbound train departed within a few hours and required about ten more to travel the 180 miles to reach its destination on the Colorado River.

"The trains are mixed—that is they haul water, freight, railway material and passengers," it was reported of this journey and, "the average speed is about twenty miles an hour."[87] That was a good rate, it was thought, since the train was stopping frequently to drop off supplies to laborers who were still employed in completing ballast work on the roadbed or installing permanent bridges and trestles over desert washes.

"Taken as a whole," the *Citizen* in Tucson concluded of the couple's trip, "the fact that this long line of road is built at all is surely a wonder to all...". After reviewing the economic advantages the railroad would bring to the territory's mining industry, the paper exclaimed about another of its very significant benefits, "A pleasure trip to Yuma! It hardly seems possible, and yet it is quite true to the observant and experienced traveler."

CHAPTER THIRTEEN

"Ask him, 'who built the Southern Pacific Railroad?' and the
child of centuries will answer, 'Crocker'."

While track-laying was suspended at Casa Grande, a permanent settlement began
to develop there. Temporary or portable buildings were replaced by site-built
structures, and the tiny population started to slowly increase. Despite that, when
a correspondent for the *Chicago Tribune* visited in October of 1879, he didn't
have much to say about the place. He did comment on the train's late arrival time
of 11:30 p.m., and the generosity of the conductor in allowing passengers to
remain in their sleeping berths until 4 a.m., at which time the coaches had to be
prepared to return to Yuma. About his only remark on the community was,
"Here we see piled up thousands of ties and heaps of rails, which in two or three
weeks more are to be used in extending the track to Tucson, the principal town in
southern Arizona, distant now seventy miles…".[1]

Three years later, Casa Grande still only had two dirt streets, one for businesses and the other for residences, each located on either side of the railroad
tracks. Among its commercial establishments, according to a local newspaper,
were a "comfortable" hotel, a stationery store, a restaurant owned by a "thoroughly Americanized Chinaman," and two saloons. There was also a blacksmith
shop, a lumber yard, and a bakery. A class of twenty students had enrolled in
school, some handsome homes were being built, and water was available from a
well only 52 feet deep.[2]

Northwest of Casa Grande at Maricopa, though, development was completely
stagnant. Within several months after the arrival of the tracks, one visitor would
say of the community which only a short while before had been predicted to have
a very bright future: "This place is a fraud, as nearly all railroad towns are. It was
a lively place until the road was built as far as Casa Grande, 26 miles east of here.

Since then the town has been gradually going down. At present there are three stores, one fruit stand, two saloons, and a hotel; and with the exception of the hotel they are all starving to death."[3]

Potential economic doldrums were of little concern to Tucson's leaders, however. When the rails finally crossed the level ground between Casa Grande and their city, people in the territory's largest settlement expected great benefits. The *Arizona Star* proclaimed even before the track-layers left Yuma, "Tucson is to be in the future, as she is now, the center of trade, enterprise and power of Arizona."[4]

The tracks should also allow for increased export of crops grown on the estimated 1,800 acres cultivated in the vicinity of Tucson, particularly along the Santa Cruz River. While this was much less farm land than existed near Phoenix, the amount would soon increase due to newly-arrived Chinese tilling more land.

Not only might more food be grown, but the types of locally produced fruits and vegetables would be altered. As the *Citizen* summarized in 1880: "John Chinaman here as in California has taken charge of the vegetable business, and instead of giving us red peppers, spinach and garlic as the Mexicans used to do, they give us a full supply of every species of vegetable grown in California, except potatoes. They also tell us that in another year they will be on hand with strawberries, raspberries, gooseberries, currents, etc…Just think of it, 'strawberries and cream,' in Tucson next year."[5]

The railroad reaching Tucson meant the city would change dramatically in many other ways. Its architecture would go from Sonoran adobe rowhouses to proper pitch-roofed Victorian homes built of wood. Its food could become more "American," as would its increasing population. The economy was expected to be transformed from one of subsistence to one which exported goods, particularly ore and cattle. Given that, the conclusion of many by this time was: "It is now a settled fact that the city of Tucson is to be the future metropolis of the great Southwest. Railroads, agriculture, mining and stock-raising will produce this result…".[6]

As the residents of Tucson waited expectantly for the railroad work to resume, the bill for laying the 182 miles of track from Yuma to Casa Grande was sent to Southern Pacific by its subsidiary company which had actually built the road. It came to approximately $9.3 million, one-half of which was to be paid in bonds, the remainder in stock.[7] The price included all labor and materials as well as sidings, maintenance buildings, and other operational necessities along with the proposed purchase of railroad cars for the company at a cost of $10,000 per mile of track laid. The actual total for the track-laying, according to a company spokesman, did not exceed $30,000 a mile,[8] and one of the ways S.P. would save a considerable amount was by obtaining its own locomotives and other rolling stock for the road.

In June of 1879, Collis Huntington ordered the first three steam engines from Schenectedy Locomotive Company in New York for the Arizona branch of the

Southern Pacific.[9] These were individually priced at $6,500, with the head lamp of each costing an additional $165.[10] The engines were eight-wheelers, and on the coal tenders Huntington instructed to be printed "S.P.R.R. of Arizona".

The Huntington Library

SOUTHERN PACIFIC LOCOMOTIVES AT YUMA

Cabooses were also on their way to the territory. The first one would arrive in Tucson a few months after the rails did, and it had been built in California, not on the east coast like the engines. "It is perfection so far as desk, lockers, swinging bunks, wash basin, water cooler and other comforts are concerned," was reported of the initial caboose, and more would be sent south.[11]

Along with ordering equipment for the new line, Huntington was desperately trying to obtain sufficient rails to allow construction to resume as soon as the intensely hot summer weather cooled off. Securing the additional railroad ties needed wouldn't be difficult, but buying the rails could be. This problem was compounded when in early June of 1879, Charles Crocker informed his New York partner that he was using the steel which the company presently had on hand in California to make needed repairs to some of their other west coast roads.[12] No more rails were thus being sent to Casa Grande. Despite that shortage, by this time the formerly pessimistic Crocker had concluded the track-laying must continue all the way through Arizona in order to make the line profitable, while also admitting that freight traffic on the S.P. was increasing nicely.[13]

Even before receiving these letters from San Francisco, Huntington had begun communicating with a half dozen east coast supply companies that more rails were urgently needed in Arizona. He had contracted for some track, while negotiating for much more, and told Crocker confidently, "I am making arrangements for rails sufficient to extend the Southern Pacific to the Rio Grande."[14]

While assuring his partner the tracks could be secured, Huntington was actually having enormous difficulties with one of his major suppliers. In July he had written them, "Our people in California want the…rails now…How soon will you ship the rails?"[15]

Due to an improving national economy and an explosion of railroad-building throughout the country, rails were very hard to obtain. One estimate was that over 10,000 miles of tracks would be laid in 1880 alone so that "everybody can have a little railroad of their own".[16]

This railroad building boom, combined with the low prices which Huntington and Crocker wanted to pay for the steel, meant they would not be at the top of their suppliers' list. These two men might be rich and powerful, but they couldn't control everything. Over the summer months and into the fall, Huntington's attempts to obtain a steady supply of rails to quickly continue the track-laying away from Casa Grande would fail. This situation did not please Crocker at all. In September, he impatiently wrote his associate, "I wish you would hurry up the steel, as when we commence work in Arizona again, we do not want to be detained for lack of material."[17]

Responding to his west coast partner, Huntington explained the problems of purchasing more track. Anxious to get working again, however, Crocker was unimpressed. "We ought to have those rails as soon as possible now," he commented on October 1st, "as the weather in November, December, and January is the best for building down south, and when I get at that job, I want to do it at the minimum expense, which is best attainable when we have material on hand and do not have to wait and feed the teams and men for waiting."[18] His goal, Crocker said in another October letter, was to reach Tucson by early in the new year.[19]

Huntington had been trying his best to apply additional pressure on his rail suppliers, especially the one which was far behind in its promised deliveries. "You are now 3 1/2 months in arrears," he wrote them angrily in September, "and our company want them very much. Mr. Crocker telegraphed this day, anxious in relation to it, and wants to know what is being done about it."[20]

The supplier replied quickly, offering a litany of excuses which Huntington found "pitiful," and he told an associate he had lost confidence in the firm's ability to deliver the ordered rails. In his response to the company, Huntington indicated the S.P. was suffering great damage because of the lack of steel, while stressing: "Please let me hear no more 'excuses', but instead that the rails are going forward daily…We need those rails badly, and if you don't let us have them promptly, there will be something you can expect to pay."[21]

Despite his threats, by the end of October not much had changed. The supplier claimed a lack of railroad cars on which to ship the tracks was impeding delivery, so Huntington arranged for that difficulty to be overcome. Rails were still not being produced and forwarded rapidly enough, and some of those that were sent west turned out to be defective. The reality of the lack of enough material was obvious. "The steel is coming at the rate of only about one car a day now," Crocker in frustration told his associate in late October, "which is very slowly, and we shall not at this rate get sufficient steel to lay the road in Arizona this winter."[22] In reply, Huntington could only offer, "I am doing all I can to get rails started but find it one of the most difficult things to do that I ever tried."[23]

While obtaining sufficient steel rails was next to impossible in the fall of 1879, ordering the rolling stock needed to operate a railroad company in the territory was not a problem. After the first three engines were obtained for the Arizona line, Crocker requested more locomotives along with 200 flat cars and 100 box cars.[24] All of them, he said, should be marked "S.P.R.R. of Arizona", and Huntington complied, paying $7,700 for each of the new steam engines.[25]

In addition to locomotives and other rolling stock for the line, the company would be ordering passenger cars. For the Arizona desert, General Superintendent Towne told Huntington, these cars should have a galvanized iron roof and contain a ventilator to combat the heat. They might also have a new interior decor, one which was lighter in tone than Southern Pacific's existing sleeping cars. Proposed to be decorated in a Colonial-style of woodwork with intricate designs and massing around the doorways and windows, Towne was pushing his reluctant boss to make this change from past company practice.[26]

Towne was making other alterations to the layout of the passenger cars as well. An extra wash stand was added to the state rooms and a hot water stove placed in another room accessible to a porter. He thought this latter improvement important "on account of so many invalids traveling and our desire to aid them with hot water as required from time to time."[27]

Along with these additions made for travelers' comfort came standard railroad items for the twenty-four berth sleeping cars. Each contained, "156 pillow slips, 156 sheets, 60 towels, 24 berth curtains, 12 spittoons, 24 mattresses, 48 pillows, 1 carpet, 1 step ladder, 1 shovel, 1 ventilator hook."[28] All of this material was acquired and soon available for the Southern Pacific of Arizona line.

As rolling stock and accessories were being easily obtained by S.P., while more rails were proving hard to come by, the residents of Tucson had grown concerned about just what the company's plans were for them. Earlier, there had been some question as to whether the line would even pass near the territory's largest community, but that rumor had been set aside to be replaced by three others. The first was speculation that Southern Pacific demanded a $150,000 bribe or they would lay their tracks thirteen miles south of Tucson.[29] Next came talk that the rails would be laid three miles north of town, a possibility the *Citizen* quickly discounted.[30]

Then, in July of 1879, the *Star* noted that another rumor was circulating, this one concerning local citizens telling visitors, "'There is some fear that the San Pedro [River], or other spot will yet beat us as the R.R. goes on'."[31] By September, based on what he was hearing from people in the territory, from San Francisco Towne was forwarding information to Huntington about this gossip. The General Superintendent said speculation in Tucson was that Southern Pacific would develop its own town along the river for roundhouses, machine and repair shops, and other railroad business, in part because it offered the easiest access to the rapidly-developing Tombstone mining district about 25 miles to the south of that location.

This new community along the San Pedro, some people in Tucson feared, would become "the great city of the territory," and Huntington was told this suspicion was turning public opinion against Southern Pacific. "Rumor has gone so far as to say that the company has purchased the property to lay out an extension town and that the surveys for the same have already been made," Towne reported.[32] This gloom, however, was somewhat typical of Tucson, one company spokesman believed. "There are croackers here," he wrote from Arizona, "who continue to assert that Tucson is doomed as soon as our road passes it…".[33]

While Towne said he agreed that a large town would eventually develop in the area along the river southeast of Tucson, he added, "I am not aware that our people have any survey of the land at or near the crossing of the San Pedro River."[34] To allay fears in Tucson and to clarify the company's intentions, an S.P. official told the *Arizona Daily Star* in October of 1879 that the San Pedro story had no basis in fact.[35] That didn't squash the rumor, however, and in a subsequent letter to Huntington, Towne wrote, "It is the generally expressed opinion of the people of Tucson that when the road reaches the San Pedro River that <u>there</u> will be located the city of the territory."[36]

Four months later the rumor was still circulating, but the *Star* pointed out an important reason why it wasn't realistic. "In the first place, a new cargo of inhabitants would have to be shipped in every year to replace the sick, dying and dead ones;" the newspaper commented cynically of the proposed river-side town, "as it has been considered from the earliest history of southern Arizona, even when the Apaches run wild, that the malarial plague of the San Pedro was by far more dangerous to life than the rifle or scalping-knife of the red devils."[37]

While the debate over the location of the future "great metropolis of the territory" raged, others in Tucson were worried about the pending arrival of more

Chinese people. As early as July of 1879, the *Star* had been complaining: "Hardly a stage arrives that does not bring one or more Chinamen to our city. Last week seven Celestial heroines arrived, which, added to the number already here, make ten in all."[38]

This increase, the newspaper assumed, would be detrimental to the community. The editor of the *Star* said these foreigners were "bringing their loathsome characteristics; establishing wash-houses in the central portion of the city, which are surrounded with cesspools of filthy, stenchy water…Their hovels or holes in which they live are anything but cleanly. Take a look into any of these dens; filth is the first thing suggested."[39] To counter this Asiatic onslaught, the newspaper recommended the Tucson City Council "establish at once such regulations as will locate the Chinese element in one section or location of the city—say for instance at the northwest corner of the city limits, where they can be entirely separated from the remainder of the population."

A few weeks later, the *Star* reprinted a comment from its afternoon competitor the *Citizen* which read, "A good deal of the trouble about the Chinese seems to grow out of their temperate habits, their determination to work for a living and their refusal to be bilked out of their wages."[40] This stance, the Tucson morning newspaper replied, was simply a weak apology for their rival's support of the importation of cheap Chinese labor into the country. The *Star* concluded it was good for the people of the city to know which newspaper "advocates the filling up of our territory with an ignorant, filthy, leperous horde of beings who may have the form of a human being but lack every element which enters into true American civilization—a horde of almost barbarians that have no higher aspirations than to eat, sleep, and consume opium…".

As the growing number of Asian people in Tucson was of concern to the editor of the *Star*, the possibility that more than one railroad might be built to the community was a cause of intense interest throughout the fall of 1879. In September, the newspaper reported that surveyors working for the Atchison, Topeka and Santa Fe Railroad were exploring for a way to connect Albuquerque with Tucson as part of its plan to build a line to Guaymas on the Gulf of California in Mexico. The proposed route ran near some rich mining areas, but also had to cross high mountain ranges and difficult river canyons through the Arizona and New Mexico territories. Despite that, the engineer in charge hoped he would find "a road of easy grade and reasonably cheap construction,"[41] and the *Star* optimistically predicted that if the line were built, Tucson would become the Denver of Arizona.[42]

Despite this A.T.&S.F. reconnaissance effort, in an interview with the *Washington Republican* at the end of October, a Southern Pacific representative downplayed the possibility that a second railroad would run to Tucson. As for the Atchison, Topeka and Santa Fe line even entering Arizona, this official said it certainly wouldn't since, instead, they could just use the S.P. tracks which would eventually extend into New Mexico. Thus, he concluded, because the A.T.&S.F. was planning to build south through New Mexico and the S.P. further eastward in Arizona, the two routes would probably meet somewhere around the village of Mesilla, 45 miles north of El Paso.[43]

Even though neither railroad had expressed any real confidence that the Atchison, Topeka and Santa Fe would be extended to Tucson, and the company by this time had already decided to lay tracks west from Albuquerque along the 35th parallel toward California, the *Arizona Daily Star* was nevertheless certain that more than one railroad would come to town. In December of 1879 they predicted it would happen, "without question"[44] and a few months later pushed for a committee of civic leaders to visit the A.T.&S.F. offices in Topeka to pursue the possibility.[45]

The idea of the two lines meeting in Tucson then slowly faded away. The routes of the Southern Pacific and the Atchison, Topeka and Santa Fe railroads were going to join somewhere within the area of the Gadsden Purchase, but it soon became obvious that point would not be in Arizona. Civic pride and boosterism by a hometown newspaper could not overcome the financial and topographical realities which both companies faced in planning a future junction of their roads.

Where exactly the meeting point would be, though, was still very much undetermined. Towne told Huntington in October of 1879 that their competitors were building a road south from Colorado into New Mexico as quickly as possible. With the S.P. track-laying effort suspended at Casa Grande, and because of the much-prized mining districts around Tombstone, he added of Southern Pacific's efforts: "It seems all important that this work in Arizona should be pushed forward with as much activity as is evinced by the A.T.&S.F. people. Every mile east of Tucson that you can build to form a junction with that road will be worth more than five times that number west thereof."[46]

Another related consideration being discussed at the same time was whether and how Southern Pacific would access those sought-after mining areas around Tombstone. Off the main line, a branch route running south near the San Pedro River was contemplated by company officials because, as former Arizona Governor A.P.K. Safford wrote Huntington in May of 1879, "The Tombstone district southeast of Tucson bids fair to become one of the richest districts on the coast."[47]

A few months later, Southern Pacific was shipping 5,000 tons of equipment to the mining area, but of course it would have to be transported overland from Casa Grande by wagon. Crocker, the former opponent of extending the line past Yuma, and then Maricopa, had decided by the end of 1879, "It is very important for us to build that road from Casa Grande to the point on the San Pedro River opposite the Tombstone mines as soon as possible."[48] The usually frugal Californian also told his east coast partner, "I suppose, of course, you are doing all you can to forward steel, but really if there is another link you can let loose and send it faster, it will be very much to our advantage, more than the difference in price."

Also by December, the prospects for a resumption of Southern Pacific track-laying were beginning to increase. Earlier press reports had indicated the work would resume by November, but rails were only trickling into Casa Grande and Crocker wrote then: "Steel is coming very slowly as yet. We are receiving more than we did, but it comes very slowly."[49] Within a few weeks, however, Huntington was sending frequent telegrams to San Francisco stating that he had been told hundreds of tons of tracks were finally on their way west. Based on this, before the end of the year he wanted to know, "When do you commence work on S.P.?"[50]

"We will commence work there as soon as there is enough steel on the way to insure us against any stoppages," Crocker responded curtly.[51] "I think it would be very prejudicial to our interests to commence work and then have to stop," he said, and added in obvious exasperation: "We have got the ties on the ground and if we had the rail, would commence immediately. Strobridge is very anxious to go down and get through before the hot weather commences. He says it will be difficult to get men to work to advantage in that hot climate in summer."

Early in the new year of 1880, Huntington was again wiring that rails were being forwarded. Twenty car loads were shipped on January 14th, he said, eighteen more two days later, and four more the next day. Because of these and other anticipated deliveries of steel, Crocker said on January 19th: "Mr. Strobridge has gone down to the front and will resume work immediately and I do hope he will not be delayed for want of material. You have no idea how much it adds to the cost of a road to have its construction stopped for lack of material while the work is progressing."[52]

This decision certainly was good news in Tucson. Even before Crocker made it official, the *Star* had announced the pending resumption of work. For its part, a *Citizen* story on the 19th proclaimed under a "Toot To-o-ot To-o-o-o-ot!" head-line that men were on their way to Casa Grande and, "Sixty days more will doubtless mark an important era in the history of Tucson."[53]

Two more months wasn't too bad, considering that people in the community had already been waiting several years for the tracks to arrive. As early as the fall of 1876, the *Citizen* had predicted that it was very likely that within three years the people of Tucson "will daily hear the cheery and energizing sound of the loco-motive whistle."[54]

A few months after that, when Los Angeles area railroad man Phineas Banning had been in Tucson in January of 1877 to lobby the Arizona legislature on behalf of Southern Pacific's request for permission to build across the territory, he also spoke to the Village Council. He pointed out the advantages which would accrue if the tracks came to town and "stated that the S.P.R.R. contemplated the extending of its road to this point and desired a right-of-way through the town and lands for depot and other purposes."[55] In response, the Council voted unanimously to donate almost 200 acres to the company, property which included the former military plaza as well as a long stretch of land along the eastern and northern borders of the village. It was agreed by everyone involved that S.P. would have the tracks completed to Tucson within five years.

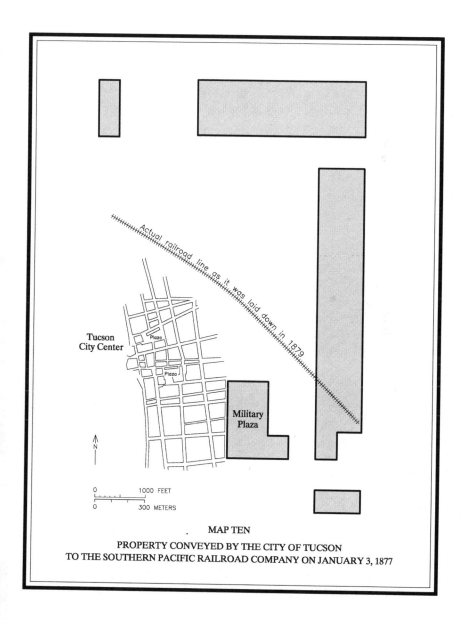

MAP TEN

**PROPERTY CONVEYED BY THE CITY OF TUCSON
TO THE SOUTHERN PACIFIC RAILROAD COMPANY ON JANUARY 3, 1877**

By November of 1878, the *Star* was hopefully announcing, "The railroad surveyors are camped on the plaza; looks as if the railroad is not far distant."[56] Based on this reconnaissance work, two possible routes to Tucson were identified, one which ran along its northern edge, the other outside its boundaries. Once S.P. officials had located the former line exactly, they approached local politicians about obtaining the property. The land transferred by the Village Council to Southern Pacific in 1877 had just been a good-will gesture, but by the spring of 1879 the railroad company knew precisely what they needed and proposed a trade.

At a City Council meeting on the 14th of May, S.P.'s chief engineer George Gray requested a 100-foot wide strip of land for tracks which would be laid in a northwest to southeast angle across the vacant northern part of the community. Gray also asked for a 350-foot wide piece of property for a passenger and freight depot, as well as twelve city blocks nearby which were needed for roundhouses, repair shops, and other maintenance facilities. The Council unanimously granted this request from the company, free of charge, with the understanding the surplus land given to S.P. earlier was to be returned.[57]

Even before this meeting was held, the *Citizen* had been very supportive of the proposal, writing: "We deem this proposition extremely fair, and do not doubt that it will be so regarded by almost everybody. It will cost the city a few hundred dollars; but we are confident that it will be able to buy the ground for this purpose, from our townsmen, at the lowest market price."[58]

To pay for the required property, Mayor James Toole and the other members of the Council called a special election for June 21st, 1879. The ballot issue was "to determine whether a sufficient amount [$10,000] of bonds shall be issued to defray the expenses attending to acquiring right-of-way for Southern Pacific Rail Road."[59] One hundred and forty male voters turned out for the election, and all but one of them supported the measure. The lone dissenter was publicly demeaned by the *Citizen* as "a man who mostly resides in Sonora [Mexico] and whose name is not on the taxroll, and it is almost certain he never paid a dollar of taxes in Arizona."[60]

After approval at the ballot box, the Tucson city government quickly proceeded to acquire the property needed to lay the tracks through town. By July 22nd, this process was almost finished and the Council authorized Mayor Toole to telegraph Gray: "Right-of-way secured complete except for one lot. This is in course of Probate and deed will be obtained to it July 30. You can send your attorney at once to examine titles."[61] In a follow-up letter, the Mayor told Gray, "It affords me pleasure to say that our whole people have heartily cooperated with the corporate authorities in accomplishing the very liberal requirements of your company, and we confidently look for the early completion of your road to

Tucson to give a new impetus and prosperity to our city."[62] Because of his important role in this process, the City Council would later name the street which ran parallel to the tracks on its south side after Mayor Toole.

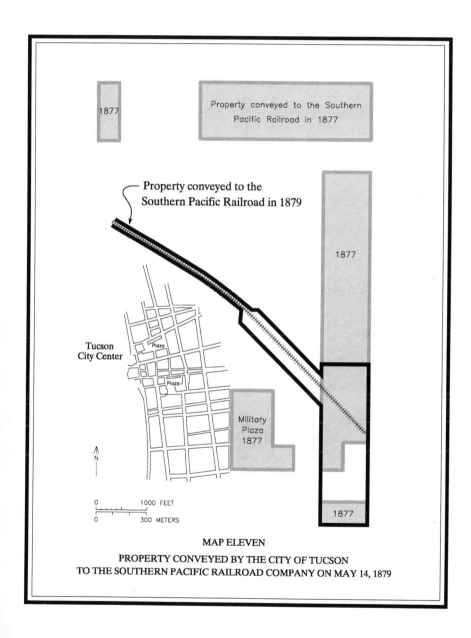

MAP ELEVEN

PROPERTY CONVEYED BY THE CITY OF TUCSON
TO THE SOUTHERN PACIFIC RAILROAD COMPANY ON MAY 14, 1879

When the railroad would actually reach Tucson, however, remained somewhat in doubt, even though work had finally resumed after a halt of eight months. Upon Strobridge's arrival in Arizona on January 23rd, grading by the Chinese laborers began immediately south from Casa Grande, and at the construction front one railroad engineer promised "to give an extraordinary long toot of [his engine's] whistle when he reaches Tucson, February 20th."[63] By January 27th, the *Star* announced: "Track-laying will commence today. About 500 men are at work now and more are arriving nightly. They expect to build from one and half to two miles per day."[64]

Tucson's other newspaper, the *Citizen*, projected a wildly optimistic future for the construction effort. "Five hundred men have been sent forward," they wrote on January 20th, "and the number will be increased to 4,000 or 5,000 and the road be pushed through to El Paso at the rate of 3 to 5 miles per day."[65]

Both newspapers' estimates of the number of men were a little high, the actual figure being 435, and more would not be on their way for quite some time. Crocker worried that construction could be delayed by a lack of rails, so he severely restricted the size of the work force. Even with that limitation, however, the track-laying progressed very rapidly over the level terrain toward Tucson.

The path the rails were to follow would again demonstrate the advantages of the Gadsden Purchase for railroad building. One company representative exclaimed of the easy grades, "It seems that Nature had provided a way for a railroad through the territory on the route selected by the Southern Pacific line with no formidable barriers in the way."[66]

The resumed work in late January went rapidly and smoothly at first, until a freak winter storm hit the southern Arizona desert. As a resident remembered years later: "Snow fell in Tucson to the depth of eight inches. Not being prepared for such an unusual display of nature, there were no jingling sleigh-bells and merry shouts of youngsters, with which snow falls are generally welcomed…".[67] One party of local pranksters did rig up an old stage coach with runners and rode it several miles out of town, but the snow melted before the group could return, so they had to walk back.

The snow fall delayed the grading and track-laying crews a day and one-half, but then they quickly pushed on. Eventually the rails passed the prominent rocky peak at Pichaco, near which water "pure and free from all alkaline substances," would be found at a depth of 280 feet.

The next construction slowdown was due to a special occasion. "We have been having China New Year," Strobridge wrote Crocker on February 10th from the end of the track, "which will account for us not doing more work for last few days."[68]

It was another factor, however, which concerned Crocker much more. In early February he told Huntington that the amount of steel in Arizona, and what was on its way west, was "only sufficient to last us eleven days at the present rate of building, and I very much fear that the material will not come along fast enough to keep us going."[69] To emphasize the point he sent a telegram to New York on the 13th which read, "Unless rails are shipped faster than they have been, we will be compelled to suspend work in Arizona."[70]

While climatic and cultural delays, along with a lack of track, slowed the work down, the people in Tucson were nevertheless growing excited. After construction had resumed the *Star* informed its readers: "The boom is at Casa Grande. It will soon be at Tucson."[71] Of the arrival of the railroad and accompanying telegraph line, the newspaper predicted: "The changes which will necessarily be wrought with the coming of these two great factors of commerce, civilization and progress cannot be estimated. To the consumer it cannot be otherwise than advantageous. To the miner and bullion-producer it will be the era of prosperity."[72]

In addition to these enormous economic benefits, the daily publication also knew there could be some drawbacks. "To the merchant and trader it may for a few months bring over competition," the *Star* warned, "but they who now are on the ground have every advantage in knowing the wants of the trade and its limit."[73] One leading merchant even went so far as to admit the same thing in a newspaper ad which read, "The coming of the Railroad and the increase of population demand an entire change of business principles...".[74]

Even though existing retailers might potentially be harmed by the cheaper freight which the railroad could supply, many new businesses in Tucson would also be established because of its arrival combined with a growing population. "No less than four new mercantile houses will be opened in the next week," the *Star* excitedly announced in February of 1880, and predicted that "this number will be trebled in two weeks, and increase in geometrical ratio as soon as the 'Angel of Progress' blasts her trumpet within the city line."[75] With slightly less rhetorical fanfare, they continued: "Already we hear of a tannery, a woolen factory, and a soap and candle factory being put up on large scales. A foundry will soon be in course of erection which will supply this market with all ordinary cast iron work. A sash and door factory is also talked of, which will make a luxurious fortune for the judicious investor. We have now one flour mill in the city, a larger one with all of the latest improvements will soon be added...".

This commercial development, however, would not be something completely new in the community. Tucson already held the distinction of being the business and population hub not only of Arizona, but of the entire area of the Gadsden Purchase. It had grown considerably from the 1860s, when it had been described as, "A city of mud-boxes, dingy and dilapidated, cracked and baked into a composite of dust and filth; littered about with broken corrals, sheds, bake-ovens, carcasses of dead animals…'."[76] Tucson was a remote frontier town with only 925 residents in 1860, 71 percent of whom were Mexican-Americans and less than 20 percent Anglo.[77] Despite that, the vast majority of property was owned by the latter group. In addition, while the Anglos were almost exclusively adventuresome males, the Mexican-American population included many long-established families.

The two segments of this isolated village differed in many ways. The Mexican diet included spicy food and a plentiful supply of beans along with tortillas. The women who daily made this flat bread in their homes "had adapted their clothing to the climate. In their *casas* they wore a low-necked and short-sleeved *camisa*, fitting neatly, with bands around the neck and arms. Over this they put a long calico skirt, always white stockings and black shoes."[78] Once they began arriving in the 1870s, however, Anglo women donned, "Eastern styles of fashion and sweltered during the day in high ruffled collar and long-sleeved white calico dresses which fell to the floor."

Josephine Brawley Hughes was one of these early Anglo women. After arriving in Tucson with her infant daughter in 1872, she became the first female public school teacher in Arizona. She additionally helped raise funds to build the first Protestant church in the community and was later active in the temperance and women's suffrage movements.

She was also the wife of L.C. Hughes, publisher of the railroad-promoting, Chinese-hating *Arizona Daily Star*. "In the early years of the *Star*" one historian wrote, "Mrs. Hughes was business manager, bookkeeper and cashier, while Mr. Hughes was editor, doing all the work, local, exchange and clipping."[79]

By the early 1870s, when Hughes and other Anglo women initially appeared in town, Tucson had over three thousand people and the Sisters of St. Joseph of Carondelet had journeyed to the community to open a school for girls. A decade later, just as the tracks arrived, under the direction of Bishop Jean Baptiste Salpointe, this Catholic order would also establish St. Mary's hospital on the west side of the Santa Cruz River.

It was mainly because of an influx of Anglo businessmen and investors, along with a rush of Mexican nationals seeking work, however, that Tucson had swelled to 7,000 people by 1880. That was more than one-sixth the territorial total of 40,400, and the Anglo, or "American", portion of the city's population had reached almost 30 percent by then. Even with their minority status, they dominated the economic, social, and political circles of the community, owning 80 percent of the businesses in central Tucson and most of the residences in the area.[80]

Despite that, Spanish remained the primary language of commerce, the Mexican population still was twice as large as the Anglo, and it was steadily increasing primarily because of immigration from south of the nearby international boundary line. Most of these new immigrants, like the Mexican-Americans already living in Tucson, found work in low-paying manual labor jobs.

There were several exceptions to this general rule, of course, and Tucson's elite did include some Mexican-Americans. One of the most prominent was Estevan Ochoa. The legislator and prosperous freight company owner was not only a successful businessman, but he and his wife would host banquets in honor of visiting dignitaries, no matter what their ethnic background. Born in Mexico and a naturalized American citizen, Ochoa co-owned the second largest firm in town, which at one time employed hundreds of people and possessed freighting equipment worth over $100,000.[81]

Along with his economic success, Ochoa was known for his kindness and generosity to the community, and his support of public education. When Tucson needed a new school, he donated a lot for it and then supervised the construction of a building paid for in part by a charity ball which raised $812. Ochoa was also famous for being Tucson's first, and only, Mexican-American mayor. In 1875, he captured the position by a lopsided total of 187 to 40.[82]

While Ochoa was included among Tucson's upper-class, the overwhelming number of Mexican-Americans in town were not. Instead, they were laborers, farm hands, miners or servants, often working for Anglo residents. It was this last group, which included bankers, merchants, and ranchers, who were the most outspoken supporters of the railroad coming to Tucson.

These were also the people who had diversified the city's religious affiliations. At first a Catholic community because of its Mexican heritage, the influx of Anglos had eventually resulted in a growing Jewish population along with a Presbyterian congregation being founded.

As the tracks approached, housing, or a lack of it, was also a topic of conversation in the community. Real estate prices were escalating rapidly, with the *Star* noting that within four months land costs for vacant property had quadrupled to $200 for a residential lot.[83] The price of homes was often around $4,000, and $100 a month was required to lease one. These factors, combined with an increasing population, resulted in there hardly being a house to buy or rent in Tucson. The situation was so critical that the *Citizen* suggested Southern Pacific be asked to leave some sleeping cars in town to serve as rooms,[84] while the *Star* pushed for the introduction of portable buildings to ease the housing crunch.[85]

While this problem was being debated, north of town the tracks continued to be laid, if somewhat sporadically. In the middle of February it was predicted the rails would arrive in Tucson within thirty days, and one railroad employee commented, "We are being worked so fast that we have barely time to eat and sleep."[86]

By the end of the month a large force of Chinese graders had moved beyond Tucson on their way farther east, a sign of both additional problems with rail delivery and also the eventual arrival of the tracks in the community. "As they passed through the town," the *Citizen* reported about this group of men, "one enthusiastic young hoodlum…expressed a wish to 'go through the crowd with a pick handle'."[87] To this violent idea the newspaper replied, "We devoutly wish he had made the attempt, for it would have given our Coroner a job, and there would have been one vagabond less on the face of the earth."

In addition to this threat of physical violence aimed at the laborers, the *Citizen* added, "One gentleman of Teutonic origin remarked, 'Vell, vot a shame dot ish. I don't like dem Chinamans von bit.' When asked why, he replied, 'Vy? Vy becaush, becaush dey don't drinks lager. Dot's vy'." About that comment, the paper dryly theorized, "He may have been in the business."[88]

Crocker had very reluctantly made the decision to relocate some of the graders from north of the city. It meant the men would have to be provided with supplies over the long and expensive distance separating them from the construction train, thus violating one of his basic track-laying principles. "Our style of building rail-road is to keep the grade and the track right along together," Crocker once summarized.[89] "It is much cheaper and better than to do a large amount of grading away on ahead, and then wait for the material." In Arizona, the Chinese laborers had to be moved, however, in order to keep them busy since the shortage of rails had resulted in another slowdown.

In early February, Crocker once more asked Huntington in desperation to hurry the shipments of steel. On the 20th he added to his previous pleas, "There is only sufficient steel on hand for five (5) days work, after which I suppose it will come along in driblets, some days none, and other days, 4 or 5 car loads."[90] Six days later Strobridge wired Huntington the simple message, "Out of steel".[91] From New York the exasperated response continued to be, "I am doing all I can to get the rails sent forward but I find it very hard work to get [one of the suppliers] to do what they have agreed to."[92]

After another halt of several days, the track-laying work did begin again, and with it the excitement started mounting in Tucson once more. As early as February 14th, the *Star* had written: "Tucson must get ready for a fitting reception of the great southern national highway…The driving of the first spike within the city limits must be solemnized as the great importance of the event demands. The general reception ought to be one in which every citizen can join. In brief, it should be celebrated as the grandest event in the history of our ancient city."[93]

Two days later, the *Citizen* called the arrival of the tracks, "The greatest event in the history of this city," and suggested "it would be quite the thing for Tucson to have a little extra Fourth of July on that occasion."[94] Then the newspaper continued, "It would be the thing for the municipality to take the lead, and we suggest that [the town] Fathers hold a meeting for that purpose." The City Council, however, did nothing.

In its next edition the *Citizen* went even further with its proposition for a welcoming ceremony. In addition to a community celebration and banquet for S.P officials, it proposed "a square meal [should] be provided for the laborers who have toiled across the deserts with pick and shovel to this distant point. Give them a taste of our good cheer, even at the sacrifice of a few bottles of [the fine French champagne] Roederer."[95]

To this, the usually anti-Asian *Star* surprisingly replied: "The *Citizen* wants to give a banquet to the heathen Chinese who are toiling across the desert with pick and shovels, and suggests that they be filled with champagne. This is worthy of the greatest consideration."[96] One of the newspaper's readers saw it differently, though, and wrote, "We do not want champagne for the heathen Chinese...".[97]

Around this same time, the *Star* spelled out specifically what it thought could be included in the community's celebration of the railroad's arrival. The military, it said, should be present to provide a proper salute, and an orator was needed to give a fitting speech. The suggestion was made that the last spike be driven by Tucson's oldest citizen and then, "In the evening a banquet could be gotten up for the officers of the road, at which all who feel like giving vent to their sentiments could be heard."[98] Despite the public pressure to act, however, the City Council still remained silent on the subject.

As the tracks approached town, however, the Southern Pacific Company did begin offering tickets to San Francisco on an excursion train which would leave Tucson shortly after the rails actually arrived. The cost for the round-trip to the Bay area was $65, which included a sleeping berth for the 57-hour one-way journey, and the schedule would be set once a definitive date for the track completion to Tucson was known.[99]

By the beginning of March, more graders had come to Tucson and had erected their tents in town. With the tracks only fourteen miles away, though, the work was again halted because of a lack of rails. Even given this close proximity, the Tucson City Council still had done nothing about organizing an arrival celebration, and the *Star* stated anxiously, "It would be well for our boom committee to be moving, or the iron horse will be in the city limits without a proper reception."[100]

The lack of arrangements for a welcoming ceremony wasn't slowing the track-layers down when they had enough steel rails. On March 4th, the men reportedly installed almost three miles of track, and they kept approaching Tucson as rapidly as possible.

Concurrently with the track-laying, plans were being made to construct a suitable depot and other needed railroad structures. To be sited on the land donated by the community, these buildings were necessary to provide service to the traveling and freight-sending public, maintain equipment, and to accommodate the hundreds of men S.P. would eventually be employing in Tucson.

According to the *Citizen*: "The round house [for locomotive repairs] will contain six stalls,"[101] but that number was very quickly increased to fifteen. Also to be built would be a machine shop, tool sheds, and a bunk house for employees, along with a brick engine house, coal sheds, blacksmith shop, and a building to store 100 tons of ice brought in from the Sierras.

Collection of Miss Roberta Niesz

THE TUCSON TRAIN STATION

Within two months after the railroad's arrival, a 200-foot long, two-story passenger depot was also completed, a structure which had wide roof overhangs on both floors and a twelve-foot platform adjoining the tracks. In the opinion of the *Star* this wooden building could be a model for people wanting to construct frame homes in Tucson instead of using adobe bricks. Company offices occupied the top floor of the depot, while on the ground level was a "spacious, well ventilated"[102] passenger waiting room measuring sixteen feet by thirty-five feet, as well as ticket and freight offices plus a space to store baggage.[103]

Also on the first floor was the general agent's office which was described as having "walls or partitions finished in redwood and pine finely polished and varnished, the ceiling is thirteen and one-half feet high and made of inch lumber painted white."[104] On the walls of this office hung four oil paintings entitled, "Wine Tasters, Reading Club, Damsel," and an unnamed country scene.

To supply water to the depot, pipes were laid from the railroad's nearby tank. This source, while also used to replenish the steam engines with water, would be employed to fight potential fires in the wooden structure as well as to dampen the dirt around the building.

Near the depot would be built a hotel, which was to be a two-story redwood structure with 60 guest rooms. "It was supplied with the latest conveniences," a local citizen later recalled, "all rooms with running water furnished by the R.R. Company Water Department. Toilets, however, were at the end of the halls, also bathrooms, for Tucson had not yet constructed sewers."[105]

Because it was being built on vacant land almost one-half mile from the community, there was at first very little other development in the vicinity of the depot. One apt description of the desolate site was as a "mesa bristling with mesquite, a race course for the swift-footed lizard," while a long-time resident remembered years later: "At that time there wasn't any buildings around in that section of the town. And across from the railroad track at that time, probably one or two adobe houses were over on the other side [of the tracks]."[106]

The few thousand feet of mostly open desert between Tucson and its depot resulted in the building being very isolated from the community. The impact of this, according to a complaint letter sent to the *Star*, meant that arriving railroad passengers would be dumped "out into that sea of dust, with no way to get down to the city except to wade in six or more inches of the all-pervading dust...".[107] In the view of the *Citizen*, "None of these patrons and railway officials can fly, and few of them can swim; that three inches of hot dust, affectionate and friendly to the last degree, is not exactly conducive to comfort...".[108] To correct this deplorable situation, both newspapers called for building sidewalks to the railroad station.

But while installing sidewalks and developing the depot grounds were still in the planning stages, the track's arrival continued to be anxiously anticipated in Tucson, in part because stage coaches remained threatened by Indian attacks. Early in 1880, a new city resident wrote home to his father in South Carolina about this situation. "The R.R. will be finished in 2 weeks," he said, then continued: "I had to travel 60 miles in a stage...When we got in the stage the citizens...said we would never get out alive in this world again for the Indians were on the war path [and] just had robbed and killed the passengers [and] driver [and] threw the U.S. Mail all over the plains and took the mules. We had 2 soldiers with us and we all had a gun, mine came in good but thank god we went through without a hair on our heads unfurled."[109]

Concerning the community where he had arrived, the newcomer wrote: "This is the best and most peaceful town I have seen since I left home. There are only 3 wooden buildings in the city, all [the rest] adobe." Of southern Arizona in general he said: "I think this is the prettiest country in the world. Every side you look here [there are] beautiful mountains. I am just carried away with Tucson."[110]

In 1879, a correspondent for the *Chicago Tribune* had disagreed, saying Tucson wasn't much to look at. He thought, though, that the place, "Improves on acquaintance, and in its evident possibilities; if it did not, a long acquaintance would not be desired by most new-comers, for its external appearance, as a whole, is dilapidated and unprepossessing."[111] The author commented that the town's one-story adobe structures looked "weatherworn and rough," the Cathedral had a "tumble-down appearance," and the unpaved streets were full of roving dogs. The city also lacked either gas or electrical service, but even given all that, the writer concluded, "Tucson improves on acquaintance".

The arrival of the tracks, of course, would enhance the community tremendously. On March 13th, 1880, under a headline which read simply, "AT LAST!!", the *Star* proclaimed, "The first regular train will arrive at Tucson at 11:55 p.m. on Saturday, March 20th; and the first train to leave Tucson will be on Sunday, the 21st, at 3 a.m."[112]

The regular passenger schedule may have been set, but that still didn't resolve the question of when dignitaries aboard the ceremonial first train would come to town. Despite that, in its edition of March 17th, the *Star* said of the construction effort: "This morning the first rail of the S.P.R.R. will be laid in Tucson, and by 12 [noon] it will reach the depot grounds and the first locomotive will crack the air with her shriek—which means more than could be expressed in a volume. Suffice it to say, steam, steel and well directed energy in the future will reign in the ancient city of Tucson."[113]

This momentous occasion, however, meant the certain demise of at least one business. As the *Citizen* noted before the first train arrived: "Tomorrow the Southern Pacific stage line will make its last passenger trip from Casa Grande. The last coach leaves today, and instead of the long, cold and dusty stage ride, travelers will come to our doors in palace sleeping cars. Progressive civilization has some luxuries after all."[114]

As the horse-drawn coaches were being phased out, the tracks actually did arrive in Tucson on the 17th. The next day it was reported that thousands of people had gone to observe the work, and: "The sight of the approach of the track-layers yesterday through the city created an enthusiasm among the natives not soon again to be witnessed. The school children were amazed and delighted, and with wonder looked at the 'big idea' and the steel path over which it carried its burden."[115]

The combination of St. Patrick's Day and the advent of the railroad proved to be too much for some in town. They celebrated mightily, but most people reserved their enthusiasm for the actual appearance of the ceremonial first train.

It was announced on the 17th, that for the official welcoming ceremony, Charles Crocker and other special guests would arrive about noon on Saturday, March 20th. The Tucson City Council finally took that notice seriously and appointed a number of committees to organize the reception event. Eight groups were formed with a total of 105 men serving, only seven of whom, however, were Mexican-Americans.[116]

In addition to this official celebration, Tucson residents were asked to participate in what was hoped would be "the grandest occasion ever witnessed in the city". They were requested to decorate their homes and illuminate them on the night of the 20th. At the same time, though, people were warned to keep children away from the tracks "as accidents are sure to occur no matter how much care is taken on the part of the railroad."[117] It was the Southern Pacific Company, however, which had earlier insisted the Tucson City Council adopt "no restrictions of the speed of locomotive and trains to less than ten miles per hour."[118]

Also on March 17th, Mayor R.N. Leatherwood had sent out telegrams announcing the coming of the railroad to his city. These went to the President of the United States, the territorial governor, and the mayors of Yuma, Los Angeles, and San Francisco. Leatherwood additionally co-signed with Bishop Salpointe a message to the Pope which read: "The Mayor of Tucson begs the honor of reminding your Holiness that this ancient and honorable pueblo was founded by the Spaniards under the sanction of the church, more than three centuries ago, and to inform your Holiness that a railroad from San Francisco, California, now connects us with the Christian world."[119]

As the Mayor was proclaiming the event around the globe, the March 19th edition of the *Star* carried a column by early mining pioneer Charles Poston entitled, "The Railroad in Tucson". In it he poetically summarized: "And now the railroad comes along, like a giant anaconda, embracing the continent in its coil, and its ponderous machinery breathes the vitality of civilization in sonorous respirations, breaking the silence of the desert and awakening the reverberations of the mountains for the first time since the planet commenced its revolutions in the universe."[120] Poston then continued, "The ancient pueblo of Tucson is roused from the lethargy of ages, and is embraced in the network of the civilized world."

Who was responsible for this transformation, Poston asked his readers, and answered rhetorically: "The typical New Zealander, in crossing this continent by the 'Southern Pacific Railroad' a thousand years hence to visit the ruins of

London, will stop at the 'Casa Grande' and ask a descendant of the Pima Indians, who built the citadel of that name, and the gentle savage will' reply in the soft dialect of his tribe, 'pimae'h' (I don't know); but ask him, 'who built the Southern Pacific Railroad?' and the child of centuries will answer, 'Crocker'."[121]

At 11 a.m. on the morning of March 20th, 1880, Charles Crocker arrived in Tucson by special train. A thirty-eight gun salute was fired, and the local Sixth Cavalry Band provided music for the thousands of people in attendance at the dusty, vacant site of the to-be-built depot. A speech welcoming the dignitaries was followed by the presentation of a silver spike to Crocker by Estevan Ochoa. The precious rail nail, he said, had been produced by a mine in Tombstone, and then to loud applause, Ochoa implored his fellow residents, "Let us put our shoulders to the oars of progress until we become the bright star in the constellation of these United States of America."[122]

One little girl who attended the ceremony on that memorable day remembered it vividly years later. "A great crowd gathered around the depot," she recalled, "and some few people were given free rides up and down the railroad yards in front of the depot. They thought it was a lot of fun."[123]

After the welcoming ceremony, Crocker and the other special guests in attendance were taken by carriage to Levin's Gardens, an entertainment center near the Santa Cruz River. This facility was located on seven acres of land, and its entrance was down a lane lined by cottonwood trees. The grounds were decorated with numerous flowers and fruit-bearing trees, and the attractions included a skating rink, shooting gallery, and bowling alley.[124]

Along with the dignitaries participating in the celebration at the Gardens, a large contingent of local residents also took part. A reception was followed by a two p.m. banquet served at tables formed in the shape of a horse shoe, and after the meal, and obligatory speeches, a grand ball was to be held for 1,200 at eight that evening. There is no record, however, that either the Chinese graders or any other railroad laborers were invited to these ceremonies.

Upon completion of the afternoon banquet, Poston was introduced as the man who would propose the toasts, each to be followed by a speech from someone representing the highlighted party. Obviously the Tucson organizing committee didn't know of his former difficult dealings with the Southern Pacific Company and apparent support for the Texas and Pacific Railroad, but on this occasion all was smiles and good cheer.

Over the course of what must have been seemingly endless hours of speech-making, Poston toasted numerous subjects. He began by raising his glass to the President of the United States, and then called for "The Prosperity of the Southern Pacific Railroad". After that salutation, Crocker provided a short reply in his unpolished fashion. He said the road would be continued until it reached the Gulf of Mexico and that the company would be fair in its dealings with its new customers. Then to prolonged applause, Crocker "expressed a very lively hope for the future of Arizona, and predicted that the most enthusiastic dreams of the early pioneers would be realized in the prosperity which was swiftly coming upon the Territory."[125]

Next came a toast to "Chained Lighting," or the telegraph line, which was followed by one for "The Health and Prosperity of the City of Tucson". The gentleman offering the response said unabashedly of the community: "Were I to picture her future as I believe, I might be charged with dealing in romance, or rambling in the realms of fancy; but from enterprises now on foot, backed by that public spirit and energy for which her citizens are renowned, at no distant day do I prophesy that Tucson, the mud town on the banks of the Santa Cruz, will be Tucson the magnificent."[126]

After this came recognition of the Army of the United States, and the Major supplying the long reply said: "Concerning the Indians, I am not one of those who wish to press the idea that the only good Indian is a dead one, although I have no exalted opinion of the race; but I think the nation owes it to itself to treat the poor miserable savages with justice and humanity, and owes to the pioneers of civilization complete protection."[127]

Toasts and rejoinders to the bench and bar, and then commerce, were followed by one to "The Prosperity of Our Sister Republic" of Mexico. That government's consul provided the reply, and the next toast, to "Extension of International Relations," was responded to in Spanish by another speaker.[128]

Those in attendance must have been growing very weary of all the speech-making by this time, but Poston just kept on. He offered his glass to "The Press," and then "Mining," which was followed by a very long speech. Next came acknowledgment of "The Pioneers," "The Postal Service," and "Education". Finally, the last toast of the afternoon was to "Absent Friends," including former Mayor Toole who was out of town.

Somewhere among all this never-ending and mostly boring talk, so the story goes, someone stood up and proudly proclaimed that the Vatican had replied to Mayor Leatherwood's earlier telegram. Who the culprit was, and what exactly he said, have long been disputed, but the crux of the humorous response was: "His Holiness, the Pope, acknowledges with appreciation receipt of your telegram informing him that the ancient city of Tucson at last has been connected by rail with the outside world and sends his benediction but, for his own satisfaction would ask, where in hell is Tucson?"[129]

Despite that prank, the *Citizen* was very serious a few days later when it reprinted an article concerning Southern Pacific officials and their decision to build eastward from California. "Say that only selfish thoughts possessed their minds, if you please, and that the only consideration which influenced them was an ambition to extend their power and wealth, and still they are entitled to credit," the story said.[130] "Most men with their years, their wealth, and with the triumph which came of first leading the iron horse across the Sierras, would have been content to retire, and for their declining years to seek such comforts as their wealth would secure. But they did not."

Some in Tucson, however, would quickly begin to complain about the company's service and the freight rates and passenger fares it charged. Before the end of the year the *Citizen* was reporting, "From the day on which the Southern Pacific Railroad opened its station at this point, there have been those who have done nothing but growl and find fault at the 'tardiness' of transportation and the excessive rates charged."[131]

For his part, Crocker had heard all of this, good and bad, before. In his view: "Whenever I have known a railroad to be built, while it is building, and while it is being proposed, the projectors of the enterprise are the best fellows in the world. 'You are going to make my land valuable, you do make it valuable' and everybody throws up his hat. But when they come to ride on the road, they think, because they have been friends of the road and have not abused it, that they ought to ride free, or near free as possible; and it is a 'great monopoly' as soon as it wants pay for serving the public."[132]

Crocker was, however, impressed by his visit to the remote town in the Arizona desert. "I found a large community at Tucson," he wrote Huntington upon his return to San Francisco, "and was surprised at finding so many people, and generally of such good standing and intellectual ability."[133] Then the former opponent of extending the tracks through the territory admitted: "We are going to have a brisk trade with that country, especially in the way of lumber and mining machinery. I met many long trains between Tucson and here on the way down and there were over 100 car loads of freight on side tracks between Los Angeles and Tucson, waiting for the completion of the road to the latter place."

CHAPTER FOURTEEN

"New Mexico may yet be able to boast the great southwestern metropolis"

Stretching all the way from Tucson to the Rio Grande was a mostly vacant, table-top flat landscape rimmed by periodic mountain ranges and wrinkled by dry desert washes. While there were a few minor natural barriers the railroad builders of 1880 would have to overcome in crossing this region, in general the terrain would make for very fast track-laying.

This route had first been proposed over thirty years before by Lt. Col. Philip St. George Cooke when he led the Mormon Battalion to California. Instead of following the San Pedro River as the Battalion had done, however, the Southern Pacific surveyors, graders, and track-layers would head almost due east from Tucson. The path they would take was along a line very similar to the direct desert cutoff Cooke had originally mentioned in 1846, even though he and his men had gone farther south in search of water.

An S.P. representative described this land in a letter to Collis Huntington at the end of 1878. "From Tucson eastward the country is generally of the same general desert character," he wrote, "but rapidly changes from having scattering bunches of grass to a country nearly covered with it. By the time the San Pedro Valley is reached, and thence eastward, the grass is very commonly as close in growth as wheat under cultivation...".[1] He continued, "Water on the surface remains rare, occasional springs and tide marshes ("Cienegas") are the only natural water found; but wells of a depth of 100 feet and less generally find water...".

A few months later this same official wrote Huntington again, providing an even more extensive overview of the area. "The Tombstone mines are situated about twenty-five miles from the survey of the railroad," he said, "in the San Pedro

River Valley. There is no doubt of the extreme richness of some of the mines located here; and the only question to be settled by time is their permanence."[2]

He thought the river valley itself was "fertile, easily irrigated, has abundance of water, and is surrounded by good grazing land, extending far into the mountains." East of there in the Sulfur Springs Valley, though, he found water for irrigation to be less abundant, and proposed artesian wells to encourage farming.

The San Simon Valley straddling the Arizona and New Mexico border was described as having few economic prospects since it was made up of gravelly grazing land. While occasional surface water was available in this vicinity, reports indicated that most of it would have to come from shallow wells.

Across the border with New Mexico was the usually dry Mimbres River, although its route had "much choice farming land, easily irrigated along its course."[3] After traversing this part of the territory and observing where the mining areas were located, the S.P. official concluded the railroad should run as far north of the Mexican boundary line as possible. Farther south was found mostly desolate desert, he said, of little economic interest to the company.

At the same time these letters were sent, S.P. Chief Engineer George Gray was also writing Huntington with his own perspective on the land which would be crossed east of Tucson. He noted the Mimbres riverbed ran "through an open valley about ten miles wide,"[4] and he believed that, despite a few spots where some "moderately heavy grading" would be required, the railroad from Tucson all the way to El Paso could be easily built.

While the prospect for rapid construction of the line to the Rio Grande was anticipated, a growing uneasiness was entering into Southern Pacific's ranks. The potential threat of direct competition from the Atchison, Topeka & Santa Fe railroad was becoming more of a possibility all the time. Not only was the company building south from Colorado with the apparent goal of reaching both Mexico City as well as Guaymas on the Gulf of California, but they were also pushing west along the 35th parallel in northern New Mexico toward Arizona and eventually California.

This type of direct business challenge from a rival was a rarity for Huntington, Crocker, and Stanford. It wasn't as if they hadn't been forewarned, however. Two years before, General Superintendent Towne had informed the three of the aggressive nature of the other firm. By October of 1879, when almost 450 men were at work on the A.T.&S.F. line in northern New Mexico, he was writing to New York that road grading had passed near Santa Fe and "from reports from all quarters, which are believed to be authentic, the work will be pushed south with all possible speed."[5]

In anticipation of the two lines crossing at some point in the area of the Gadsden Purchase, engineer Gray had by this time spelled out options for the junction. He focused on the areas around El Paso along with the small town of Mesilla in eastern New Mexico. He also told Huntington that from the center of that territory the Southern Pacific tracks could either run through Mesilla or head straight for the Texas community.

By the time S.P. reached Tucson in March of 1880, their railroad competitors were hiring one hundred more track-layers in New Mexico. Because of the rapid pace of southbound construction by the Atchison, Topeka & Santa Fe, the potential junction point was moving ever westward, a prospect which greatly worried Charles Crocker. After meeting with an engineer for the A.T.&S.F., he said the company "proposes to cross our road somewhere near the Mimbres, but I am decidedly of the opinion that if they build through there, they will go nearer Tucson, tapping the Tombstone Mining District. If they do, they will hurt us very much…".[6] Thus, he stressed, "They are going to be very serious competitors for that business against us."

Leland Stanford agreed with his San Francisco partner. "The control of the Tombstone District is an important matter, judging from what I hear," he wrote.[7] To insure that Southern Pacific exclusively got that business, in early April of 1880, Stanford urged Huntington to send rails west rapidly, no matter what the cost, so that track-laying wouldn't be slowed again.

On the east coast, however, Huntington wasn't too concerned about the threat of competition from the A.T.&S.F. He ridiculed their idea of building a railroad to Guaymas, said he understood the firm's financing was on shaky ground, and thought the company would probably break up soon. Just in case it didn't, he also wanted to pay a premium price for rails to guarantee no further delays in the construction work, while also commenting, "I am disposed to think that if we push on rapidly to Mesilla, the Atchison, Topeka & Santa Fe will connect with us there…".[8]

While the three longtime business partners were contemplating what would happen when their rails eventually reached toward New Mexico and the Rio Grande, track-laying continued away from Tucson. The Chinese graders who had been moved eastward through town in February of 1880 had done heavy labor along Cienega Creek and then retreated to meet up with the construction train as it rolled forward.

As the railroad workmen departed the city, they left behind a community brimming with confidence for the future. "No matter what may be said to the contrary, every day is establishing the fact beyond question that Tucson is now, and will be, the great center of trade and manufacturing industry of Southern Arizona," offered the *Arizona Daily Star*.[9] "The railroad is with us, and it is proving the great vitalizer of this ancient settlement…We are growing on all sides, and Tucson is, and will be, the metropolis of Arizona."

This economic boom, the newspaper wrote, wasn't only theoretical, but practical. In less than a month after the tracks arrived, $4,000 in daily freight business was being conducted. These deliveries one day included: "8 cars of general merchandise, 2 flour, 4 barley, 2 hay, 4 lumber, 22 R.R. material for end of road, 2 hay for R.R. Co."[10] Some while later it was even reported that "a special refrigerator car containing eighty-four barrels of Anheuser beer" had arrived in town.[11]

Crocker was pleased by this commerce, but continued to express concern about the future potential for competition in the Arizona market. "The fact is business is increasing very rapidly at Tucson," he wrote in April, "and if the Atchison, Topeka & Santa Fe road don't steal it from us, we will have a very profitable trade there."[12] A few days later he rejoiced that, "The earnings since we reached Tucson have been immense, and it will continue right along."[13] For his part Huntington called the Arizona business "very gratifying news to me."[14]

It wasn't only freight, though, which was coming to Tucson. Passengers in larger numbers than expected were arriving and departing, with $500 being collected daily from the sale of about 40 tickets. Among those making the trip to town was Leland Stanford, who came for a quick visit in April. After journeying to the construction front, he returned to Tucson where he was met by Mayor Leatherwood and others. The party then rode in carriages out to the mission church of San Xavier del Bac, "which was most enjoyable to all concerned," according to the *Star*. "After visiting the church in all its apartments," the newspaper continued, "Governor Stanford visited the [Tohono O'odham] village and secured a lot of native pottery, which he carried as relics."[15]

Before the end of the year an even more important person used the new railroad system to get to Tucson. In October, the President of the United States, Rutherford B. Hayes, arrived by train on his way around the country. The man who in 1877 had agreed that Southern Pacific could utilize its bridge across the Colorado River to enter Arizona, was now riding over the very rails which that political decision had helped implement.

To continue the rapid population increase and economic growth which was occurring in Tucson, the southern transcontinental railroad across the Gadsden Purchase needed to be finished, and to accomplish that goal the track-layers were moving swiftly eastward. By early April of 1880 they had reached Cienega Creek, twenty-eight miles from town, where the path of the railroad required the existing stage coach stop to be demolished because the rails ran right through it. A switching station with two side tracks would soon be opened at this point, called "Pantano," and by May 1st regular passenger service had begun. Trains departed Tucson at 7 a.m. for the two-hour trip and returned at 4:30 in the afternoon.

Within a few months a small community developed at Pantano. Among other buildings there was a 1,600 square-foot depot, a post office, and a Southern

Pacific Railroad hotel. Initially, this last establishment served many customers and was promoted as having both a fine restaurant which advertised that "prompt, courteous attention will be given to all," along with a corral where plenty of hay and grain were available for animals.[16]

The freighting firm of Tully and Ochoa also built a storehouse at Pantano for goods to be transported to nearby mining camps. In addition, they opened a small retail shop, along with a blacksmith and carpentry business. While the population of the settlement originally was quite small, according to the *Star*, "Pantano is bound to be a place of much more importance than is generally conceded…[it] bids fair to bloom into a full-grown city before many months, unless the place takes to cramps."[17]

The new community quickly became a destination for Tucson residents seeking a little relief from the rising desert temperatures. By the end of May a Sunday excursion train had taken a carload of holiday-seekers out to the station at Pantano where they enjoyed a dance and other activities before returning home.[18]

As some city people were relaxing along Cienega Creek, the Southern Pacific graders and track-layers kept moving toward the San Pedro River. Crocker had ordered more men to the front but also told Huntington, "You must not expect much progress for the next 40 miles, as there is some quite heavy work, which at the very best, will detain us from going on as fast as we have been accustomed to."[19]

After the natural obstacles near the San Pedro River were surmounted, however, and if enough rails were available, Crocker assumed it should be easy work from there all the way to El Paso. "There will be no difficulty in reaching the boundary of Texas by one year from today, if we have the steel," he predicted confidently at the end of April of 1880.[20] By June he had moved the target date to December 1st, or the new year at the very latest.[21] Forecasting the workers could lay two to three miles of track every day all the way to the Rio Grande, he later wrote, "I guess it will be about as tall [a] railroad building as has been done anywhere in our history."[22]

In Arizona, however, even though the graders and track-layers were within a few miles of the proposed town site of Benson by the 13th of May, they were not moving rapidly due to the undulating terrain in the San Pedro River Valley. Benson, probably named after a friend of Crocker's, was the planned railroad community which some Tucsonans feared would replace them as the great city of the Southwest because it was a natural point for a branch line running to the Tombstone mining district. A reporter for a Los Angeles newspaper anticipated that the site would be "where the great town is to be located. Everybody is getting ready to go there."[23]

The location of Benson was seemingly ideal. Situated less than a mile west of the San Pedro River, according to the *Star*, "The spot is well selected, being on high ground above the miasmas [vaporous emanations of the atmosphere] of the valley, overlooking a beautiful tract of country, and free from all danger of malarial influences."[24]

Despite these apparent advantages, the *Citizen* wasn't worried by the threatened competition to Tucson. "There is nothing there to build a town," they wrote disdainfully of Benson. "It is an unhealthy location to begin with: has no agriculture to speak of and can never be more than a shipping station for the mines, with a precarious population of a few hundred. We are told that the railroad is going to do wonders for this imaginary town. Now we should like for some one to tell us where railroads have built a town."[25]

While it might not build towns, the Southern Pacific Railroad Company did have a 160-acre community laid out on a bluff above the narrow but perennial San Pedro River. Benson was divided into blocks of thirty-two lots, each measuring 25 by 150 feet. Every block was split by a center alleyway, and the north-south roads were numbered one through eight. The east-west streets were named after either rivers or mountain ranges in the vicinity, such as Gila, Dragoon, Huachuca, and Patagonia.[26]

With the thermometer hitting 106 degrees in Tucson during early June, but with slightly cooler temperatures near the San Pedro, S.P. announced a sale of Benson town lots for later in the month. Paying $2 for a round trip train ticket, potential buyers could spend most of a day traveling to and returning from the site as well as partaking in an auction. The terms of sale would be one-third cash at the time of purchase, with the balance due within one year. A monthly interest rate of one percent would be charged on loans made by the railroad company.[27]

After the auction, Benson grew quickly. "Within six months," it was reported, the town "had four stores plus a number of small shops, the two-story Benson Hotel...and the usual complement of saloons."[28]

Even before the sale of lots at Benson was held, the forecasts for the future of Tombstone, 25 miles to the south, had been growing wildly. The mining district, according to the *N.Y. Commercial Bulletin*: "Is now attracting more attention than any other in the territory. It is only two years since it was discovered, and already a town of about 3,000 inhabitants has been built there, and it is predicted that it will contain a population of 40,000 before a year from this time."[29]

No matter how impressive the outlook for the mining town appeared to some, not everyone was paying it much attention. As a letter written to the *Citizen* a week after the railroad arrived in Tucson commented: "Mayor Leatherwood of Tucson has sent telegrams to the Pope, the President and all the boys, but Mayor Randall of Tombstone didn't get any. He was up Saturday night last until quite late waiting for it, but was finally compelled to retire without it. Tombstone ain't of any importance in Tucson any away, but when the railroad reaches us, we will send a message to Mayor Leatherwood 'C.O.D.' which will occupy a little of his time to peruse."[30]

Disregarding the good-natured ribbing between the two communities, and because of the apparently bright prospects for the mining district, Huntington had decided Southern Pacific should lay branch tracks to Tombstone off its main line. "If one tenth of what I hear of the Tombstone mines is true," he wrote in early May, "it will pay very well to build this road...".[31]

For his part, Crocker at first opposed the idea. "It would undoubtedly be a profitable enterprise to build a road down to those mines," he thought, "but I do not think we care to stop our forward movement towards the Gulf [of Mexico] in order to build branch lines now."[32] After considering it some more, Crocker quickly changed his mind. Assuming the work could be done without interfering with the main line track-laying, by May of 1880 he had concluded, "I am rather inclined to think it will be a paying road in the course of a short time, if built cheaply."[33] It wasn't until the end of the year, though, that steps were tentatively taken to actually accomplish the idea when Crocker said he would have a survey of the route prepared.[34]

Long before the decision to lay S.P. tracks to Tombstone had been made, though never to be implemented, potential conflicts between Apache Indians and the railroad workers laboring east of the San Pedro River developed. By the end of May, U.S. Cavalry troops were patrolling in the mountains south of the tracks to offer protection, and, "The men working at the front have also been provided by the [Southern Pacific] company with arms and ammunition."[35]

Even if this move was strictly precautionary, very real problems were occurring just across the New Mexico line. The *Star* reported that citizens in the mining towns of Silver City and Shakespeare were near starvation because supplies weren't reaching the communities due to Indian raids on freight wagon trains. Despite that, no actual conflicts were ever reported with the railroad workers, and the track-laying proceeded eastward at a rapid pace after leaving the Benson area.

Ignoring increasing summertime temperatures, the railroad effort moved forward, and this time there was no question of stopping the work. As the labor continued through the eastern Arizona desert, Crocker and Huntington were debating several topics. One concern was the eventual termination point of the line. While Huntington had some thoughts of ending it at Galveston in Texas, Crocker was pushing for New Orleans, and that would be the final choice.[36]

To get to the Louisiana port city, Crocker supported going through El Paso, even though that wasn't technically necessary. He thought for business purposes, "It might be well to touch the Mexican territory as nearly as we can."[37] For his part, Superintendent Towne had a much more ambitious proposal for trade from south of the border. Referring back to some of the ideas floated at the time of the Gadsden Purchase, he favored the United States annexing all the northern states of Mexico for an appropriate amount of compensation.

Of more pressing concern to Crocker at the time, though, was the growing threat being posed by the Atchison, Topeka & Santa Fe Railroad. That company was rapidly building its line southward, and Crocker continually reminded his New York partner of the possible problems their rivals could cause them. "I hope you will not forget that the A.T.&S.F. road, if they build through, will injure us very much," he said in one June letter to Huntington,[38] while in another written the next day he commented, "I would dislike very much to have them go forward toward Tombstone, and in fact go beyond the point where they will reach our line."[39] If their competitors did build to the mining district Crocker feared: "They will prevent us from making any money, and we will prevent them from making any. It would certainly be suicidal on both sides."[40]

To minimize competition between the two roads, Crocker proposed an agreement which would establish a junction point as well as address other issues. The roads were less than 500 miles apart, and he was hoping the meeting place could be at Mesilla, but based on the rate the A.T.&S.F. was laying tracks, he soon concluded it would probably be somewhere west of there instead. No matter where that point was, however, Crocker had decided the two companies needed to come to terms or "if we don't make an arrangement, we will both make a great mistake."[41]

Crocker also thought Huntington wasn't taking the other company seriously enough. "I very much fear that you are underrating these men and do not give them credit for the energy and persistence which they are showing," he wrote in late June of 1880.[42] "They are the only ones that I have feared, or that I now fear…". A week later he commented, "These people have more power and money than you have given them credit for. I hope you will not get tired of my eternal dinging on this subject, but this thing is the one subject that gives me more uneasiness than anything else connected with our R.R. affairs, and I assure you they will cut our business all to pieces if they get into that mining country down there, and our earnings will be regulated back to almost nothing."[43]

For his part, Huntington remained rather flippant toward the men behind the A.T.&S.F. In July he said of them: "I did think last winter they would come to grief before this time, but they seem to be stronger now than then. Still, I cannot believe that any set of people that have been slashing around as they have, will ever make a perfect success, and I believe they will come to grief sooner or later."[44] Despite that opinion, Huntington agreed to meet with his competitors to discuss a junction point for the rails, along with other topics, but was not finding A.T.&S.F. officials very cooperative concerning even setting up a time to talk.

The company the two veteran railroad builders were dealing with was spearheaded by a pair of younger men as aggressive and forceful as they were. Both had been born in Vermont, and while one began his railroad career as a station agent in Milton, Wisconsin, the other later graduated from the academy there.

In 1877, as vice-president and general manager of the Atchison, Topeka and Santa Fe Railroad, forty-year old William B. Strong had assumed responsibility for its expansion program. At that time the company had less than 800 miles of track, but in the next twelve years would add over 6,000 more. The former small-town Wisconsin station agent successfully oversaw this rapid growth, and according to one historian, "Strong's extraordinary achievements were in part made possible by his own great ambitions, his fighting determination and his powerful leadership…".[45]

To assist him with the road building effort, Strong could rely on engineer Albert Robinson, who was seven years younger than he was. First employed by the A.T.&S.F. in 1871, before the end of the decade Robinson was partially responsible for the switchback project through the Raton Pass. This engineering feat allowed the company's tracks to enter New Mexico from Colorado and thus opened up both the Southwest and southern California to them. Called "one of the greatest railroad builders this country has produced,"[46] Robinson was a perfect match to implement the dreams of Strong. Combined, these two men had the enthusiasm, drive, and financial resources to match that of their more experienced Southern Pacific rivals.

While potential competition with S.P. for the freight traffic from Tombstone and other points in Arizona was looming, actual storm clouds were building over the territory. In late July and then again in the middle of August of 1880, fierce thunderstorms rolled across the desert. As the *Citizen* noted of this common summertime occurrence, "When it does rain in Arizona, it rains so hard that dry beds of creeks suddenly become bank full of water, and the fall is so great that it seems to carry everything before it."[47]

The impact of these cloudbursts was serious damage to the Southern Pacific track work already completed. The first storm washed out a considerable length of rails near Pantano, causing the train from Benson to be delayed and requiring a large effort to repair the line.

The rain in August was even worse. "Such a complete wreck the waters must lately have caused along the railroad track," the *Star* wrote, "can only be imagined from the debris of all kinds, scattered in the greatest profusion and confusion, all along the course the raging waters took; railroad ties are strewed around by the hundred for a long distance, trees of immense growth have been uprooted and carried down the current as though they had been willow wands."[48]

The result was over 6,000-feet of track between Pantano and Tucson being washed away, but the damage was quickly fixed. Shortly afterward, however, another storm arrived and destroyed the repair work just completed, thus halting all train traffic. After two hundred men and more material were sent to correct the problems again, they managed to improvise a temporary solution by which passengers could be transferred by a handcar across a jerry-rigged road.

The cost of these repairs was estimated to be $25,000 at a minimum, but at least no one had lost their life because of the flooding damage to the tracks. For his part, Crocker's concise conclusion regarding the violent summer thunderstorms in the desert was, "I guess it is a feature of that country."[49]

Even as Southern Pacific officials had to contend with these washout problems, to which their initial "build it cheap" philosophy may have contributed, the graders and track-layers kept moving ever eastward. The work was progressing rapidly with often around two miles of rails a day being put down.

By early September another station site had been selected at a strategic place along the road. Located in the Sulfur Springs Valley of eastern Arizona, the *Star* thought this new settlement held great economic promise since it would be a supply point for two nearby military posts. "Large warehouses will be erected by the Government and private companies," the newspaper offered, "and altogether Sulphur Springs Valley has a prosperous future in view. The S.P.R.R. Co. have named the new station Willcox,"[50] after an army general then stationed at Prescott, Arizona.

Within a year, an apparent source of revenue for the railroad company, as well as a possible supply of fuel for their steam engines, had been discovered nearby. "Coal has been found on the San Carlos Indian Reservation north of Willcox Station," Crocker wrote his New York partner, "very near the southerly line of the reservation, and only a few miles inside of it."[51] To benefit the Indians, the reservation's agent was trying to make arrangements to collect a royalty on any mined coal, but Crocker said, "The citizens of Arizona are moving in the matter, and getting up a petition to have the line of the reservation moved so as to exclude the coal from it…".

A few days later, he elaborated further on the situation while also imploring his east-coast associate to use his lobbying skills in Washington to help resolve the issue. "The fact is that the Indian Reservation is located in a mining region," Crocker wrote, "and that there is a great deal of mining wealth within it. Certainly this coal is of no benefit to the Indians, and to tax the people of Arizona a royalty on every ton of coal burned by them would be, I think, wrong in principle and is a matter that the government ought not for a moment to entertain."[52]

The topic was still being discussed between the two partners in May of 1881, when Crocker wrote that he was confident he could "get most of the citizens of Arizona and New Mexico to sign petitions to have this land returned to the public domain."[53] Not only would the people of the two territories participate, but Crocker believed officials of the Atchison, Topeka & Santa Fe line would also help since they were "in the same fix as ours…", concerning access to the mining area.

Well before the Arizona coal controversy had occurred, Towne and Crocker made it clear they wanted to be ready to accommodate the increased business which would result when the S.P. and A.T.&S.F. lines met somewhere in New Mexico. "Order immediately ten, ten wheel locomotives, two hundred flat cars and one hundred box cars," Crocker wired Huntington at the end of June of 1880, "…and send them forward as quick as possible."[54] It wasn't only freight traffic he was thinking about; he also wanted twelve passenger coaches, six smoking cars and six first-class sleepers, all to be delivered "as soon as we connect with the Topeka road".

By November, as debate continued over where the junction with the A.T.&S.F. would take place, Towne was asking for even more rolling stock. He urged his boss to "order at an early day for 20 more 10 wheel engines, of the same size as the last ordered, together with 200 box cars and 400 flats, all of which should be marked S.P. of N.M."[55]

Where and when the meeting point of the two railroads was to be located and reached, however, still hadn't been determined late in the year. In the summer of 1880, even before the tracks were east of Willcox, speculation and rumor had intensified about the possibilities. In June, Crocker told a New Mexico newspaper that he anticipated the connection would be made just west of El Paso, if the Atchison, Topeka & Santa Fe could put down tracks as fast as his company would.[56] Late the following month he wrote Huntington that Mesilla would be acceptable, but he expected the actual spot to be further west.[57]

From New Mexico, the *Mesilla News* made no secret of where it thought the junction point should be. In July of 1879, they had written of the A.T.&S.F. line, which was building south from the Colorado border and nearing Albuquerque, "They will then most likely come down the Rio Grande to control the future great trade of the valley to Mesilla and cross the Southern Pacific here and then strike to Guaymas…".[58]

By October of 1880, the *News* reported: "And now the cry is Ho! for Mesilla. The race between the two constructing transcontinental railroads wages hotter and hotter to see which will be the first to reach Mesilla on the Rio Grande."[59] A few weeks later, however, they admitted the competing railroads would probably connect thirty miles west of the river.[60]

To determine the location of the junction, in the fall of 1880 leading officials of both companies met in Boston and the result was a memorandum of agreement. While no exact conclusion was reached, according to Huntington the A.T.&S.F. representatives said they would not build across the S.P. line. He further added, obviously still underestimating the men he was dealing with, "We agreed to this memorandum of contract, thinking it would give them time to learn the whole situation of matters on that side, and that as soon as they did, they would hardly think of building through [to California] on the 35th parallel, or building the Guaymas road."[61]

Just in case the A.T.&S.F. decided to continue pushing toward Mexico, though, Huntington had earlier asked a favor of Ulysses S. Grant. The Civil War hero and two-term President of the United States wrote a letter to the president of Mexico extolling the virtues of the Southern Pacific company.[62] At the same time, Huntington himself suggested the Mexican government should "hold everything in abeyance until such time as they could make thorough surveys so that they would know which were the best routes to build on," in the northern part of the country.[63] Based on these actions, he thought the A.T.&S.F. thrust south of the border could be delayed for "a couple of years".

Despite taking these precautionary steps to slow the competition, Huntington still didn't realize the financial strength of his rivals. By the time of the October meeting in Boston between the two companies, "Money was no longer lacking [for the A.T.&S.F.], for the splendid increase of earnings, the successful handling of the company's lands and the sound management of the Santa Fe Company had now secured for it abundant credit," observed one commentator.[64]

As the negotiating game over a junction point and other issues continued between the two railroads, the S.P. track had crossed the San Simon Valley of eastern Arizona, where water was available seventy-two feet below the surface. The rate of track-laying was very rapid at this point, with one report stating, "On the 24th [of August] there [were] 12,200 feet of steel rails laid; on the 25th, 11,600; and the 26th, 12,800—over two miles and the greatest distance ever laid in one day by the Southern Pacific…".[65]

After spanning this level terrain, the company's construction train was finally approaching New Mexico. The pace of work near the territorial border, however, would be slowed due "to the rock cutting and heavy grades, which occasioned much blasting and hard work."[66] It wasn't until about September 20th that the boundary between the two territories was actually crossed. Even after that, the effort remained impeded because of the difficult grading which needed to be done, but expectations were that things would pick up again shortly.

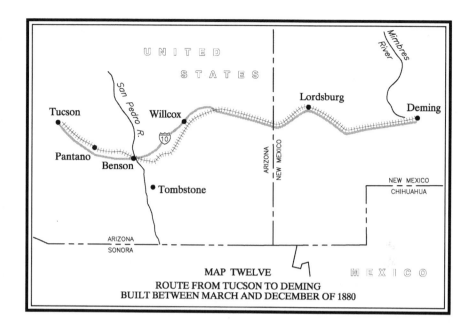

MAP TWELVE
ROUTE FROM TUCSON TO DEMING
BUILT BETWEEN MARCH AND DECEMBER OF 1880

The political and economic groundwork for building the line into New Mexico had started being laid a few years before. Beginning in March of 1877, Los Angeles area railroad man Phineas Banning had visited on behalf of the Southern Pacific Company, and Territorial Governor Samuel B. Axtell was soon corresponding with Huntington to proclaim the territory's advantages. "We have copper, lead, silver, coal and iron in quantities," Axtell wrote, "and some gold in places and some small leads of gold bearing quartz. We have also a good stock country, [and] an excellent country for sheep. We also have quite a large population, probably 120,000, [and] all of this must make business for R.R.s."[67]

In a later letter to New York, Axtell expanded on his anticipation for the railroad reaching New Mexico. He stated, "I believe it will settle the Indian question and the uncivilized border warfare, introduce families and make and protect homes for them."[68]

While extolling the virtues of his territory and proclaiming its great need for a railroad, Axtell also asked Huntington for a favor. "Now if you have confidence in my integrity and ability," he said, "I wish you to use your influence to have me continued as Governor of the Territory...If you will do this for me, I shall feel under renewed personal obligation to you."[69]

A native of Ohio and an attorney, Axtell had moved to California two years after the gold rush of 1849. There he was elected twice to Congress and in 1874

gained an appointment from President Grant as governor of Utah. The next year
he left that post, but quickly obtained the same position in New Mexico. Axtell
was a big supporter of railroads eventually reaching the remote territory and was
in frequent communication with Huntington about this possibility.

To accommodate and encourage railroad construction in New Mexico, by
early 1878 the territorial legislature had approved a bill similar to that adopted
the previous year in Arizona. Axtell noted there had been only one slight amendment. "It relates to the liability of owners of stock found upon the track and
causing injury to the [rail]road," he wrote Huntington.[70] Within a few weeks of
the bill's passage, however, it wasn't Southern Pacific but rather the Atchison,
Topeka & Santa Fe which was taking advantage of the new law by initially incorporating in the territory.

As he promoted development proposals for New Mexico, the Governor's own
job was in jeopardy. By August of 1878, he was being investigated by the Hayes
administration for something unrelated to railroading, and he asked Huntington
again for help in retaining his appointment. It was to no avail. The following
month Axtell was removed from his position.

Around this same time, Huntington wrote his west coast partners, "I think
you should at once organize a company in New Mexico to build from the end of
the Arizona road to El Paso."[71] The response from San Francisco was, "We will
go on at once to organize" such a subsidiary, "…to construct a road connecting
with the Southern Pacific Railroad of Arizona and running thence to some point
on the Rio Grande and near the town of El Paso, following as near as may be the
thirty-second parallel of north latitude."[72]

It wasn't until April 14th of 1879, however, that the Southern Pacific Railroad
of New Mexico was actually incorporated. Five directors were named, two of
whom were from the territory, but, as president of the company, Crocker's son
controlled 99 percent of its 2,000 shares. To finance the venture, ten million
dollars of capital stock was approved.

Just as in Arizona, the newspapers of southern New Mexico were jubilant over
the expectations for prosperity which they thought the two railroads would bring
the region. Shortly after the Atchison, Topeka & Santa Fe had entered the territory from Colorado, the *Thirty-Four* in Las Cruces exclaimed, "Southern New
Mexico must begin to wake up. Young and vigorous life blood is being injected
into the arterial system of the Territory, and old-fogyism must take a back seat.
The [rail]road will certainly not stop at [Las] Vegas [New Mexico], but proceed at
once to the Rio Grande, and our people must be ready to meet it, if they would
reap the full measure of benefits to be derived from its advent."[73]

As for the impact which the Southern Pacific would have on New Mexico
when it combined with the A.T.&S.F., one local newspaper believed the financial

rewards these roads could offer the territory would be incredible. "Railroads, capital, immigration, manufactures and enterprise are pushing fast for New Mexico,"[74] they wrote, while predicting one result around Mesilla would be that, "When there are railroad facilities, the wine and brandy interest of that section will become very important."

It wasn't only the exportation of agricultural and other products which excited people in New Mexico. One visitor to the territory predicted: "I expect to see the patient and health seeker from all parts of the Union and Europe flock here to snatch their failing bodies, as it were, from the grave; make happy homes and live to a good old age. I expect to see millions of people on your beautiful Rio Grande valleys, all healthy, happy and prosperous."[75]

After the Southern Pacific graders and track-layers had worked through the difficult terrain along the Arizona—New Mexico border, rapid progress resumed across the level land of the Gadsden Purchase. By October of 1880, the rails had reached a point just north of the silver mining camp at Shakespeare, and there a new community would develop. Named Lordsburg after Tucson merchant Charles H. Lord, the first Southern Pacific passenger train arrived on the 18th of the month.

The tiny community initially consisted of only railroad buildings, and the first family to live in town was the Ownbys. They operated the post office, provided meals for railroad workers and passengers, and remained in Lordsburg the rest of their lives.[76]

The continental divide ran east of the new town, but because of the very level topography, it was an unnoticeable summit in the area. A Southern Pacific official had written of this portion of New Mexico, "From the continental divide to the Rio Mimbres is a gentle slope in open valley dotted with isolated buttes…There are no bluffs or mesas approaching the Rio Mimbres on either side to exceed 15 feet in height."[77]

While the Southern Pacific track-laying moved swiftly eastward into New Mexico, a decision about where exactly the junction with the Atchison, Topeka & Santa Fe line should be located still had not been finalized. Superintendent Towne, representing the S.P., recommended a point to General Manager Strong of the A.T.&S.F., and Stanford suggested the place be called "Deming," Mrs. Charles Crocker's maiden name. A meeting at that location between company officials was arranged, but the precise spot, according to Towne, would be determined mainly by one factor. "Water, of course," he wrote Huntington, "will be the principal thing that will influence them in selecting the point."[78]

To finalize an approximate junction site, on December 16, 1880, chief engineer Gray of the S.P. met with engineer Robinson of the A.T.&S.F. at a spot ten miles east of the Rio Mimbres. Before then, however, the A.T.&S.F. had made a major decision: Once their track-layers, moving south from Albuquerque, reached a place called Rincon, their line would split. One route would go southwest to a junction with the Southern Pacific tracks near the Rio Mimbres, while the other leg of the "reverse Y" headed toward El Paso.

Crocker was very unhappy about that move by his competitors, saying he hoped it would be abandoned and they would only meet the S.P. at El Paso since that would insure more freight business for Southern Pacific. In addition, he argued, an agreement over the general location of the junction point had already been finalized in Boston, and this new decision showed that the Atchison, Topeka & Santa Fe was not fulfilling its part of the bargain. "You will also notice that they are pushing their road almost parallel with ours," he wrote Huntington of the A.T.&S.F. route southwest of Rincon, "…and that they will probably join our road some fifteen(15) miles west of where they ought to connect with us, under a fair interpretation of the contract."[79] Based on that, Crocker concluded the agreement was no longer binding.

For his part, Huntington still wanted a compromise. "I expect to see the Atchison, Topeka & Santa Fe people this week," he told his San Francisco partner just after the New Year of 1881, "and will then see if we can agree upon the point of junction."[80]

This wasn't the only contentious disagreement between the two companies. What intentions the A.T.&S.F. had for extending their line to Tombstone as well as into Mexico also remained uncertain. Based on his efforts to negotiate a settlement of these issues with them, Huntington had concluded of his rivals: "I do not think it is worthwhile to pay much attention to them. I think they are going their own way for anything we can do; although I [will] still try in every way I can to harmonize our and their interest in these roads. They are on a very high horse at this time, and for that matter, have been for some months past."[81]

As these disputes were occurring, Southern Pacific's construction rate was again reduced by a lack of rails. The Atchison, Topeka & Santa Fe track-laying was also going much slower than expected. They not only had a shortage of steel, but cold weather in northern New Mexico caused delays in the shipment of other needed materials and their workers even staged a brief strike for better food.

Ignoring these problems, settlers and speculators began arriving in the area of the supposed meeting point of the two railroads. They established a tent city on the east side of the Mimbres River, and called it "New Chicago" in hopes it would also become a railroad center like its midwestern namesake. Some of the tents in the newly-born community served as businesses and had door plates which announced, "Dancehall," "Lodging," or the most popular, "Saloon".[82]

While Southern Pacific's rails soon reached this area, with service officially beginning on December 15th of 1880, the arrival of the A.T.&S.F. was still three months away. Writing from New York, Huntington said of the uncertainty over the junction point: "It is very difficult to learn just what the Atchison, Topeka & Santa Fe people are doing in the way of closing up the gap between their road and ours. From the talk here, it would seem that they were more anxious about building to El Paso…Although I cannot see how their interest would be against an early connection with us at some point near Deming."[83]

As their tracks moved down from Rincon, the A.T.&S.F. line unexpectedly swung farther west than anticipated by the residents of the infant settlement east of the Mimbres River. Southern Pacific eventually laid out another town some miles west of "New Chicago," and the tents of the original community were simply picked up and moved to "Deming", the actual junction point of the two railroads.

Within weeks, two hundred or so inhabitants were living and conducting business in tents and frame buildings hurriedly erected at the new town site. The shops included "thirteen saloons, two groceries, two Chinese laundries, one barber shop, one restaurant, one butcher shop, and one cigar store."[84] The people who established the place were a rough bunch, and one commentator said of them, "Deming morals are not to be discussed in a newspaper—till she has some."[85]

On March 8, 1881, the Atchison, Topeka & Santa Fe tracks finally reached Deming. Another silver spike ceremony was arranged for 3:45 p.m. and some minor officials from both companies were on hand to witness the connection which completed the nation's second transcontinental railroad. Engineer O'Neil at the controls of A.T.&S.F. locomotive 503 was the first over the junction, and that was about it for the celebration. As one New Mexico newspaper commented, however, "Quite a company of eastern notables have gone out to witness the event, among whom is Miss Longfellow, a daughter of the poet."[86]

Unlike the first meeting of transcontinental tracks in 1869 at Promontory in Utah, this occasion received very little national attention. The *New York Times* mentioned it in one paragraph in its "General Railway Notes" of March 10th, and the *New York Tribune* had the same coverage on the 18th. The Arizona legislature, though, did send their congratulations, calling it "an event which will mark a new era in the prosperity of our Territory…".[87]

Interestingly, London's *Railway Times* gave the connection of the two lines a little more notice and wrote: "This month witnesses the opening of the new route to the Pacific, an event which is probably of as much significance in American railroad history as anything which has occurred in railroad construction since the opening of the first transcontinental line twelve years ago…The opening of the new route, while of great value to general commerce, is also calculated to promote the development of a vast region of the Southwest and Pacific coast, and the opening up of Mexico's resources."[88]

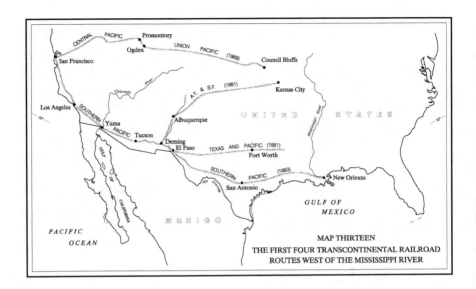

MAP THIRTEEN
THE FIRST FOUR TRANSCONTINENTAL RAILROAD
ROUTES WEST OF THE MISSISSIPPI RIVER

Despite the general lack of national publicity, local people assumed great things lay in store for the new community of Deming. As one newspaper in Las Cruces noted in an article under "A New Mexican Metropolis" headline: "It is the opinion of a great many observant people in this southern country that New Mexico may yet be able to boast the great southwestern metropolis. It is stated that the two railroad companies are determined to make an important point of Deming and will erect there roundhouses and machine shops; that the natural location of the town could not be better, being in the midst of as fine a grazing section as is to be found anywhere, with plenty of water at a depth of a few feet, and surrounded by rich mining districts on all sides...".[89] Thus, the paper concluded, "If these statements are true, we may yet look for the great business center in New Mexico."

Even though the future had yet to decide that issue, the country's second transcontinental railroad line had at last finally been completed. It wasn't the southern route which James Gadsden and Jefferson Davis had sought and fought for almost thirty years earlier, but at least it was finished.

This new cross-country road ran from Kansas City to Deming, then turned toward Tucson and points further west. The cost of traveling over this route naturally depended upon the class of ticket and the accommodations secured. For first-class passengers the price from Kansas City to Los Angeles was $105, with sleeping berths being slightly extra. The lowest fare between these destinations was for "emigrants" and cost $47.50.[90]

On their way west, these passengers would pass through the Gadsden Purchase. To accomplish the feat of providing a second transcontinental band of steel, the 219 miles between Tucson and the new station at Deming had been connected with rails by the Southern Pacific Railroad Company in a period of less than nine months in 1880. Despite some construction and supply problems, the rate of track-laying had again demonstrated the topographical advantages of building a railroad through the area acquired from Mexico in 1854.

As the *Boston Herald* concluded of the new transcontinental line even before it opened for business: "The southern way will without question be the favorite winter route to the Pacific. Tourists for pleasure…have shrunk from the hardships of the bleak journey across the snowy plains of the Union Pacific route, with its threatening delays from the furious storms that often block the way and bury the trains in their terrible drifts. But hereafter they may make the journey through the warm air and perpetual sunshine of New Mexico and Arizona direct to Southern California…".[91]

CHAPTER FIFTEEN

"A certain barbarism disappears before the advance of the locomotive"

Within days of the establishment of the track connection at Deming, the two railroad companies had each identified a square-mile of land which they would use. Since after leaving "New Chicago" the squatters had already occupied some of this property, it meant their tents and shacks had to be moved a second time.

A Post Office located in a box car soon opened, but eventually an appropriate shanty was erected for it. A weekly newspaper was also quickly founded and called the *Deming Headlight* because the publisher was fascinated with the lamps of the steam engines. At $3 per year, the one-page paper was printed on a foot-powered press.[1]

To encourage development, the railroad companies laid out a town site. According to one report, residential lots measuring 75 by 140 feet would cost from $500 if on a corner, down to $125 for land at a distance from the tracks.[2] Those amounts, someone joked about the new and remote community, indicated the companies seemed "as if they were learning El Paso tricks,"[3] while another critic commented of the asking prices, "Judging from present appearances, as many cents would cover the value and have a good margin to spare."[4]

A month after the transcontinental line opened, Southern Pacific already had made significant improvements. "The S.P. has six miles of a perfect network of tracks, spurs, etc.," one newspaper reported, "and when both roads have completed their arrangements the railway yard at Deming will be the largest west of Chicago."[5] Southern Pacific would also soon erect two transfer sheds "of Oregon pine plank and redwood lumber," and its 300-foot long freight building was nearing completion. In addition, a 50,000-gallon water tank was finished, and a 15-stall roundhouse was under construction.

A combination union depot and hotel was also being built. Located between the two main lines of track, the structure would contain the usual assortment of railroad necessities, but additionally included a clock in the S.P. section set to west coast time and one in the A.T.&S.F. office running on mountain time.

Described as a 13,000 square foot building, the depot had a lengthy second floor which contained a 100-room Harvey House hotel. Broad verandahs lined both sides of the station, and there was a 750-foot long platform next to the tracks on which to store freight.[6] The hotel was considered an outstanding establishment and was "furnished at an expense of $10,000 by Fred Harvey, and is first-class in all its appointments," remarked a visitor.[7]

Irrespective of its fine train station and hotel, however, the community quickly became known as a wild town. By April of 1881, according to one account, "Deming was almost under siege from a band of lawless brigands who were making it uncomfortable for area residents and the traveling public at best, and sometimes even downright dangerous."[8]

A county grand jury put the situation in Deming in more polite terms. "There seems to be a very bad state of affairs existing in the southern part of this county," they determined, "near the border of Old Mexico. It almost seems that a law abiding citizen can hardly live there with any safety to himself or property. There seems to be a band of men living in that section of the county, who live by robbing and stealing, and defy the authorities."[9]

To restore order, and because the grand jury determined "such a state of affairs seriously effect[s] the prosperity of our county,"[10] the sheriff paid a visit to Deming accompanied by two deputies, one of whom was Dan Tucker. Within days some sort of order had been established and the sheriff departed, leaving Tucker behind. The double-barrel shotgun toting deputy quickly gained a reputation as someone who gave no quarter, and it was soon reported, "The most perfect order now prevails at Deming".[11]

While Tucker was helping to instill civility in the new community, further north in the New Mexico territory, another famous act of the west was playing itself out. "The trial of [Billy the] Kid for the murder of sheriff Brady began yesterday," a territorial newspaper wrote of William Bonney on April 9th, 1881.[12] "The jury was enpanelled and the evidence all got in…There appears, from the evidence, to be no doubt of a conviction of murder in the first degree."

After the guilty verdict and death sentence were handed down a few days later, it was decided: "Kid will be taken to Lincoln under strong guard…Kid will be chained in an ambulance and the guard will be strong enough to prevent his being either mobbed or rescued."[13] The jail at Lincoln, however, couldn't hold the Kid, and he escaped after killing the guards and eventually ended up in Fort Sumner, New Mexico. He was tracked down there by Sheriff Pat Garrett on July

14th. The two met late at night in the dimly lit bedroom of a small home, the armed Kid in his stocking feet. According to the sheriff: "I felt sure he had now recognized me, but fortunately he drew back from the bed at noticing my movement, and although he had his pistol pointed at my breast, he delayed to fire, and asked in Spanish, "Quien es? Quien es?' [Who is it?] This gave me time to bring mine to bear on him, and the moment I did so I pulled the trigger and he received his death wound, for the ball struck him in the left breast and pierced his heart."[14]

Garrett wasn't the only lawman during 1881 etching his name into posterity. Later that year, under the headline, "A Street Fight", the *Rio Grande Republican* in Las Cruces, New Mexico, reprinted an article which said: "The liveliest street battle that ever occurred in Tombstone took place at 2:30 p.m. today [October 26th], resulting in the death of three persons and the wounding of two others, one probably fatally. For some time past several cowboys have been in town, and the fight was between City Marshall Virgil Earp, his two brothers, Morgan and Wyatt Earp, and Doc Holliday on one side, and Ike and Billy Clanton and Frank and Tom McLowery on the other."[15] Thus began a lengthy account of the incident which became known to history as the "Shoot-Out at the O.K. Corral".

As that gunplay was occurring in the Arizona territory, how the lawlessness in Deming was being handled continued to be graphically portrayed for the public. According to a report from late November of 1881: "Three weeks ago a cowboy rode his horse defiantly over the depot hotel platform, and was about to ride into the dining room, when he dropped off his horse with a charge of buckshot in his back…The cowboy was buried without ceremony. He is indebted to Deputy Sheriff Tucker for his change of abode, and ten other roughs are similarly indebted to that officer, who is still in the harness, and promises to rid the locality of the hateful element before long."[16]

Even if this was simply a sensationalized account of the deputy sheriff's exploits, the writer did include a detailed description of the new community and its surroundings. "I find Deming on a perfectly flat country," he wrote, "stretching away off in the distance to the point where it meets the sky. But here and there, in every direction, great black mountains, in lumps and in ranges, rise up suddenly out of the flat, and look as if they had been accidentally left by some range of mountains which had moved away. In these barren lumps is the hope of this part of the territory. They are rich in gold, silver, copper and lead."[17]

On the level terrain around the town, the writer said, was unlimited grazing land but no surface water. Shallow wells, though, could be drilled. While sandstorms were an occasional problem, the climate of the area was usually delightful. All in all, the anticipation was that "the complete occupation of this part of the territory is only a question of time."[18] Based on that the author concluded, "Evidently the railroads anticipate a good future for Deming."

After a year, however, the little town still hadn't gotten much bigger, but its future continued to look bright. By 1882, Deming had "twenty-eight business houses, covering all the various branches of business incident to and which make a live town. Its population is American," according to one report.[19] Despite the lack of rapid growth, it was stated assuredly, "There are here men of enterprise that can make the town what they wish it to be, with the aid of the railroads, and it is certain that they will do their part...".[20]

While that future had yet to be determined, in December of 1880 the Southern Pacific graders and track-layers had kept right on working after passing Deming. What route they were going to take from there to reach the Rio Grande and El Paso had been debated by company officials for quite some time and had only recently been decided.

People in Mesilla had originally assumed the Southern Pacific rails would pass through their community, and they also once hoped the junction with the Atchison, Topeka & Santa Fe could take place in their town. "Mesilla is fortunate to be on the direct route of the main line," the *Mesilla News* optimistically stated in the summer of 1879, while anticipating the rails would arrive by January of 1881.[21]

During July of 1880, though, Charles Crocker was writing Collis Huntington that there were two choices east of Deming. "Whether we will go by way of Mesilla, or go direct to El Paso" he said were the options. "It will be fourteen (14) miles shorter to go direct, and I do not know of any good reason for our going around by way of Mesilla, still you always seemed to favor that route."[22]

The final decision was put off until November, when Leland Stanford wired New York: "Grading will be completed this week to a point where we must determine whether we take line direct to El Paso or go by way of Mesilla. My judgment is in favor of direct route as it is of better grade, easier to construct, and is about fourteen miles less distance."[23]

With the two west coast partners in agreement, the choice was made. Southern Pacific's tracks would bypass Mesilla to the south and head straight for the Rio Grande a few miles above El Paso. It was still possible, though, that the Atchison, Topeka and Santa Fe line coming down from Rincon would lay steel through the small community.

Even if home to a population of less than two thousand, Mesilla was the largest settlement in the region, as well as the county seat of government. It contained two churches, three hotels, a telegraph office, and a weekly newspaper. It also had six stores, a variety of craftsmen, three lawyers, three doctors, and a school teacher. According to one account, "The town is built in the Mexican style around a central square or plaza, in the center of which stands the town pump and on one side the Catholic church; the hotels, stores, court house, post office and the saloons occupying [the] other three sides."[24]

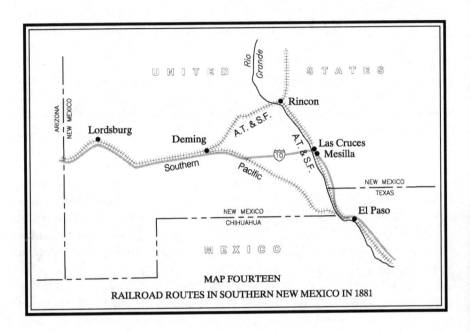

MAP FOURTEEN
RAILROAD ROUTES IN SOUTHERN NEW MEXICO IN 1881

A few miles north of Mesilla, and founded about the same time, was the slightly smaller community of Las Cruces. "It has a population of fifteen hundred souls," a local newspaper reported in 1880, "ninety percent of whom are Mexicans. The town is laid off in [the] American style, with streets crossing each other at right angles, and half a block in the center of the town has been left vacant, so as to form a public square...".[25] The town's shops and services were very similar to those in Mesilla, and the buildings of both were made of adobe.

One of the oldest businesses in Las Cruces as the railroad era approached was a retail establishment co-founded by Julius Freudenthal. He had emigrated to the United States from Prussia in 1856 and joined with his nephew in opening a store. After Julius left the area in the 1860s, his sons Morris and Phoebus entered the business, the former continuing with it until the end of the century while the latter started his own store in 1882. Phoebus was also later involved with the establishment of Las Cruces College, which eventually became New Mexico State University.[26]

Around 1878, the two brothers were joined by their cousin Samuel, who had journeyed by railroad from New York to the end of the line in Colorado. From there, he rode a stagecoach for days to reach Las Cruces, of which he wrote years later: "Everything was expensive, excepting Mexican labor, which was certainly cheap enough. This, more than likely, was sufficient to account for the terribly low standard of living of the poorer Mexicans."[27]

Remembering early Las Cruces, Samuel Freudenthal recalled: "It was the custom of the American population on Saturday night to repair to the Schaublins, a big-hearted German couple who operated a flour mill. There we would dance and drink the native wine until late hours."[28] Freudenthal also contracted malaria while in town, which put him in bed for some time, but a remedy of quinine and whiskey soon had him back on his feet.

The two communities of Mesilla and Las Cruces shared a mild climate and a setting near towering mountains which provided magnificent scenes. In glowing terms, the agricultural advantages of the area were also exclaimed by its inhabitants. "Wheat, barley, and corn are adapted to the soil and grow well; while of fruits there is an endless variety," a newspaper stated.[29] "The finest of apples, peaches, pears, plums, apricots and figs are the leading varieties. Pecans can be profitably grown."

These fruits, however, were not the reason why the region was well known. "By far the most important product of the Mesilla Valley is the grape" was stated in 1880.[30] "It is, without exaggeration, the best table grape in the world, finely flavored and very sweet." Based on this belief, it was "confidently expected that the wine will shortly take its place along with the Spanish, French and other celebrated wines of the world."

Given all of these advantages, locals thought it possible that the great metropolis of the southwest could develop in their area. "The Mesilla Valley…is destined to become one of the most thickly populated sections of New Mexico…," was predicted by one newspaper, "and when the iron horse shall come thundering along with his numerous train of enterprising settlers we expect to see a large and prosperous city spring up somewhere," in the vicinity.[31]

The decision by Southern Pacific officials to bypass Mesilla, however, meant their tracks would head directly for El Paso. While S.P. may have ignored the community, the Atchison, Topeka, and Santa Fe was building south from Rincon, destined for west Texas. They intended to stop somewhere in the area, and it came down to a choice between Mesilla and Las Cruces as to where that spot would be.

At first, surveyors for the A.T.&S.F. planned to run their rails through Mesilla. However, according to accounts from that era, the owners of the land designated for the depot and tracks: "Refused to sell, declaring that they wanted nothing to do with the railroad. It is rumored that this attitude was taken in an effort to force the Santa Fe to pay more for the land than it was actually worth."[32]

Based on that cold reception, and with the encouragement of citizens from Las Cruces, the railroad men decided to look elsewhere for their depot location. Several businessmen quickly formed the Las Cruces Town Company and offered the needed land on property just west of their community. This proposition was quickly accepted.

The estimates of the tracks' potential impact on the small town were similar to those elsewhere throughout the Gadsden Purchase. "When the locomotive reaches Las Cruces," a local newspaper speculated as the construction work approached, "then will the town 'boom' in earnest. The little stir here now is only a 'starter'."[33]

Thus, on April 6, 1881, when the first train arrived, the citizens of Las Cruces celebrated mightily. One young boy remembered years later: "Hundreds of people thronged into the town, coming from miles around. The tracks had to be cleared of people before the train could come to a stop. The curious had to satisfy the urge to touch the engine, which resulted in greasy fingers."[34]

The economic effect on the community was dramatic. The property which had been set aside for the railroad company soon boasted a depot and new residences. One of the town's hotels, the Rio Grande, was remodeled with a barber shop and saloon being added. In addition, according to an historian, "The approach of the railroad had a great impact on the saloonkeepers of Las Cruces. In January 1881, *Newman's Thirty-Four* [newspaper] reported that the number of saloons was beginning to increase and that 'every available room is being sought after and adorned with all kinds of bar fixtures…'. Editor Simeon H. Newman wrote, 'There are eighteen saloons and five dance halls in full blast every night…'."[35]

While the railroad brought rapid change to Las Cruces, the results nearby were just about as predictable. "Mesilla, the dominant community in southern New Mexico prior to the 1880s," stated one commentary on the village, "was unable to attract or hold onto key political, economic, and social institutions, and fell into a period of destabilization and decline."[36] Late in 1881 it was written, "In Mesilla business is duller than ever before known,"[37] and by the next year the county seat of government had been moved to Las Cruces.[38] Over the next century, the population of Mesilla would hardly vary.

New Mexico State University Library

THE RIO GRANDE HOTEL IN LAS CRUCES

As the A.T.&S.F. workers had been moving toward Las Cruces, after leaving Deming Southern Pacific's track-layers quickly crossed the flat land of eastern New Mexico, and by February 24th of 1881 were within 13.5 miles of El Paso. Grading near the Rio Grande would be difficult and time consuming, however, and a bridge over the river still had to be built. Based on that, Crocker estimated it would be May 1st before the Texas town had train service.[39]

With their rails moving ever eastward, several issues continued to be debated by S.P. officials. The first was how to deal with potential competition for business in Arizona from the Atchison, Topeka and Santa Fe line. General Superintendent Towne favored a pooling plan to allow both companies to use the S.P. track from Deming to Benson, which would maximize the freight carried at the highest rate possible.

Crocker agreed with that approach, but added that if their competitor decided, instead, to build its own line into Arizona to connect at Benson with the tracks they were already laying north from Guaymas in Mexico, "It will be a 'fight from the word go'."[40] He also repeated his earlier pledge to build to Tombstone as soon as possible once he heard of the other company's putting down rails west of Deming. In response, Huntington said he would do what he could to prevent any competition for the Tombstone mining district business, but didn't hold out much hope for success.

Before any agreement could be reached with the A.T.&S.F. for joint use of the road west from Deming, a Santa Fe official was complaining to S.P. about the exorbitant freight rates it was charging over that line. In one of the first typewritten letters contained in Huntington's files, on May 10, 1881, he was informed that, while it cost $600 to ship a carload of beer all the way from St. Louis to Deming, Southern Pacific charged $400 more to get it the few hundred miles from there to Tucson.[41] For commercial reasons such as that, William Strong of the A.T.&S.F. was sent to San Francisco to negotiate a shared track settlement with Crocker and Towne.

Eventually, an agreement was reached which allowed for joint use of the line from Deming to Benson. For a pre-established rental amount, the A.T.&S.F. could use this 174 miles of track until either party gave two year's notice to terminate the contract.[42]

This arrangement permitted the Atchison, Topeka & Santa Fe Railroad to quickly lay steel south from Benson past the Tombstone area and they would soon connect it with their tracks in northern Mexico. Even though Huntington had tried to stop them while Crocker continuously threatened retaliation, by October of 1882, the A.T.&S.F. had installed rails off the main S.P. line to join with their own tracks running north from Guaymas. While this line didn't reach Tombstone, it did serve the mines in the general vicinity. The supposed silver wealth of the area, however, proved to be elusive. By 1884, the Tombstone veins were dwindling out, and the mines also flooded, thus making additional work too expensive. The town which had been the focus of so much speculation for so many years was soon returned to obscurity.

Another issue facing Southern Pacific as their tracks moved toward El Paso was how much total rolling stock should be purchased for the new lines in the two territories. Towne had reported in January of 1881 that the Arizona subsidiary had forty-seven engines, mostly ten-wheel locomotives manufactured in Schnectady, New York.[43] The New Mexico branch of the company had twenty more steam engines and Towne now asked Huntington to order an additional thirteen for Arizona and twenty for New Mexico to bring the total to 100. This was quickly done and delivery of all of them was expected by November.[44]

Towne also wrote New York indicating he had received a job offer from the Northern Pacific Railroad Company and was considering it. Having been hired by Huntington twelve years earlier at an annual salary of $13,000, the 53-year old Towne was hoping for more financial security. With some trepidation, however, he admitted to Huntington that Crocker had once told him, "No man in [our] service would be favorably considered who uses other offers to get an increase of salary."[45]

Even before he received Towne's letter, Huntington had heard rumors that the General Superintendent might be leaving. He told Stanford, however: "I think we can afford to give him what he would ask, as he is always fair...I think it is a very important matter, and hope his connection with us and our interest will not be severed until I know what is needed to retain him."[46]

Another concern to the partners was how, exactly, they were going to build across Texas. As in Arizona and New Mexico, they had no specific legal authority to lay tracks to either Fort Worth or to New Orleans via San Antonio. In this case, though, the Texas legislature wasn't expected to be very accommodating since there were already several railroad companies operating in the state, including their former nemesis for the southern transcontinental route, the Texas and Pacific Company.

Despite that situation, Crocker didn't think it should be much of an issue for the S.P. to just build a few miles of track into El Paso after crossing the Rio Grande. "I do not suppose that anybody would interfere with our building it," he wrote Huntington, "except the A.T.&S.F. people."[47]

To overcome the legal hurdle of laying tracks through all of Texas, a variety of choices was possible. One was to buy out or consolidate with a company which already had the required right-of-way. Another was to reach an agreement with the Texas and Pacific on determining a meeting point somewhere east of El Paso.

Stanford considered speed of construction to be an important factor in making a decision about which option to pursue. He told Huntington he wanted to finish the project to New Orleans quickly because once "our line is completed through to the Gulf of Mexico, we will have the shortest line for all the country west of the Rocky Mountains to [the] tide water on the eastern coast, and the cheapest route for all that section of country to Europe."[48]

Their old rival, the Texas and Pacific Railroad, was still trying to thwart that possibility, however. Because of failing health, Tom Scott had sold his interest in the company for $3.5 million and died soon afterward.[49] Under new leadership, the T.&P. had begun laying tracks from Fort Worth heading toward the Rio Grande and was also taking a much more aggressive approach about the Southern Pacific Company's work in Arizona and New Mexico.

In the spring of 1881, the Texas and Pacific board of directors adopted a resolution which read: "Without the semblance of authority of law, the Southern Pacific Railroad Company…have partially constructed, and are now constructing a line of railroad across the Territory of New Mexico through the land grant of the Texas & Pacific Railway Company, derived from the United States Government, under an act of the Congress of the United States…".[50] To correct this illegal action, the resolution continued, "The Texas & Pacific Railway Company claim all the improvements, fixtures and structures, railroad and railroad material, [and] equipment thus placed on its land grant and right-of-way, and will assert its rights thereto in the proper forum." The board also approved a similar motion for Southern Pacific's work in Arizona.

In response, Huntington wrote Crocker, "I do not know as there is any way to get any better title to our right-of-way through Arizona and New Mexico than we have."[51] Despite that opinion, he suggested that possibly a lawsuit might be in order to verify S.P.'s claim to the land on which its tracks had been constructed.

For his part, an apparently nervous Crocker believed Congress should be asked to adopt legislation which would give Southern Pacific clear ownership of the land. He also thought an agreement to build a joint line with the T.&P. about 100 miles east from El Paso might settle the issue. No matter how it was resolved, though, he stated emphatically, "I do not believe the Texas & Pacific can steal our road through New Mexico and Arizona."[52]

Huntington agreed and added, "My own opinion is that this move to contest our rights west of the Rio Grande is got up as a basis to negotiate on our stopping at the Rio Grande…".[53] He felt confident that once the S.P. had laid a few hundred miles of track into Texas, this threat would quietly disappear.

Things didn't exactly work out that way. The Texas and Pacific Company filed a lawsuit against the S.P., claiming the tracks its competitor had laid down through Arizona and New Mexico actually belonged to them. To resolve the dispute, the two companies finally agreed to joint use of 82-miles of track east from El Paso, while Southern Pacific could also legally claim the federal land grant through the Gadsden Purchase which a decade before had originally been awarded its rival.[54]

The prospects for Southern Pacific actually obtaining the rights to the twenty sections of government land which were to be provided for each mile of track built in the two territories still seemed possible in 1881. Huntington, however, had always said his company could implement the project without a subsidy, so Congress killed that chance in 1885.[55] Concerning another Congressional action, it wasn't until 1894 that it finally gave legal authority for S.P. to operate across the military reservation of Fort Yuma in California.[56]

To reach El Paso would also be more time consuming than expected because of the difficult terrain along the Rio Grande, combined with a shortage of men. As Crocker explained in an early March 1881 letter, "The work from the 'Mesa' down to the river has been very heavy, and our force has been light, and we have been unable to increase it, consequently it has held us."[57] Then, commenting on the short distance to the community from where the bridge would be built, he continued, "We expect to reach the river and commence construction on the bridge about the middle of this month, and while the bridge is being built, we can do the grading between the bridge and El Paso, about 4 miles, which is also heavy work."

Disregarding those problems, excitement in El Paso and throughout the region was growing. As the track-laying work proceeded, a Las Cruces newspaper wrote about the Texas community, "People here are almost all more or less crazy on the subject of the future of this town."[58] Another local newspaper in April reported: "The iron horse of the S.P. now waters at the Rio Grande five miles from El Paso…The material for the bridge at that point is arriving and within the next ten days the locomotive will walk across the river dry-shod."[59]

Southern Pacific's tracks weren't the only ones approaching the community, of course. The Atchison, Topeka & Santa Fe line was also grading its route into town from Las Cruces, and early estimates were that they would arrive first. The companies had originally agreed to share two tracks into El Paso, but the A.T.&S.F. wanted to own them both and lease one to their competitors. Southern Pacific officials rejected that proposal and decided instead to spend an additional $25,000 to lay their own rails.[60]

To approach El Paso from the north, surveyors from both companies had chosen a route which cut through the military reservation of Fort Bliss. Although the United States Army had been in the area since 1849, this particular 135-acre post was purchased and occupied only a few years before the railroad's arrival.[61]

For the Southern Pacific Company, this meant the laying of its rails across the land of the Gadsden Purchase would be bookended by military property, and problems. Just as with Fort Yuma in California, S.P. was going to have difficulty in obtaining permission to build across Fort Bliss in Texas. Crocker had been to the construction front in early April of 1881 and wrote New York, "The authorities at Fort Bliss, after having expressed themselves as not objecting to our grading on our line, which lies back of all their buildings on the reservation, refused to allow us to strike a pick until we get authority from the War Department."[62]

Crocker noted that the A.T.&S.F. company was also working its way into El Paso and had already graded a line through Fort Bliss. He thus assumed they must have received federal permission and reported with annoyance that their route was built directly across the fort's parade ground "and right between the principal buildings of the Post. They really damage the Post, whereas our line would not."[63]

Despite that difference, Crocker wired Huntington, "The commander at military reservation [at] El Paso has informed [project foreman] J.H. Strobridge that he will not be allowed to enter the reservation until full authority is given from Washington…Much delay will result if permission is withheld."[64]

Based on that *deja vu* situation, one of the company's lobbyists immediately went to see the Secretary of War and reported he might "be able to get them to keep hands off".[65] Two meetings with new President Garfield were also held, and by April 18th, Huntington could write: "I telegraphed you some days since that the Government had authorized us to build through the grounds at Fort Bliss, or rather, they would not interfere with our building. I have also telegraphed you since that I thought you had better hurry up the work there, as the Texas & Pacific people are no doubt doing all they can to get us estopped. You know how uncertain white men are."[66]

With that military hurdle out of the way, by the end of April Crocker was anticipating the tracks would enter El Paso within three weeks. On May 9th he wrote: "We crossed the bridge with the track yesterday, and Strobridge will pass through El Paso the latter part of this week."[67] The first S.P. train actually arrived on May 19th, and according to one Texas newspaper a week later: "Since it reached El Paso a large immigration has been pouring into that place, principally from California and Arizona. Every train that arrives brings hundreds of people, and the population is increasing with marvelous rapidity."[68] Not to be outdone, by June 11th the A.T.&S.F. line had also reached the community.

When the S.P. rails entered El Paso, something unknown on the track-laying project up until then occurred: For the first time since they began grading the road east from Yuma thirty months before, the Chinese employees of S.P. called a strike and intentionally stopped working. Crocker saw the influence of the Texas and Pacific Company behind this action and added, "Strobridge thinks it is for higher wages, as they have struck and are not at work, though they have said nothing as yet."[69] He continued, "I had in contemplation the idea of raising their wages in order to get more men down there…".

Their meager $26 a month salary was only one of the problems facing the Chinese. Although not substantiated, it had earlier been reported that their employer was looking to get rid of all of them. According to the *Citizen* in Tucson, "The Southern Pacific Railroad people are endeavoring by all possible means to replace their Chinese help by white labor, but white men are not easily obtainable, strange as this proposition may sound."[70]

That, though, would not happen in the short term. Much to Crocker's and Strobridge's satisfaction, since the Chinese worked cheaper than white men, they eventually finished the S.P. route across Texas. In general, though, they were not hired after that as maintenance workers on the line through the Gadsden Purchase. Those jobs primarily went to Mexican-Americans.

Fear of losing their grading jobs with Southern Pacific was only one obstacle among many facing the Chinese. In 1882 a federal Exclusion Law was passed which prohibited most additional Chinese immigration into the United States for the next 10 years.[71] After that period was up, a new law was enacted which continued the immigration ban, while also requiring Chinese laborers to obtain a residency permit, without which they could be deported.[72]

Of course, none of that was of any importance to the residents of El Paso in the spring of 1881. The tiny town was booming in growth, and between May and June the number of people had doubled to reach 1,500.[73] Sensing something special, a local banker commented on the community: "Plenty of room here for a big city…It is the natural pass from East to West, North to South, and it may become a mining center."[74]

The speedy influx of people, obviously, came with a predictable price. While the cost of most commodities fell considerably because of the arrival of the railroad, housing became much more expensive. Mere shacks were renting for $100 a month, while vastly overpriced vacant lots sold for $500 or more.[75] At the same time, local boosters bemoaned the fact that the lack of affordable housing was keeping an even larger number of new residents away from El Paso.[76]

On the other hand, almost every other item was cheaper because of the railroad. Even with that advantage, a common Mexican-American laborer who earned only $9 a week still had difficulty in finding affordable housing, while buying eggs at 30 cents a dozen, butter at 38 cents per pound, and a chicken for 35 cents.[77]

While there were some potential economic pitfalls, the future of the place appeared promising to many people. "El Paso will grow because it can have no successful competition for the southwestern and Mexican trade," the local *Lone Star* newspaper claimed in October of 1881.[78] Reflecting similar sentiments expressed previously by other publications across the entire width of the Gadsden Purchase, it added: "Some city of supreme importance must grow up in the southwest. The railroad connections of El Paso with the east and the Pacific coast will, of necessity, secure for it this supremacy."

Within a year of the arrival of the tracks, El Paso had grown considerably larger and one commentator wrote at the time, "Today the city numbers 3,000 or over, and has many fine wood buildings, and some handsome blocks of brick and stone. What caused the increase?" the author asked rhetorically. "Why railroads, and the confidence that this is to be the railroad center west of the Missouri River," he answered.[79]

Five years after the railroad's arrival, businessman Samuel Freudenthal was living in El Paso, by then a community of almost 10,000 residents, most of whom were Anglos. He wrote of the place: "Saloons and gambling dens were located on every block. In the more respectable of these emporiums, one met the political and social leaders of the city. All great questions of the day were discussed and settled before the bar. One saloon had a sign which read: 'If drinking interferes with your business, quit business'."[80]

In that same year of 1886, the Indian wars of the southwest finally came to an end. The railroad had indeed allowed many more soldiers to be sent to the region, and the last band of marauding Apaches eventually surrendered. In a symbolic sign of the times, they were shipped out of Arizona by train.

Long before that, Southern Pacific's tracks had continued progressing into Texas. On December 1st, 1881, at Sierra Blanca, eighty-two miles east of El Paso, they met the Texas & Pacific line moving west from Fort Worth, thus forming the nation's third transcontinental railroad line.

This route, which ran from Los Angeles through Arizona, New Mexico and central Texas, was somewhat similar to that advocated almost thirty-five years earlier by James Gadsden and other supporters of a southern cross-country railroad. Perhaps remembering that, *The Daily Picayune* in New Orleans ran a story about the junction of the two roads entitled, "The Southern Overland Route Completed".[81]

The last-spike ceremony marking this event, however, was less than memorable. The Texas and Pacific official who was supposed to be present was delayed, so the act was accomplished using an ordinary spike driven into a pre-drilled hole by a woman in attendance. In its view, an El Paso newspaper concluded, "What should have been made a memorable occasion in the history of this city was, by some inexplicable lack of appreciation of its importance, allowed to pass without even a demonstration."[82]

Southern Pacific wasn't satisfied with just that route across Texas. Having obtained the needed right-of-way, it kept pushing its own tracks toward New Orleans and, on January 12, 1883, made the connection. Thus it had completed the nation's fourth transcontinental line and the third to be finished within less than two years.

To commemorate the inauguration of this latest cross-country route, General Superintendent Towne, who had remained with the company, had circulars prepared. They advertised ship passage from Havre, France to New Orleans, followed by a train trip to San Francisco, all for $65.[83] It was stated that if competition for this traffic warranted it, the price could be cut as low as $30.

By 1883, the availability of numerous transcontinental railroads was a concern to Charles Crocker. Even though he had been partially responsible for all of them built up to that time, he said of future routes, such as the one then being implemented by the Atchison, Topeka & Santa Fe line along the 35th parallel from Albuquerque to Los Angeles: "I fear the country is to suffer from too many railroads; there is not enough through business for all the lines that will be opened to California. Some of them will have to develop a local business if they expect to prosper."[84]

By that point in time, Southern Pacific officials themselves had contemplated providing service to other than long-distance railroad markets. A month before their tracks entered El Paso, Huntington had written Crocker: "In looking on the map, it would seem that it would pay for us to build a railroad from Yuma to the head of the Gulf [of California]....".[85] Several weeks later his west coast associate replied to the idea: "I would state that I have been thinking of that for some time. We are rather short of good engineers [to survey the route] but I guess we can do some talking on the subject, and get it into the papers, which I will do."[86] It would be another three decades, though, before even a portion of that line was finally constructed by the federal government.

This was just one of several instances where the golden prospects anticipated for the Gadsden Purchase because of the arrival of the railroad didn't materialize as predicted. After an initial burst of business in Tucson, the failure of the Tombstone mines, combined with a severe drought, resulted in a long economic depression. Between 1880 and 1900 the population of the community would hardly increase, and one observer noted: "The coming of the railroad caused considerable activity in a business way but it did not last long. Between 1880 and 1884, there was some growth but at the same time, some failures…We stood practically still from 1884 and 1896—a period of 12 years. During that time, I don't believe there was a single house built in Tucson. Everybody was downhearted, discouraged and disgusted."[87]

One of the casualties of this economic slump was Estevan Ochoa's freighting business. Within a few years of the train's arrival in Tucson, his company had been shut down, destroyed in part by the very railroad competition which his 1877 Arizona legislation had helped to create. Ochoa retired quietly, and eventually went to visit his mother in New Mexico, where he died in Las Cruces on October 27, 1888, at the age of 57.

It wasn't only small, local companies which suffered during this period. The Southern Pacific and other railroad lines owned by Huntington, Stanford and Crocker were also hurting. As the latter said in 1888, "Our systems of railroads, and we have over five thousand miles of road now, this last year we made only a million and a quarter in round numbers."[88]

Even given the economic highs and lows which followed the track's arrival in the Gadsden Purchase, the three men who had been primarily responsible for building the railroad through it saw the project as a very beneficial enterprise. In the end, Charles Crocker, Collis Huntington, and Leland Stanford had spent approximately $18,000 a mile in laying tracks across Arizona, and another $21,000 per mile in New Mexico.[89] Those, of course, were phenomenally low prices when compared to the high cost of over $100,000 for every mile which was paid to build the first transcontinental railroad. In addition to the huge savings, though, the three partners believed this southern cross-country route, and other railroad lines, were very important for business and society. Not only would their own personal wealth increase, but the country as a whole could be improved.

Prior to the tracks reaching Tucson, Leland Stanford had said: "Arizona is an illustration of the influence railroads produce. Before the construction of the

Southern Pacific railroad to that territory, no substantial progress was made there. The mines were known to be rich and abundant, but supplies could not be obtained at reasonable rates, nor could the minerals be reduced or shipped to market at paying prices; besides, the Indians had possession of the land and roamed over it at pleasure, preventing settlement and development."[90] The railroad, Stanford knew, would change all of that.

In a more general way, Collis Huntington remarked on the same topic: "There is no question in my mind on the subject of the beneficial effect of railroads on a community. Intercommunication of people brings improvements, and a knowledge of the arts and sciences, as well as an influence upon public morality. A certain barbarism disappears before the advance of the locomotive."[91]

For his part, Charles Crocker saw things in much the same way. "The educational and political conditions of the people are benefited and improved by the railroad," he believed.[92] In more specific economic terms Crocker concluded: "As to the effect on the country tributary to the road, I can say it advanced the value of land and afforded a great deal cheaper transportation...Large communities have grown up on account of the railroad facilities which they enjoy...".

EPILOGUE

South of Yuma, the land lies level; huge fields of lettuce and other vegetables grow along either side of rural U.S. Highway 95. Early in the new millennium of the 21st century, dozens of Mexican migrant farm workers are bent over under a cool, blue-black fall morning sky, weeding some of the fields while in others long jets of water particles spray out of hoses to irrigate the neatly planted produce.

A small gaming casino on the Cocopah Indian Reservation next to the road is being replaced by a larger, more elaborate structure. A nearby billboard displays the American flag, along with the words, "God Bless America," while another sign gives a toll-free number to contact the United States Border Patrol.

Somewhere unseen to the west of the highway is the Colorado River. By this point in its long journey south, it has been drained of most of its water, and what remains is high in salt content. Further upstream the river has been dammed several times in order to generate electricity for the bright lights of ever-expanding desert cities, irrigate endless farm fields, and supply drinking water to millions of people throughout the southwestern United States. Having surrendered much of its vitality, by the time it passes Yuma, the river has lost most of its original character.

Below the international border the Colorado relinquishes even more of its water to agricultural irrigation, so that it no longer empties into the Gulf of California. Instead, it just disappears into Mexican marsh lands, a victim of overuse.

In a fortified border crossing with surveillance cameras targeted at automobiles driving into Mexico, Highway 95 ends abruptly in the town of San Luis, Arizona. Because of the oddly configured boundary line along the Colorado River, Mexico is both south and west of the American community. Spanish is the language heard on the main street of San Luis, and its grocery stores are filled with items popular on the other side of the border.

A few minutes north of there is the tiny settlement of Gadsden. Founded around 1914 in the pre-highway era, it was located to take advantage of a United States Government Reclamation Service railroad, "The Valley Line". Those tracks connected the farmland north of the international boundary with the main Southern Pacific line running east and west through Yuma. The rails allowed locally grown produce to be shipped to market anywhere in the United States. These crops were raised on once barren desert which had been transformed at the cost of millions of federal tax dollars into lush gardens by the addition of Colorado River water.

The community of Gadsden was created when three real estate partners purchased a 30-acre block of land, cleared it, subdivided the property into lots, and named it after the Gadsden Purchase.[1] Initially, the place was prosperous, having restaurants which served "splendid meals," a butcher shop, a bank, a drug store and a large mercantile store.[2] It also offered its residents a barber shop, pool hall, bowling alley, and a movie theater. Five cotton gins were located in the area, along with two churches, a woman's club, an elementary school, and even a local newspaper was available weekly. Electricity, though, wouldn't be provided to the residents until 1930.

The *Sentinel* in Yuma wrote shortly after the community's founding: "Gadsden is the liveliest little town in the southwest, and nothing on earth can keep it from rising to the dignity of a prosperous city within five years. Such is the optimistic spirit of Gadsden citizens."[3] The hopeful prediction was that 10,000 people might live there by 1920.

That future, of course, was not to be. The highway was paved from Yuma to Gadsden in 1921, and life became different. With the eventual common availability of the automobile, which allowed people to easily commute, came change. Residents began moving away, and the small town shrank in size.

Today Gadsden has less than one thousand residents. A used car lot and used furniture store now line the highway. Nearby is Sam's Market which contains the typical assortment of snacks and cold drinks, along with cassettes of Mexican music. Just down the road is a tiny brick post office building which serves zip code 85336. Next to the highway are also a Kingdom Hall of the Jehovah's Witnesses and a small park with large eucalyptus trees, a baseball backstop, and soccer goals.

Along both sides of the roadway sits the town's residential area, containing a mix of single family homes, mobile homes, and trailers. Dilapidated vehicles and other junk litter the landscape as dogs jog through nearby plowed farm fields.

Back a block from the highway is an elementary school built in 1953. It now serves modern day students, who wear standardized uniforms as they run around on the playground during recess.

On nearby U.S. Highway 95, drivers speeding along at over 50 m.p.h. quickly pass through Gadsden on their way to Yuma or San Luis. They see mostly a short blur of old buildings as they go by the tiny, mostly-forgotten place.

Those heading south, however, may notice a road marker, but probably won't recognize the historic significance it has relating to the obscure events of 1853 and 1854 which greatly affected the land they are passing through. Just outside of Gadsden, Arizona, the sign announces it is four miles to "Old Mexico".

Notes

Introduction

1. Chronic, *Roadside Geology of Arizona*, 46.
2. Roscoe Willson, "The Surveyors Were Sober," *Arizona Republic*, August 29, 1965, "Arizona Days and Ways" magazine, 26-27.

Chapter One

1. Cotterill, "The Beginnings of Railroads in the Southwest," 322-324.
2. Ibid., 326.
3. "A Sketch of the Early Life of General James Gadsden," *Charleston Mercury*, October 7, 1848, "James Gadsden papers" collection, University of South Carolina Library.
4. Ibid.
5. Jackson to John Caldwell Calhoun, August 10, 1818, *The Papers of Andrew Jackson*, Moser, Hoth, and Hoemann (eds.), vol. 4.
6. Derrick, *Centennial History of South Carolina Railroad*, 138.
7. Ibid., 139.
8. Cotterill, "Southern Railroads and Western Trade, 1840-1850," 431.
9. Cotterill, "Early Agitation for a Pacific Railroad, 1845-1850," 396.
10. DeBow, "Col. Gadsden's Report," 27.
11. Gadsden to Lewis Shanks, September 17, 1845, "James Gadsden papers" collection, New York Public Library.
12. Ibid.
13. DeBow, "Commercial Spirit at the South," 131.

14. Gadsden to Calhoun, March 6, 1846, *The Papers of John C. Calhoun*, Wilson (ed.), vol. 22.

15. DeBow, "Internal Improvements".

16. Senate Document, "Memorial of A. Whitney," 29th Cong., 1st sess., No. 161, 5.

17. DeBow, "Additional Remarks by the Editor on the Proposed Southern and Northern Routes Across the Continent to the Pacific," 485.

18. DeBow, "Atlantic and Pacific Railroad," 478.

Chapter Two

1. Goetzmann, *Army Explorations in the American West, 1803-1863*, 127.

2. Bigler and Bagley, *Army of Israel: Mormon Battalion Narratives*, 147.

3. Ibid., 145.

4. Golder, *The March of the Mormon Battalion*, 183.

5. Ibid., 184.

6. Cooke, "Report of Lieut. Col. P. St. George Cooke of his March from Santa Fe, New Mexico to San Diego, Upper California," in Emory, *Notes of a Military Reconnaissance from Fort Leavenworth, in Missouri, to San Diego, in California*, 561.

7. Bigler and Bagley, *Army of Israel*, 177.

8. Anonymous, "Sketch of part of the march & wagon road of Lt. Colonel Cooke, from Santa Fe to the Pacific Ocean, 1846-7".

9. Bigler and Bagley, *Army of Israel*, 158.

10. Ibid.

11. Golder, *The March of the Mormon Battalion*, 195.

12. Bigler and Bagley, *Army of Israel*, 162.

13. Ibid, 163.

14. Cooke, "Report of Lieut. Col. P. St. George Cooke," 415.

15. Goetzmann, *Army Explorations*, 130.

16. Ibid., 134.

17. Johnston, "Journal of Captain A.R. Johnston," in Emory, *Notes of a Military Reconnaissance from Fort Leavenworth, in Missouri, to San Diego, in California*, 572.

18. Ibid., 573.

19. Emory, *Notes of a Military Reconnaissance*, 61.

20. Johnston, "Journal of Captain A.R. Johnston," 579.

21. Emory, *Notes of a Military Reconnaissance,* 65.

22. Johnston, "Journal of Captain A.R. Johnston," 590.

23. Ibid.

24. Emory, *Notes of a Military Reconnaissance*, 75.

25. Ibid., 81.

26. Johnston, "Journal of Captain A.R. Johnston," 599.

27. Ibid., 598.

28. Ibid., 602.

29. Emory, *Notes of a Military Reconnaissance*, 132.

30. Johnston, "Journal of Captain A.R. Johnston," 601.

31. Emory, *Notes of a Military Reconnaissance*, 83.

32. Ibid., 84.

33. Ibid.

34. Johnston, "Journal of Captain A.R. Johnston," 602.

35. Emory, *Notes of a Military Reconnaissance*, 99.

36. Johnston, "Journal of Captain A.R. Johnston," 614.

37. Goetzmann, *Army Explorations*, 139-140.

38. Johnston, "Journal of Captain A.R. Johnston," 614.

Chapter Three

1. Gadsden to Calhoun, February 13, 1847, *The Papers of John C. Calhoun*, Wilson (ed.), vol. 24.

2. Gadsden to Calhoun, January 23, 1848, *The Papers of John C. Calhoun*, Wilson (ed.), vol. 25.

3. Buchanan to Trist, April 15, 1847, Senate Executive Document, 30th Cong., 1st sess., No. 52, 86.

4. Ohrt, *Defiant Peacemaker*, 14.

5. Buchanan to Trist, October 25, 1847, Senate Executive Document, 30th Cong., 1st sess., No. 52, 94-95.

6. Trist to Buchanan, September 4, 1847, Senate Executive Document, 30th Cong., 1st sess., No. 52, 199.

7. Ibid., 196.

8. Emory, *Report on the United States and Mexican Boundary Survey*, vol. 1, 41.

9. Buchanan to Trist, July 13, 1847, Senate Executive Document, 30th Cong., 1st sess., No. 52, 90.

10. Trist to Buchanan, September 27, 1847 and P.S. dated September 28, 1847, Senate Executive Document, 30th Cong., 1st sess., No. 52, 201-203.

11. Buchanan to Trist, October 6, 1847 and October 25, 1847, Senate Executive Document, 30th Cong., 1st sess., No. 52, 91-95.

12. Ohrt, *Defiant Peacemaker*, 137.

13. Ibid., 140.

14. Ibid., 142.

15. Trist to Buchanan, January 25, 1848, Senate Executive Document, 30th Cong., 1st sess., No. 52, 289.

16. "Treaty of peace, friendship, limits and settlement between the United States of America and the Mexican republic, concluded at Guadalupe Hidalgo, on the 2nd day of February, in the year 1848," Senate Executive Document, 30th Cong., 1st sess., No. 52, 45.

17. Ibid., Article XI, 50.

18. Trist to Buchanan, January 25, 1848, Senate Executive Document, 30th Cong., 1st sess., No. 52, 293.

19. Ohrt, *Defiant Peacemaker*, 145.

20. Mahin, *Olive Branch and Sword*, 157.

21. Hammond, *The Treaty of Guadalupe Hidalgo*, 16.

22. Ibid., 14.

23. Wallace, *The Great Reconnaissance*, 7.

24. Senate Executive Document, "Report of A.B. Gray to the United States Senate," 33rd Cong., 2nd sess., No. 55, 2.

25. Bartlett, *Personal Narrative of Explorations and Incidents*, vol. 1, 190.

26. Ibid., 213.

27. Ibid., 215.

28. Ibid., 188.

29. Senate Executive Document, "Report of A.B. Gray," 27.

30. Bartlett, *Personal Narrative*, vol. 2, 565-575.

31. Ibid., 570.

32. Ibid., 571.

33. Wallace, *The Great Reconnaissance*, 27.

34. Emory, *Report on the United States and Mexican Boundary Survey*, 17.

35. Bartlett, *Personal Narrative*, vol. 2, 161.

36. Ibid., 189.

37. Ibid., 296.

38. Ibid., 298.

39. Ibid., 298-299.

40. Norris, Milligan, and Faulk, *William H. Emory: Soldier-Scientist*, 139.

41. Senate Executive Document, "Report of A.B. Gray," 3.

Chapter Four

1. DeBow, "Communication Between the Atlantic and Pacific Oceans," 20.

2. Ibid., 21.

3. Ibid., 29.

4. Ibid., 36.

5. Ibid.

6. Ibid., 29.

7. Cotterill, "The National Railroad Convention in St. Louis, 1849," 208.

8. Ibid., 214.

9. Cotterill, "Memphis Railroad Convention," 86.

10. Ibid., 91.

11. Ibid., 92.

12. Ibid.

13. DeBow, "The Memphis Convention—Intercommunication Between the Oceans," 221.

14. Ibid., 219.

15. Ibid., 229.

16. Russel, *Improvement of Communication with the Pacific Coast*, 25.

17. Ibid.

18. Senate Miscellaneous Documents, "Memorial of a Committee Appointed at a Railroad Convention," 32nd Cong., 2nd sess., No. 5, 7.

19. Senate Reports, "Report on the Memorial of Robert Mills for a Railroad Connection with the Pacific Ocean," 32nd Cong., 1st sess., No. 344, 9.

20. Senate Miscellaneous Documents, "Memorial of the Legislative Assembly of New Mexico," 32nd Cong., 2nd sess., No. 36, 1.

21. Russel, *Improvement of Communication with the Pacific Coast*, 101.

22. Appendix to the Congressional Globe, "Speech of Hon. V.E. Howard of Texas in the House of Representatives, July 6, 1852," 32nd Cong., 1st sess., 777.

23. "The Gadsden Treaty and Mr. Bartlett," a letter from John Russell Bartlett, *Charleston Daily Courier*, April 22, 1854.

24. Ibid.

25. Derrick, *Centennial History of South Carolina Railroad*, 219.

26. "Southern Emigration to California," letter from Gadsden in Shreveport, Louisiana *Caddo Gazette*, January 24, 1852, reprinted in *Charleston Courier*, February 7, 1852.

Chapter Five

1. Carson (ed.), "William Carr Lane Diary," October, 1964, 282.

2. Rippy, "The Boundary of New Mexico and the Gadsden Treaty," 728.

3. Ibid., 735.

4. Garber, *The Gadsden Treaty*, 37.

5. Ibid., 49.

6. Gadsden to Davis, May 9, 14, and 23, 1853, Crist (ed.), *The Papers of Jefferson Davis*, vol. 5, 198.

7. Marcy to Gadsden, July 15, 1853, Diplomatic Instructions of the Department of State, 1801-1906: Mexico.

8. Ibid.

9. Bonilla to Gadsden, August 31, 1853, Dispatches from United States Ministers to Mexico, 1823-1906.

10. Ibid., Gadsden to Bonilla, September 1, 1853.

11. Ibid., Bonilla to Gadsden, November 15, 1853.

12. Ibid., Gadsden to Marcy, November 18, 1853.

13. Ibid., Communication No. 14 from Gadsden, November 19, 1853.

14. Ibid., Communication No. 15 from Gadsden, December 4, 1853.

15. Wyllys, "William Walker's Invasion of Sonora, 1854," 63.

16. Bonilla to Gadsden, October 18, 1853, Dispatches from United States Ministers to Mexico, 1823-1906.

17. Ibid., "Memoranda," written by Gadsden, n.d.

18. Ibid.

19. Ibid., Bonilla to Gadsden, November 30, 1853.

20. Ibid., Gadsden to Marcy, November 3, 1853.

21. Marcy, "Memorandum of Instructions," October 22, 1853, Diplomatic Instructions of the Department of State, 1801-1906: Special Missions.

22. Ibid.

23. Garber, *The Gadsden Treaty*, 94-96.

24. Ibid., 94-97.

25. Ibid., 98-101.

26. Rippy, "A Ray of Light on the Gadsden Treaty," 240.

27. Ibid., 238.

28. Ibid., 239.

29. Garber, *The Gadsden Treaty*, 103.

30. "Latest Intelligence," *New York Daily Times*, January 9, 1854.

31. "Latest Intelligence," *New York Daily Times*, January 10, 1854.

32. "Later from Mexico," *Daily Picayune*, January 13, 1854.

33. "The Mexican Treaty," *New York Daily Times*, January 18, 1854.

34. "The News," *Chicago Daily Tribune*, January 19, 1854.

35. "The Important Treaty," *Richmond Enquirer*, January 18, 1854, reprinted in *New York Herald*, January 20, 1854.

36. "Return of Gen. Gadsden to Charleston, en route to Washington," *Charleston Daily Courier*, January 21, 1854.

37. "Latest Intelligence," *New York Daily Times*, January 19, 1854.

38. "The Treaty with Mexico," *New York Daily Times*, January 20, 1854.

39. "Important from Mexico," *New York Herald*, January 20, 1854.

Chapter Six

1.   Albright, *Official Explorations for Pacific Railroads*, 38.

2.   Ibid., 6.

3.   Russel, *Improvement of Communication with the Pacific Coast*, 174.

4.   Davis to Parke, December 9, 1853, Crist (ed.), *The Papers of Jefferson Davis*, vol. 5, 50.

5.   Parke, *Reports of Explorations for that Portion of a Railway Route Near the Thirty-Second Parallel of Latitude*, 7.

6.   Ibid., 8.

7.   Ibid.

8.   Ibid., 10.

9.   Ibid., 11.

10. Ibid., 15.

11. Ibid., 16.

12. Ibid., 17.

13. Ibid., 22.

14. "Historical Sketch of the Different Pacific Railroad Schemes," *Frank Leslie's Illustrated Newspaper*, December 15, 1855.

15. Bailey (ed.), *The A.B. Gray Report*, 220.

16. Ibid., 177.

17. Ibid., 179.

18. Ibid., 68.

19. Ibid., 202.

20. Ibid., 204.

21. Ibid., 208.

22. Ibid., 211.

23. Ibid., 213.

24. Ibid., 83.

25. Ibid., 90. While some historians believe the community of Ajo was named after the Spanish word for the wild garlic which grows in the area, Gray's comment offers another possibility.

26. Ibid., 216.

27. Ibid., 91.

28. Ibid., 221.

29. Ibid.

30. Ibid., 223.

31. Ibid., 92-93.

32. Ibid., 215.

Chapter Seven

1. Garber, *The Gadsden Treaty*, 112-113.

2. "The Mexican Treaty," *New York Daily Times*, January 28, 1854.

3. Senate Executive Journal, 33rd Cong., 1st sess., March 15, 1854, 266.

4. "Latest Intelligence," *New York Daily Times*, March 22, 1854.

5. Ibid., "From Washington".

6. "Miscellaneous Matters," *New York Daily Times*, March 25, 1854.

7. Senate Executive Journal, 33rd Cong., 1st sess., April 3, 1854, 276.

8. Ibid., April 4, 1854, 278-279.

9. Ibid., April 5, 1854, 280.

10. "Latest Intelligence," *New York Daily Times*, April 6, 1854.

11. "Important Movements in Washington," *New York Herald*, April 6, 1854.

12. "Letter from Washington," (*Philadelphia*) *Public Ledger*, April 11, 1854.

13. Senate Executive Journal, 33rd Cong., 1st sess., April 10, 1854, 284.

14. Ibid., April 12, 1854, 289.

15. Ibid., 290-291.

16. Ibid., 291-292.

17. Garber, *The Gadsden Treaty*, 125.

18. Senate Executive Journal, 33rd Cong., 1st sess., April 17, 1854, 300-301.

19. Russel, *Improvement of Communication with the Pacific Coast*, 147.

20. "Letter from Washington," (*Philadelphia*) *Public Ledger*, April 19, 1854.

21. "Rejection of the Gadsden Treaty," *New York Daily Times*, April 18, 1854.

22. DeBow, "The Great Southern Convention at Charleston," 409.

23. "Latest Intelligence," *New York Daily Times*, April 19, 1854.

24. Senate Executive Journal, 33rd Cong., 1st sess., April 25, 1854, 310.

25. Ibid., 311.

26. Schmidt, "The Gadsden Purchase and the Southern Pacific Railroad," 17.

27. Untitled, *New York Daily Tribune*, April 28, 1854.

28. "From Washington", *New York Daily Times*, April 28, 1854.

29. "Washington Correspondence," *Charleston Daily Courier*, May 10, 1854.

30. Untitled, *Detroit Free Press*, May 4, 1854.

31. Gadsden to Marcy, June 17, 1854, Dispatches from United States Ministers to Mexico, 1823-1906.

32. Ibid.

33. Ibid.

34. Ibid., Gadsden to Marcy, June 9, 1854.

35. Ibid.

36. Congressional Globe, 33rd Cong., 1st sess., June 28, 1854, 1562.

37. Ibid., 1564.

38. Ibid.

39. "From Washington," *Chicago Daily Tribune*, June 30, 1854.

Chapter Eight

1. Philip Gadsden to his sister Jane, July 4, 1854, "Gadsden family papers" collection, South Carolina Historical Society, 3.

2. Ibid., 1.

3. Philip Gadsden to his mother, July 19, 1854, 4.

4. Philip Gadsden to his mother, December 1, 1854, 1.

5. Philip Gadsden to his sister, June 20, 1854, 1.

6. Philip Gadsden to his brother, November 3, 1854, 3.

7. Philip Gadsden to his mother, August 6, 1854, 5.

8. Ibid., 4.

9. Philip Gadsden to his mother, July 19, 1854, 1.

10. Philip Gadsden to his sister, June 20, 1854, 3.

11. Philip Gadsden to his mother, December 4, 1854, 4.

12. Philip Gadsden to his mother, August 6, 1854, 8.

13. Gadsden to Davis, July 19, 1854, Crist (ed.), *The Papers of Jefferson Davis*, vol. 5, 78.

14. Philip Gadsden to his mother, July 19, 1854, 5.

15. Philip Gadsden to his mother, December 1, 1854, 1.

16. Philip Gadsden to his mother, December 4, 1854, 3.

17. Philip Gadsden to his sister, June 4, 1855, 1.

18. Werner (ed.), *Encyclopedia of Mexico*, 794.

19. Garber, *The Gadsden Treaty*, 167.

20. DeBow, "Southern Commercial Convention at New Orleans," 520.

21. Ibid., 525.

22. Goetzmann, *Army Explorations in the American West*, Chapter 7.

23. Albright, *Official Explorations for Pacific Railroads*, 122-123.

24. Parke, map labeled "From the Pimas Villages to Fort Fillmore".

25. Emory, *Report of the United States and Mexican Boundary Survey*, 51.

26. Goetzmann, *Army Explorations in the American West*, 267-272. See also Norris, Milligan, and Faulk, *William H. Emory: Soldier-Scientist*, 152.

27. Davis to William Cannon, December 7, 1855, Crist (ed.), *The Papers of Jefferson Davis*, vol. 5, 142.

28. Goetzmann, *Army Explorations in the American West*, 300.

29. Emory, *Report of the United States and Mexican Boundary Survey*, 93.

30. Ibid.

31. Ibid., 51.

32. Ibid., 95.

33. Ibid.

34. Michler, "Report of Lieut. Michler," in Emory, *Report of the United States and Mexican Boundary Survey*, 102.

35. Ibid., 115.

36. Ibid., 121.

37. Ibid., 118.

38. Poston, *Building a State in Apache Land*, 48.

39. Poston, *Apache-Land*, 128.

40. Poston, *Building a State in Apache Land*, 46.

41. Michler, "Report of Lieut. Michler," 123.

42. Sacks, "The Origins of Fort Buchanan—Myth and Fact," 216.

43. Ibid., 221.

44. Kirkland, "Turning over the Gadsden Purchase to United States government."

Chapter Nine

1. "Transatlantic Sketches—A Rice Plantation," *Illustrated London News*, June 19, 1858, "James Gadsden papers" collection, University of South Carolina Library.

2. Ibid.

3. Ibid.

4. "Obituary," *New York Times*, December 28, 1858.

5. Judah, *A Practical Plan for Building the Pacific Railroad*, 3.

6. Ibid., 15.

7. Ibid., 20.

8. Russel, *Improvement of Communication with the Pacific Coast*, 226.

9. Davis, *Speech of the Hon. Jefferson Davis of Mississippi on the Pacific Railroad Bill*, 1.

10. "Pacific Railroad," *American Railroad Journal*, January 14, 1860.

11. Crocker, "Facts gathered from the lips of Charles Crocker," 5.

12. Ibid., 7.

13. Ibid., 6.

14. Russel, *Improvement of Communication with the Pacific Coast*, 287.

15. Willey, *The Tucson Meteorites*, 25.

16. Bailey (ed.), *The A.B. Gray Report*, xi.

17. Russel, *Improvement of Communication with the Pacific Coast*, 296.

18. Ambrose, *Nothing Like It in the World*, 107.

19. Ibid., 367.

20. Mowry, *Memoir of the Proposed Territory of Arizona*, 19.

21. Ibid., 26.

22. Ibid., 18.

23. Ibid.

24. Ibid., 22.

25. Goodwin, "Speech to the first Arizona Territorial Legislature," 6.

26. Ibid.

27. McCormick, *Arizona: Its Resources and Prospects*, 5-6.

28. Ibid., 19.

29. Clever, *New Mexico: Her Resources; Her Necessities*, 40.

30. Ibid., 45.

Chapter Ten

1. Pumpelly, *Across America and Asia*, 1.

2. Ibid.

3. Ibid., 4.

4. Ibid., 5.

5. Ibid., 9.

6. Ibid., 38-39.

7. Ibid., 10.

8. Williams, "The Territorial Governors of Arizona—Anson Peacely-Killen Safford," 71.

9. Pumpelly, *Across America and Asia*, 34.

10. Ibid., 48.

11. Ibid., 30-31.

12. McCormick, "Message of Governor McCormick to the Fifth Legislative Assembly of Arizona".

13. *New York Tribune* quoted in "The 32nd Parallel Railroad," *Weekly Arizonan*, April 30, 1870.

14. Haney, "A Congressional History of Railways in the United States," 123.

15. "An Act supplementary to an Act entitled 'An Act to incorporate the Texas Pacific Railroad Company'," 42nd Cong., 2nd sess., Statutes at large, Chap.132, 17 Stat. 59.

16. Woodward, *Reunion and Reaction*, 85.

17. Boehringer, "Josephine Brawley Hughes," 98.

18. Ibid., 101.

19. Huntington to Hopkins, October 8, 1875. "The Collis P. Huntington papers, 1866-1901". All following citations involving Southern Pacific company officials are from this source unless otherwise noted.

20. George Gray, chief engineer for the Southern Pacific Railroad Company, to Huntington, November 18, 1875.

21. Huntington to David Colton, a major San Francisco business associate of the four Southern Pacific partners, December 16, 1875.

22. Huntington to Hopkins, December 10, 1875.

23. Huntington to Hopkins, January 13, 1876.

24. Huntington to Hopkins, January 22, 1876.

25. "The Southern Pacific," *Arizona Weekly Citizen*, January 29, 1876.

26. Huntington to Hopkins, February 12, 1876.

27. Huntington to Hopkins, February 19, 1876.

28. Towne to Huntington, cipher telegram, February 1, 1876.

29. Gray to Huntington, February 16, 1876.

30. Gray to Huntington, May 6, 1876.

31. Huntington to Crocker, June 10, 1876.

32. Huntington to Colton, July 5, 1876.

33. Huntington to Colton, July 28, 1876.

34. "Railway Progress," *Arizona Weekly Citizen*, August 5, 1876.

35. "Railway to Yuma and Eastward," *Arizona Weekly Citizen*, September 23, 1876.

36. Colton to Huntington, cipher telegram, October 23, 1876.

37. Yuma Village Council, Minutes of meeting, October 24, 1876.

38. Yuma Village Council, Minutes of meeting, November 20, 1876.

39. "The Southern Pacific Railroad," *Arizona Sentinel*, December 30, 1876.

40. Huntington to Hopkins, January 20, 1877.

41. "An act granting to railroads the right-of-way through the public lands of the United States," 43rd Cong., 2nd sess., Statutes at large, Chap. 152, 18 Stat. 482.

42. Congressional Record, 43rd Cong., 2nd sess., January 12, 1875, 405.

43. "Governor's Message," *Arizona Weekly Citizen*, January 6, 1877.

44. Lockwood, "Don Estevan Ochoa".

45. "General Phineas Banning and Our Territory," *Arizona Weekly Citizen*, February 17, 1877.

46. Cowdery, "The Planning of a Transcontinental Railroad," 100. See also Williams, "The Territorial Governors of Arizona—Anson Peacely-Killen Safford," 81.

47. Colton to Huntington, cipher telegram, February 2, 1877.

48. Arizona Territorial Legislature, "An Act to secure the construction and operation of certain railroad and telegraph lines".

49. Poston to Huntington, January 29, 1877.

50. Crocker to Huntington, March 16, 1877.

51. Crocker to Huntington, April 20, 1877.

52. Crocker to Huntington, April 25, 1877.

53. Huntington to Crocker, March 28, 1877.

54. Huntington to Crocker, April 12, 1877.

55. Crocker to Huntington, April 20, 1877.

56. Crocker to Huntington, May 9, 1877.

57. Ibid.

58. Huntington to Colton, May 17, 1877.

59. "Railway East of Yuma," *Arizona Weekly Citizen*, April 28, 1877.

60. Untitled, *Arizona Sentinel*, June 2, 1877.

61. Ibid.

62. Crocker to Huntington, May 25, 1877.

63. Huntington to Colton, June 1, 1877.

64. Hopkins to Huntington, July 21, 1877.

65. "Railway Matters," *Arizona Weekly Citizen*, July 28, 1877.

66. Crocker to Huntington, cipher telegram, August 22, 1877.

67. Myrick, *Railroads of Arizona*, 22-23.

68. Crocker to Huntington, cipher telegram, August 23, 1877.

69. Telegram from Adjutant General E.D. Townsend to Major General McDowell, August 22, 1877, part of Crocker to Huntington, August 24, 1877.

70. Crocker to Huntington, September 8, 1877.

71. Colton to Huntington, cipher telegram, September 20, 1877.

72. Huntington to Colton, September 21, 1877.

73. Crocker to Huntington, September 25, 1877.

74. "Railroads Coming," *Arizona Weekly Star*, September 13, 1877.

75. *New York Herald*, September 16, 1877, quoted in "Progress of the Southern Transcontinental Line," *Arizona Weekly Star*, September 27, 1877.

76. Crocker to Huntington, September 30, 1877.

Chapter Eleven

1. Crocker to Huntington, cipher telegram, October 1, 1877.

2. Crocker to Huntington, cipher telegram, October 5, 1877.

3. Yuma Village Council, Minutes of meeting, October 5, 1877.

4. *Arizona Sentinel*, October 6, 1877, quoted in "Railroad Matters," *Arizona Weekly Citizen*, October 13, 1877.

5. Huntington to Colton, October 10, 1877.

6. Ibid.

7. Ibid.

8. Ibid.

9. Crocker to Huntington, October 10, 1877.

10. "Southern Pacific Railway, etc.," *Arizona Weekly Citizen*, October 27, 1877.

11. Woodward, *Reunion and Reaction*, 234.

12. "Objects of the Southern Pacific," *Arizona Weekly Citizen*, September 29, 1877, and "Railway Encouragement," December 21, 1877.

13. "Yuma Items," *Arizona Weekly Citizen*, November 16, 1877.

14. "The Railroad Route," *Arizona Weekly Star*, October 11, 1877.

15. Ibid.

16. Colton to Huntington, October 13, 1877.

17. Towne to Huntington, November 9, 1877.

18. Gray to Huntington, November 10, 1877.

19. Crocker to Huntington, December 11, 1877.

20. Towne to Huntington, January 7, 1878.

21. Huntington to Crocker, January 19, 1878.

22. Colton to Huntington, cipher telegram, January 18, 1878.

23. "Southern Pacific Mirage," *Arizona Sentinel*, January 26, 1878.

24. Ibid.

25. Huntington, *Remarks of C.P. Huntington*, 6.

26. Evans, *Collis Potter Huntington*, 258.

27. "Why Did We Do It?" *Arizona Sentinel*, February 2, 1878.

28. "Remarks on Railway Advancement," *Arizona Weekly Citizen*, February 15, 1878.

29. "On Railway Advancement," *Arizona Sentinel*, February 23, 1878.

30. Crocker to Huntington, February 12, 1878.

31. Huntington to Crocker, March 2, 1878.

32. Crocker to Huntington, March 18, 1878.

33. Crocker to Huntington, March 4, 1878.

34. Crocker to Huntington, March 18, 1878.

35. Colton to Huntington, March 29, 1878.

36. Crocker to Huntington, April 4, 1878.

37. Huntington to Colton, April 6, 1878.

38. Huntington to Crocker, April 12, 1878.

39. Berton, *A Voyage on the Colorado*, 13.

40. Ibid., 25.

41. Ibid., 26.

42. Ibid., 29.

43. Ibid., 30.

44. Ibid., 91-92.

45. "David Neahr" advertisement, *Arizona Sentinel*, November 9, 1878.

46. Berton, *A Voyage on the Colorado*, 26.

47. "Yuma and the Railroad," *Arizona Sentinel*, April 13, 1878.

48. "Cheering Railroad News," *Arizona Weekly Citizen*, May 10, 1878.

49. Huntington to Stanford, May 27, 1878.

50. Poston to William J. Osborne, July 10, 1878, part of Osborne to Crocker, July 11, 1878.

51. Osborne to Crocker, July 3, 1878.

52. "In San Francisco," *Arizona Weekly Citizen*, July 19, 1878.

53. Huntington to Colton, September 17, 1878.

54. *San Francisco Bulletin*, letter of August 28, 1878, quoted in "Railroad Wanted," *Arizona Weekly Citizen*, September 21, 1878.

55. Untitled, *Arizona Weekly Citizen*, September 21, 1878.

56. "The Live Arizona Railroad," *Arizona Sentinel*, October 12, 1878, and "Railroad Coming," *Arizona Weekly Citizen*, October 19, 1878.

57. "The Live Arizona Railroad," *Arizona Sentinel*, October 12, 1878.

58. Charles F. Crocker, son of Charles Crocker, to Huntington, October 10, 1878.

59. Huntington to Stanford, October 23, 1878.

60. Stanford to Huntington, November 2, 1878.

61. Huntington to Stanford, October 29, 1878.

62. Huntington to Crocker, October 28, 1878.

63. Ibid.

64. Crocker, "Facts gathered from the lips of Charles Crocker," 49.

65. "Southern Pacific Railway Affairs," *Arizona Weekly Citizen*, November 2, 1878.

66. *Arizona Sentinel*, quoted in "Railroad Progress," *Arizona Weekly Citizen*, November 2, 1878.

67. Charles F. Crocker to Huntington, November 9, 1878.

68. Huntington to Crocker, November 22, 1878.

69. "Railroad Matters," *Arizona Sentinel*, November 23, 1878.

70. Ibid.

71. Norwood, "The Texas Pacific Railway Contrasted with a Real Southern Pacific R.R.," 16.

Chapter Twelve

1. "The Southern Pacific Railroad," *Arizona Weekly Citizen*, November 30, 1878.

2. Ibid.

3. Stanford to Huntington, November 20, 1878.

4. "Trip to the 'Front,' No. II," *Arizona Sentinel*, December 7, 1878.

5. "A Trip to the S.P.R.R. 'Front'," *Arizona Sentinel*, November 30, 1878.

6. Ibid.

7. Ibid.

8. Ibid.

9. Ibid.

10. "A Trip from the Railroad Front," *Arizona Sentinel*, January 4, 1879.

11. "A Trip to the S.P.R.R. 'Front'," *Arizona Sentinel*, November 30, 1878.

12. Ibid.

13. Ibid.

14. "Trip to the 'Front,' No. II," *Arizona Sentinel*, December 7, 1878.

15. "A Trip to the S.P.R.R. 'Front'," *Arizona Sentinel*, November 30, 1878.

16. Stanford to Huntington, November 20, 1878.

17. Charles F. Crocker to Huntington, November 23, 1878.

18. Steiner, *Fusang: The Chinese Who Built America*, 129.

19. Williams, *A Great & Shining Road*, 96.

20. Steiner, *Fusang: The Chinese Who Built America*, 132.

21. Ambrose, *Nothing Like It In the World*, 164.

22. Williams, *A Great & Shining Road*, 98.

23. Stevenson, *The Amateur Emigrant*, 130.

24. Fong, "Sojourners and Settlers," 234.

25. Strobridge to Crocker, December 4, 1878, part of Crocker to Huntington, December 5, 1878.

26. Crocker to Huntington, December 10, 1878.

27. Ibid.

28. Crocker to Huntington, January 4, 1879.

29. Charles F. Crocker to Huntington, January 2, 1879.

30. Crocker to Huntington, January 4, 1879.

31. Untitled, *Arizona Sentinel*, December 21, 1878.

32. "Telegraphic—Progress of the Railroad," *Arizona Star*, January 12, 1879.

33. Crocker to Huntington, January 20, 1879.

34. Untitled, *New York Tribune*, January 20, 1879, part of Simonton, of the office of the New York Associated Press, to Huntington, January 20, 1879.

35. Crocker to Huntington, February 25, 1879.

36. Crocker to Huntington, January 22, 1879.

37. Crocker to Huntington, March 14, 1879.

38. Huntington to Crocker, March 27, 1879.

39. Stanford to Huntington, April 3, 1879.

40. Crocker to Huntington, January 24, 1879.

41. Towne to Huntington, January 28, 1879.

42. Crocker to Huntington, February 7, 1879.

43. Crocker to Huntington, February 6, 1879.

44. "Child Killed in Yuma," *Arizona Sentinel*, February 1, 1879.

45. Crocker to Huntington, February 7, 1879.

46. Ibid.

47. "Southern Pacific Railroad Matters," *Arizona Sentinel*, March 1, 1879.

48. Frémont to Crocker, January 20, 1879, part of Crocker to Huntington, January 27, 1879.

49. "Railroads and the Legislature," *Arizona Star*, February 20, 1879.

50. Charles Sherrill, Washington lobbyist for the S.P., to Huntington, February 5, 1879.

51. "An act granting to railroads the right-of-way through the public lands of the United States," 43rd Cong., 2nd sess., Statutes at large, Chap. 152, 18 Stat. 482.

52. "The Southern Pacific," *Arizona Weekly Citizen*, February 1, 1879.

53. Ibid.

54. Huntington to Crocker, February 1, 1879 and February 14, 1879.

55. "Railroads and Mining," *Arizona Sentinel*, March 22, 1879.

56. Crocker to Huntington, February 17, 1879.

57. Crocker to Huntington, March 8, 1879.

58. Crocker to Huntington, April 4, 1879.

59. "Railroad Gossip," *Arizona Sentinel*, April 12, 1879.

60. Kupel, "Roadside Rest," 348.

61. *Arizona Sentinel*, May 10, 1879, reprinted in "Yuma Items," *Daily Arizona Citizen*, May 12, 1879.

62. "Southern Pacific Railroad Ticket Rates in Effect March 31st, 1879," contained in the Huntington papers.

63. Hodge, *1877—Arizona As It Is*, 153.

64. William Hood, assistant to George Gray and future chief engineer of the Central Pacific Railroad, to Huntington, March 20, 1879.

65. *Chicago Tribune*, reprinted in "Southern Arizona," *Daily Arizona Citizen*, April 21, 1879.

66. Towne to Huntington, December 21, 1878.

67. "Maricopa," *Arizona Sentinel*, April 26, 1879.

68. Hood to Huntington, December 13, 1878.

69. J.H. Hammond, written from the San Carlos Indian Agency, to Towne, March 22, 1879, part of Towne to Huntington, April 5, 1879.

70. Hodge, *1877—Arizona As It Is*, 161.

71. *Mining and Scientific Press*, reprinted in "Prescott, Phoenix and Maricopa," *Arizona Sentinel*, May 24, 1879.

72. Southern Pacific promotional flyer, dated March 1, 1879, contained in the Huntington papers.

73. *San Francisco Bulletin*, April 1, 1879, reprinted in "Visions of the Desert," *Arizona Star*, May 1, 1879.

74. "The Pioneer Excursion," *Arizona Sentinel*, May 17, 1879.

75. Crocker to Huntington, May 17, 1879.

76. "'All Rail' to Tucson!" *Arizona Sentinel*, April 26, 1879.

77. "Railroad Probabilities," *Arizona Star*, May 1, 1879.

78. Crocker to Gates, a New York assistant of Huntington, cipher telegram, May 13, 1879.

79. Crocker to Huntington, May 17, 1879.

80. *L.A. Commercial*, reprinted in "Casa Grande," *Arizona Sentinel*, May 31, 1879.

81. Tipton, "Men Out of China," 354.

82. Hodge, *1877—Arizona As It Is*, 151.

83. Fong, "Sojourners and Settlers," 234. See also Wang, "The First Chinese in Tucson," 372.

84. "Casa Grande," *Arizona Sentinel*, May 31, 1879.

85. "S.P.R.R.," *Arizona Sentinel*, May 24, 1879.

86. Ibid.

87. "Trip to Yuma," *Arizona Citizen*, May 29, 1879.

Chapter Thirteen

1.   "Arizona," *Chicago Tribune*, November 15, 1879.

2.   "Casa Grande," *The Pinal Drill*, October 21, 1882.

3.   "Correspondence," *Thirty-Four*, February 11, 1880.

4.   "Our City," *Arizona Weekly Star*, September 19, 1878.

5.   Untitled, *Daily Arizona Citizen*, April 5, 1880.

6.   "Tucson," *Arizona Daily Star*, February 7, 1879.

7.   Charles F. Crocker to Huntington, September 20, 1879.

8.   "The Southern Pacific," *Arizona Daily Star*, October 25, 1879.

9.   Huntington to Schenectedy Locomotive Company, letterpress document, June 7, 1879.

10. Huntington to Towne, letterpress document, September 11, 1879.

11. "Railroad Items," *Arizona Daily Star*, May 30, 1880.

12. Crocker to Huntington, June 6, 1879.

13. Crocker to Huntington, June 7, 1879.

14. Huntington to Crocker, June 10, 1879.

15. Huntington to Albany & Rensselar Steel and Iron Company, letterpress document, July 9, 1879.

16. "The Boom for 1880," *Daily Arizona Citizen*, January 23, 1880.

17. Crocker to Huntington, September 16, 1879.

18. Crocker to Huntington, October 1, 1879.

19. Crocker to Huntington, October 8, 1879.

20. Huntington to Albany & Rensselar Steel and Iron Company, letterpress document, September 16, 1879.

21. Huntington to Albany & Rensselar Steel and Iron Company, letterpress document, September 24, 1879.

22. Crocker to Huntington, October 27, 1879.

23. Huntington to Crocker, November 3, 1879.

24. Crocker to Huntington, October 30, 1879.

25. Huntington to Crocker, November 7, 1879.

26. Towne to Huntington, August 28, 1880.

27. Towne to Huntington, March 24, 1881.

28. Towne to Huntington, March 28, 1881.

29. "The Railroad," *Arizona Weekly Star*, November 28, 1878.

30. "The Railroad Depot," *Daily Arizona Citizen*, May 26, 1879.

31. "Timely Suggestions for Tucson," *Arizona Daily Star*, July 23, 1879.

32. Thomas Cash, traveling agent for S.P., quoted in Towne to Huntington, September 10, 1879.

33. Ibid.

34. Towne to Huntington, September 10, 1879.

35. "A Chief Engineer," *Arizona Daily Star*, October 14, 1879.

36. Towne to Huntington, October 20, 1879.

37. "The San Pedro Ghost," *Arizona Daily Star*, February 11, 1880.

38. "The Chinese in Tucson," *Arizona Daily Star*, July 9, 1879.

39. Ibid.

40. "Chinese Cheap Labor," *Arizona Daily Star*, July 20, 1879.

41. "A.T.&S.F.R.R." *Arizona Daily Star*, September 30, 1879.

42. "Atchison, Topeka & Santa Fe Railroad," *Arizona Daily Star*, October 7, 1879.

43. *Washington Republican*, reprinted in "The Southern Pacific," *Arizona Daily Star*, October 25, 1879.

44. "The Atchison, Topeka & Santa Fe Survey," *Arizona Daily Star*, December 5, 1879.

45. "A.T.&S.F." *Arizona Daily Star*, February 12, 1880.

46. Towne to Huntington, October 20, 1879.

47. Safford to Huntington, May 27, 1879.

48. Crocker to Huntington, December 11, 1879.

49. Crocker to Huntington, November 13, 1879.

50. Huntington to Crocker, December 8, 1879.

51. Crocker to Huntington, December 16, 1879.

52. Crocker to Huntington, January 19, 1880.

53. "Toot To-o-ot To-o-o-o-ot!" *Daily Arizona Citizen*, January 19, 1880.

54. "Railway to Yuma and Eastward," *Arizona Weekly Citizen*, September 23, 1876.

55. Tucson Village Council, Minutes of special meeting, January 2, 1877.

56. Untitled, *Arizona Weekly Star*, November 7, 1878.

57. Tucson City Council, Minutes of special meeting, May 14, 1879.

58. Untitled, *Daily Arizona Citizen*, May 10, 1879.

59. Tucson City Council, Minutes of special meeting, May 22, 1879.

60. Untitled, *Daily Arizona Citizen*, June 21, 1879.

61. Tucson City Council, Minutes of special meeting, July 22, 1879.

62. Toole to Gray, July 24, 1879, Arizona Historical Society Library.

63. "Railroad Jottings," *Arizona Sentinel*, January 24, 1880.

64. "The Southern Pacific," *Arizona Daily Star*, January 27, 1880.

65. "Railroad News," *Daily Arizona Citizen*, January 20, 1880.

66. "The Southern Pacific," *Arizona Daily Star*, October 25, 1879.

67. Hughes, *St. Johns Herald*, February 1, 1894.

68. Strobridge to Crocker, February 10, 1880, part of Crocker to Huntington, February 11, 1880.

69. Crocker to Huntington, February 11, 1880.

70. Crocker to Huntington, February 13, 1880.

71. Untitled, *Arizona Daily Star*, February 4, 1880.

72. "Railroad," *Arizona Daily Star*, January 27, 1880.

73. Ibid.

74. "L. Zeckendorf & Co." advertisement, *Arizona Daily Star*, March 10, 1880.

75. "Home Industry," *Arizona Daily Star*, February 11, 1880.

76. Browne, *Adventures in the Apache Country*, 131.

77. Sheridan, *Los Tucsonenses*, 37.

78. Purcell, *Life and Leisure in Tucson Before 1880*, 54.

79. Boehringer, "Josephine Brawley Hughes," 104.

80. Sheridan, *Los Tucsonenses*, 82.

81. Ibid., 43.

82. Ibid., 45.

83. "Tucson Real Estate," *Arizona Daily Star*, March 6, 1880.

84. "Touching an Excursion," *Daily Arizona Citizen*, February 17, 1880.

85. "Portable Buildings," *Arizona Daily Star*, February 18, 1880.

86. Untitled, *Arizona Daily Star*, February 25, 1880.

87. Untitled, *Daily Arizona Citizen*, February 24, 1880.

88. Ibid.

89. Crocker to Huntington, March 8, 1881.

90. Crocker to Huntington, February 20, 1880.

91. Strobridge to Huntington, February 26, 1880.

92. Huntington to Crocker, January 27, 1880.

93. "Railroad Reception," *Arizona Daily Star*, February 14, 1880.

94. "Celebrate," *Daily Arizona Citizen*, February 16, 1880.

95. Untitled, *Daily Arizona Citizen*, February 17, 1880.

96. Untitled, *Arizona Daily Star*, February 18, 1880.

97. "The Railroad Jubilee," *Arizona Daily Star*, February 20, 1880.

98. Untitled, *Arizona Daily Star*, February 17, 1880.

99. Untitled, *Daily Arizona Citizen*, February 20, 1880, and "Southern Pacific Railroad" advertisement, *Arizona Daily Star*, March 10, 1880.

100. Untitled, *Arizona Daily Star*, March 2, 1880.

101. "The New Depot," *Daily Arizona Citizen*, March 5, 1880.

102. Untitled, *Arizona Daily Star*, May 16, 1880.

103. "The Tucson Railroad Depot," *Arizona Daily Star*, May 21, 1880.

104. Ibid.

105. Wheeler, "History and Information of Hotels in Tucson of Early Days".

106. Drachman, Harry Arizona and Florence E., oral interview, 54.

107. "Sidewalk to the Depot," *Arizona Daily Star*, May 21, 1880.

108. "We Don't Want Any Sidewalks," *Daily Arizona Citizen*, May 14, 1880.

109. Corbett, letter to his father dated 14/80.

110. Ibid.

111. "Arizona," *Chicago Tribune*, December 5, 1879.

112. "AT LAST!" *Arizona Daily Star*, March 13, 1880.

113. "Railroad," *Arizona Daily Star*, March 17, 1880.

114. "Last Trip," *Daily Arizona Citizen*, March 18, 1880.

115. Untitled, *Arizona Daily Star*, March 18, 1880.

116. Sheridan, *Los Tucsonenses*, 56.

117. "Caution," *Arizona Daily Star*, March 19, 1880.

118. Tucson City Council, Minutes of special meeting, May 14, 1879.

119. "Congratulations," *Arizona Daily Star*, March 19, 1880.

120. "The Railroad in Tucson," *Arizona Daily Star*, March 19, 1880.

121. Ibid.

122. "Reception," *Arizona Daily Star*, March 21, 1880.

123. Romero, Mrs. Cruz Tellez reminiscences.

124. Purcell, *Life and Leisure in Tucson Before 1880*, 119-121.

125. "Reception," *Arizona Daily Star*, March 21, 1880.

126. Ibid.

127. Ibid.

128. Ibid.

129. Myrick, *Railroads of Arizona*, 54.

130. "The Railroad at Tucson—The Southern Pacific Railroad Company," *Daily Arizona Citizen*, March 23, 1880.

131. "Railroad Matters," *Daily Arizona Citizen*, December 14, 1880.

132. Crocker, "Facts gathered from the lips of Charles Crocker," 38.

133. Crocker to Huntington, March 23, 1880.

Chapter Fourteen

1. Hood to Huntington, December 13, 1878.

2. Hood to Huntington, March 20, 1879.

3. Ibid.

4. Gray to Huntington, March 11, 1879.

5. Towne to Huntington, October 20, 1879.

6. Crocker to Huntington, March 24, 1880.

7. Stanford to Huntington, April 3, 1880.

8. Huntington to Crocker, April 5, 1880.

9. "Our City," *Arizona Daily Star*, May 16, 1880.

10. "Railroad Business," *Arizona Daily Star*, April 6, 1880.

11. "Railroad Items," *Arizona Daily Star*, May 28, 1880.

12. Crocker to Huntington, April 16, 1880.

13. Crocker to Huntington, April 19, 1880.

14. Huntington to Crocker, April 24, 1880.

15. "Railroad Magnates," *Arizona Daily Star*, April 8, 1880.

16. "Dunbar Hotel" advertisement, *Arizona Daily Star*, June 11, 1880.

17. "Pantano," *Arizona Daily Star*, July 14, 1880.

18. "Railroad Items," *Arizona Daily Star*, May 25, 1880.

19. Crocker to Huntington, April 22, 1880.

20. Ibid.

21. Crocker to Huntington, June 1, 1880.

22. Crocker to Huntington, July 20, 1880.

23. "San Pedro Town," *Daily Arizona Citizen*, April 9, 1880.

24. "Benson City," *Arizona Daily Star*, April 21, 1880.

25. "San Pedro Town," *Daily Arizona Citizen*, April 9, 1880.

26. "Benson City," *Arizona Daily Star*, April 21, 1880.

27. "Auction sale" advertisement, *Arizona Daily Star*, June 15, 1880.

28. Myrick, *Railroads of Arizona*, 58.

29. *N.Y. Commercial Bulletin*, reprinted in "Advantages of the Railroad," *Daily Arizona Citizen*, March 29, 1880.

30. "Neglected," *Arizona Weekly Citizen*, March 27, 1880.

31. Huntington to Crocker, May 6, 1880.

32. Crocker to Huntington, May 17, 1880.

33. Crocker to Huntington, May 26, 1880.

34. Crocker to Huntington, December 24, 1880.

35. "Railroad Items," *Arizona Daily Star*, May 30, 1880.

36. Crocker to Huntington, June 5, 1880.

37. Crocker to Huntington, July 26, 1880.

38. Crocker to Huntington, June 23, 1880.

39. Crocker to Huntington, June 24, 1880.

40. Crocker to Huntington, June 30, 1880.

41. Crocker to Huntington, July 20, 1880.

42. Crocker to Huntington, June 24, 1880.

43. Crocker to Huntington, July 2, 1880.

44. Huntington to Crocker, July 2, 1880.

45. Bradley, *The Story of the Santa Fe*, 146.

46. Ibid, 207.

47. Untitled, *Daily Arizona Citizen*, July 26, 1880.

48. "Devastation," *Arizona Daily Star*, August 27, 1880.

49. Crocker to Huntington, August 19, 1880.

50. "Railroad Items," *Arizona Daily Star*, September 9, 1880.

51. Crocker to Huntington, April 15, 1881.

52. Crocker to Huntington, April 19, 1881.

53. Crocker to Huntington, May 18, 1881.

54. Crocker to Huntington, June 30, 1880.

55. Towne to Huntington, November 3, 1880.

56. *Santa Fe New Mexican*, reprinted in "At the Other Side," *Daily Arizona Citizen*, July 1, 1880.

57. Crocker to Huntington, July 26, 1880.

58. "On to the Rio Grande," *Mesilla News*, July 12, 1879.

59. "Ho! for Mesilla," *Mesilla News*, October 2, 1880.

60. "South of Snow Line—The New Pacific Route," *Mesilla News*, October 23, 1880.

61. Huntington to Stanford, October 9, 1880.

62. Grant to Diaz, May 21, 1880, part of the Huntington papers.

63. Huntington to Crocker, May 25, 1880.

64. Bradley, *The Story of the Santa Fe*, 206.

65. "The Railroad Building," *Arizona Daily Star*, September 5, 1880.

66. "Railroad News," *Arizona Daily Star*, September 22, 1880.

67. Axtell to Huntington, March 22, 1877.

68. Axtell to Huntington, April 16, 1877.

69. Axtell to Huntington, March 22, 1877.

70. Axtell to Huntington, January 30, 1878.

71. Huntington to Colton, September 17, 1878.

72. Colton to Huntington, cipher telegram, September 25, 1878.

73. "What the Railroad is Doing," *Thirty-Four*, January 8, 1879.

74. "A Great Southwest," *Mesilla News*, May 31, 1879.

75. "Great Southwest," *Mesilla News*, April 5, 1879.

76. "The Day New Mexico's First Train Came Through Lordsburg," *Lordsburg Liberal*, November 14, 1947.

77. Gray to Huntington, March 11, 1879.

78. Towne to Huntington, November 19, 1880.

79. Crocker to Huntington, December 24, 1880.

80. Huntington to Crocker, January 3, 1881.

81. Huntington to Crocker, January 24, 1881.

82. "Pennington History of Early Deming Portrays Life of Pioneer Settlers," *Deming Sun*, November 21, 1957.

83. Huntington to Crocker, February 4, 1881.

84. "Something More About Deming," *Newman's Thirty-Four*, March 16, 1881.

85. Chase, *The Editor's Run in New Mexico and Colorado*, 127.

86. Untitled, *Newman's Semi-Weekly*, March 9, 1881.

87. "The Roads Joined," *Daily Alta California*, March 9, 1881.

88. "American Notes," *The Railway Times*, March 26, 1881, 283.

89. "A New Mexican Metropolis," *Newman's Semi-Weekly*, March 16, 1881.

90. "Fares Over the Southern Route," *Newman's Semi-Weekly*, March 26, 1881.

91. *Boston Herald*, reprinted in "Our Railroad System," *Daily Arizona Citizen*, December 2, 1880.

Chapter Fifteen

1. Chase, *The Editor's Run in New Mexico and Colorado*, 126.

2. "Something More About Deming," *Newman's Semi-Weekly*, March 16, 1881.

3.   Ibid.

4.   Chase, *The Editor's Run in New Mexico and Colorado*, 128.

5.   "Deming's Buildings," *Newman's Semi-Weekly*, April 6, 1881.

6.   Roman, "Southern Pacific and Santa Fe Railroads," 6.

7.   Chase, *The Editor's Run in New Mexico and Colorado*, 125.

8.   Alexander, *Dangerous Dan Tucker*, 71.

9.   Ibid., 74.

10. Ibid., 75.

11. Ibid.

12. Untitled, *Newman's Semi-Weekly*, April 9, 1881.

13. Untitled, *Newman's Semi-Weekly*, April 16, 1881.

14. "Kid the Killer Killed," *Rio Grande Republican*, July 23, 1881.

15. *San Francisco Chronicle*, October 27, 1881, reprinted in "A Street Fight," *Rio Grande Republican*, November 5, 1881.

16. Chase, *The Editor's Run in New Mexico and Colorado*, 127.

17. Ibid., 123.

18. Ibid., 124.

19. Anonymous, "Deming in 1882".

20. Ibid.

21. *Mesilla News*, reprinted in "The Southern Pacific Railroad," *Arizona Daily Star*, August 7, 1879.

22. Crocker to Huntington, July 7, 1880.

23. Stanford to Huntington, November 8, 1880.

24. "Mesilla," *Thirty-Four*, March 17, 1880.

25. "Las Cruces," *Thirty-Four*, March 10, 1880.

26. Price, *Mesilla Valley Pioneers*, 110.

27. Freudenthal, "Narrative of Samuel J. Freudenthal," 5.

28. Ibid.

29. "The Mesilla Valley," *Thirty-Four*, February 25, 1880.

30. Ibid.

31. Ibid.

32. Historical Data Committee of the Centennial—1949, "A History of Las Cruces and the Mesilla Valley," 85.

33. Untitled, *Newman's Semi-Weekly*, March 9, 1881.

34. Price, *Mesilla Valley Pioneers*, 44.

35. Neilson, "Comunidad: Community Life in a Southwestern Town," 73.

36. Ibid., 231.

37. "Las Cruces Items," *Lone Star*, October 19, 1881.

38. Price, *Mesilla Valley Pioneers*, 43.

39. Crocker to Huntington, March 7, 1881.

40. Crocker to Huntington, April 30, 1881.

41. T. Jefferson Coolidge, President of the A.T.&S.F. Railroad, to Huntington, May 10, 1881-two letters.

42. Bradley, *The Story of the Santa Fe*, 225.

43. Towne to Huntington, January 19, 1881.

44. Huntington to Schenectady Locomotive Company, letterpress document, January 29, 1881.

45. Towne to Huntington, May 9, 1881.

46. Huntington to Stanford, April 9, 1881.

47. Crocker to Huntington, January 8, 1881.

48. Stanford to Huntington, February 1, 1881.

49. Reed, *A History of the Texas Railroads,* 365.

50. Jay Gould, New York financier and President of the Texas and Pacific Railroad, to Charles F. Crocker, April 22, 1881, contained in Charles F. Crocker to Huntington, May 4, 1881.

51. Huntington to Crocker, May 3, 1881.

52. Crocker to Huntington, May 13, 1881.

53. Huntington to Crocker, May 12, 1881.

54. Myrick, *Railroads of Arizona*, 175.

55. Ibid.

56. Ibid., 27.

57. Crocker to Huntington, March 8, 1881.

58. "Editorial Correspondence," *Newman's Thirty-Four*, February 23, 1881.

59. Untitled, *Newman's Semi-Weekly*, April 6, 1881.

60. Untitled, *Newman's Semi-Weekly*, April 16, 1881.

61. Mills, *Forty Years at El Paso, 1858-1898*, 194.

62. Crocker to Huntington, April 9, 1881.

63. Ibid.

64. Crocker to Huntington, cipher telegram, April 6, 1881.

65. T. Wilson Shellabarger to Huntington, April 9, 1881.

66. Huntington to Crocker, April 18, 1881.

67. Crocker to Huntington, May 9, 1881.

68. "El Paso and Its Growth," *Dallas Weekly Herald*, May 26, 1881.

69. Crocker to Huntington, May 20, 1881.

70. "Railroad News," *Daily Arizona Citizen*, November 16, 1880.

71. Chang, *The Chinese in America*, 132.

72. Ibid., 136.

73. O'Malley, "A History of El Paso Since 1860," 44.

74. García, *Desert Immigrants*, 14.

75. "The Real Estate Question," *Lone Star*, October 19, 1881, and "Town Lots for Sale" advertisement, *Lone Star*, October 22, 1881.

76. "The Real Estate Question," *Lone Star*, October 19, 1881.

77. "Wanted, Cheap Living," *Lone Star*, October 10, 1881.

78. Ibid.

79. Chase, *The Editor's Run in New Mexico and Colorado*, 192.

80. Freudenthal, "El Paso Merchant and Civic Leader," 1.

81. "The Southern Overland Route Completed," *The Daily Picayune*, December 4, 1881.

82. Untitled, *Lone Star*, December 3, 1881.

83. "Railroad Competition," *Mesilla News*, January 13, 1883.

84. "Southern Pacific," *The Railroad Gazette*, February 2, 1883.

85. Huntington to Crocker, April 18, 1881.

86. Crocker to Huntington, May 11, 1881.

87. Drachman, Mose, "Reminiscences of Mose Drachman".

88. Crocker, "Facts gathered from the lips of Charles Crocker," 43.

89. Mercer, *Railroads and Land Grant Policy*, 157.

90. "Arizona and the Railroad," *Arizona Daily Star*, October 28, 1879.

91. Huntington, "Huntington autobiographical notes", contained in the Huntington Papers, series IV, reel 1.

92. Crocker, "Facts gathered from the lips of Charles Crocker," 40 and 42.

Epilogue

1. Anonymous, "A short history of the Gadsden Purchase," 5.

2. "Gadsden, The Border Community," *Arizona Sentinel*, March 18, 1915.

3. Ibid.

BIBLIOGRAPHY

Books and Reports

Albright, George L. *Official Explorations for Pacific Railroads, 1853-1855.* Berkeley: University of California Press, 1921.

Alexander, Bob. *Dangerous Dan Tucker: New Mexico's Deadly Lawman.* Silver City, New Mexico: High-Lonesome Books, 2001.

Ambrose, Stephen E. *Nothing Like It in the World.* New York: Simon & Schuster, 2000.

Bailey, L.R. (ed.) *The A.B. Gray Report.* Los Angeles: Westernlore Press, 1963.

Bartlett, John Russell. *Personal Narrative of Explorations and Incidents in Texas, New Mexico, California, Sonora, and Chihuahua.* Two volumes. New York: D. Appleton & Company, 1854.

Berton, Francis. *A Voyage on the Colorado—1878.* Translated and edited by Charles N. Rudkin. Los Angeles: Glen Dawson, 1953.

Bigler, David L. and Will Bagley (eds.) *Army of Israel: Mormon Battalion Narratives.* Spokane, Washington: Arthur H. Clark Company, 2000.

Bloom, John Porter (ed.) *The Treaty of Guadalupe Hidalgo, 1848, Papers of the Sesquicentennial Symposium, 1848-1998.* Las Cruces, New Mexico: Yucca Tree Press, 1998.

Bradley, Glenn D. *The Story of the Santa Fe*. Boston: The Gorham Press, 1920.

Browne, J. Ross. *Adventures in the Apache Country: A Tour Through Arizona and Sonora*. New York: Harper & Brothers, 1869.

Chang, Iris. *The Chinese in America*. New York: Viking Penguin, 2003.

Chase, C.M. *The Editor's Run in New Mexico and Colorado*. 1882. Reprint. Fort Davis, Texas: Frontier Book Company, 1968.

Chronic, Halka. *Roadside Geology of Arizona*. Missoula, Montana: Mountain Press Publishing Company, 1983.

Clever, Charles P. *New Mexico: Her Resources; Her Necessities for Railroad Communication with the Atlantic and Pacific States; Her Great Future*. Washington, D.C.: McGill and Witherow, Printers, 1868.

Cowdery, Richard B. "The Planning of a Transcontinental Railroad Through Southern Arizona, 1838-1870". Master's thesis, University of Arizona, 1948.

Crist, Lynda Lasswell (ed.) *The Papers of Jefferson Davis*, Vol. 5. Baton Rouge: Louisiana State University Press, 1985.

Davis, Jefferson. *Speech of the Hon. Jefferson Davis of Mississippi on the Pacific Railroad Bill*. Baltimore: John Murphy and Co., Printer, 1859.

Derrick, Samuel M. *Centennial History of South Carolina Railroad*. Spartanburg, South Carolina: The Reprint Company, 1975.

Deverell, William. *Railroad Crossing: Californians and the Railroad, 1850-1910*. Berkeley: University of California Press, 1994.

Emory, William H. *Notes of a Military Reconnaissance from Fort Leavenworth, in Missouri, to San Diego, in California*. Washington, D.C.: Wendell and Van Benthuysen, Printers, 1848.

_____. *Report on the United States and Mexican Boundary Survey*, Vol. 1. Washington, D.C.: A.O.P. Nicholson, Printer, 1857.

Evans, Cerinda. *Collis Potter Huntington*, Vol. 1. New Port News, Virginia: The Mariners' Museum, 1954.

Farish, Thomas Edwin. *History of Arizona*, Vol. 1. San Francisco: Filmer Brothers Electrotype Company, 1915.

Faulk, Odie B. *Too Far North:Too Far South*. Los Angeles: Westernlore Press, 1967.

Freudenthal, Samuel J. "El Paso Merchant and Civic Leader". *Southwestern Studies*, Vol. 3, no. 3, monograph No. 11. El Paso: Texas Western College Press, 1965.

Garber, Paul N. *The Gadsden Treaty*. 1923. Reprint. Gloucester, MA.: Peter Smith, 1959.

García, Mario. *Desert Immigrants:The Mexicans of El Paso, 1880-1920*. New Haven: Yale University Press, 1981.

Goetzmann, William H. *Army Explorations in the American West, 1803-1863*. New Haven: Yale University Press, 1959.

Golder, Frank A. *The March of the Mormon Battalion*. New York and London: The Century Company, 1928.

Hammond, George P. (ed.) *The Treaty of Guadalupe Hidalgo, February Second 1848*. San Francisco: Grabhorn Press, 1949.

Haney, Lewis H. "A Congressional History of Railways in the United States, 1850-1887". Madison: *Bulletin of the University of Wisconsin*, No. 342, January, 1910.

Hinton, Richard J. *The Handbook to Arizona*. San Francisco: Payot, Ypham & Co. and New York: American News Company, 1878.

Hodge, Hiram. *1877—Arizona As It Is*. 1877. Reprint. Chicago: Rio Grande Press, 1962, published as *1877—Arizona As It Was*.

Huntington, Collis P. *Remarks of C.P. Huntington before the Committee on the Pacific Railroads.* Washington, D.C.: Judd and Detweiler, Printer, January 31, 1878.

Judah, T.D. *A Practical Plan for Building the Pacific Railroad.* Washington, D.C.: Henry Polkinhorn, Printer, 1857.

Lander, Ernest M., Jr. *Reluctant Imperialists: Calhoun, the South Carolinians, and the Mexican War.* Baton Rouge: Louisiana State University Press, 1980.

Mahin, Dean B. *Olive Branch and Sword: The United States and Mexico, 1845-1848.* Jefferson, North Carolina and London: McFarland & Company, Inc., 1997.

McCormick, Richard C. *Arizona: Its Resources and Prospects, A Letter to the Editor of the New York Tribune.* New York: D. Van Nostrand, 1865.

Mercer, Lloyd J. *Railroads and Land Grant Policy: a Study in Government Intervention.* New York: Academic Press, 1982.

Mills, W.W. *Forty Years at El Paso, 1858-1898.* El Paso, Texas: Carl Hertzog, 1962.

Moser, Harold D., David R. Hoth, and George H. Hoemann (eds.) *The Papers of Andrew Jackson,* Vol. 4. Knoxville: The University of Tennessee Press, 1994.

Mowry, Sylvester. *Memoir of the Proposed Territory of Arizona.* Washington, D.C.: Henry Polkinhorn, Printer, 1857.

Myrick, David F. *Railroads of Arizona, vol. 1, the southern roads.* Berkeley, California: Howell-North Books, 1975.

_____. *New Mexico's Railroads.* Revised edition. Albuquerque: University of New Mexico Press, 1990.

Neilson, John C. "Communidad: Community Life in a Southwestern Town, Las Cruces, New Mexico, 1880-1890". Master's thesis, New Mexico State University, 1988.

Norris, L. David, James C. Milligan, and Odie B. Faulk. *William H. Emory: Soldier—Scientist*. Tucson: University of Arizona Press, 1998.

O'Malley, Catherine B. "A History of El Paso Since 1860". Thesis, University of Southern California, 1939.

Ohrt, Wallace. *Defiant Peacemaker: Nicholas Trist in the Mexican War*. College Station: Texas A&M University Press, 1997.

Owen, Gordon. *Las Cruces, New Mexico, 1849-1999: Multi-Cultural Crossroads*. Las Cruces: Red Sky Publishing, 1999.

Parke, John G. *Report of Explorations for that Portion of a Railway Route Near the Thirty-Second Parallel of Latitude, Lying Between Dona Ana, on the Rio Grande, and Pima Villages, on the Gila*. Washington: Corps of Topographical Engineers, 1855.

Poston, Charles D. *Apache-Land*. San Francisco: A.L. Bancroft & Company, Printers, 1878.

————. *Building a State in Apache Land*. 1894. Reprint. Tempe, Arizona: Aztec Press, 1963.

Price, Paxon P. *Mesilla Valley Pioneers, 1823-1912*. Las Cruces, New Mexico: Yucca Tree Press, 1995.

Pumpelly, Raphael. *Across America and Asia: Notes of a Five Year Journey Around the World and of Residence in Arizona, Japan and China*. New York: Leypoldt & Holt, 1870.

Purcell, Margaret. "Life and Leisure in Tucson Before 1880". Thesis, University of Arizona, 1969.

Reed, S.G. *A History of the Texas Railroads*. 2nd ed. Houston: St. Clair Publishing Company, 1941.

Russel, Robert R. *Improvement of Communication with the Pacific Coast as an Issue in American Politics, 1783-1864*. Cedar Rapids, Iowa: Torch Press, 1948.

Sheridan, Thomas. *Los Tucsonenses: The Mexican Community in Tucson, 1854-1941*. Tucson: University of Arizona Press, 1986.

Steiner, Stan. *Fusang: The Chinese Who Built America*. New York: Harper & Row, 1979.

Stevenson, Robert Louis. *The Amateur Emigrant*. 1895. Reprint. London: Hogarth Press, 1984.

Wallace, Edward S. *The Great Reconnaissance*. Boston and Toronto: Little, Brown and Company, 1955.

Werner, Michael (ed.) *Encyclopedia of Mexico: History, Society & Culture*, Vol. 2, M-Z. Chicago and London: Fitzroy Dearborn Publishers, 2001.

Williams, John Hoyt. *A Great & Shining Road*. New York: Times Books, 1988.

Willey, Richard R. *The Tucson Meteorites*. Tucson: University of Arizona Press, 1997.

Wilson, Clyde N. (ed.) *The Papers of John C. Calhoun*, Vols. 22, 24, and 25. Columbia: The University of South Carolina Press, 1983.

Woodward, C. Vann. *Reunion and Reaction: The Compromise of 1877 and the End of Reconstruction*. Boston: Little, Brown and Company, 1951.

Yenne, Bill. *Southern Pacific*. New York: Bonanza Books, 1988.

Journal Articles

Boehringer, C. Louise. "Josephine Brawley Hughes—Crusader, State Builder," *Arizona Historical Review* 2 (January, 1930): 98-107.

Carson, William G.B. (ed.) "William Carr Lane, Diary," *New Mexico Historical Review* 39 (July, 1964): 181-234.

_____. "William Carr Lane, Diary," *New Mexico Historical Review* 39 (October, 1964): 274-332.

Cotterill, Robert S. "Southern Railroads and Western Trade, 1840-50," *Mississippi Valley Historical Review* 3 (March, 1917): 427-441.

_____. "Memphis Railroad Convention, 1849," *Tennessee Historical Magazine* 4 (June, 1918): 83-94.

_____. "The National Railroad Convention in St. Louis, 1849," *Missouri Historical Review* 12 (July, 1918): 203-215.

_____. "Early Agitation for a Pacific Railroad, 1845-50," *Mississippi Valley Historical Review* 5 (March, 1919): 396-414.

_____. "The Beginnings of Railroads in the Southwest," *Mississippi Valley Historical Review* 8 (March, 1922): 318-326.

DeBow, J.D.B. "Col. Gadsden's Report," *The Commercial Review* 1 (January, 1846): 27-32.

_____. "Commercial Spirit at the South," *The Commercial Review* 2 (July, 1846): 119-132.

_____. "Internal Improvements," *The Commercial Review* 3 (May, 1847): 447.

_____. "Atlantic and Pacific Railroad," *The Commercial Review* 3 (June, 1847): 475-484.

_____. "Additional Remarks by the Editor on the Projected Southern and Northern Routes across the Continent to the Pacific," *The Commercial Review* 3 (June, 1847): 485-496.

_____. "Communication Between the Atlantic and Pacific Oceans," *DeBow's Commercial Review* 7 (July, 1849): 1-37.

_____. "The Memphis Convention—Intercommunication Between the Oceans," *The Commercial Review* 2 (New Series) (March, 1850): 217-232.

_____. "The Great Southern Convention at Charleston," *DeBow's Review* 4 (New Series) (October, 1854): 398-410.

_____. "Southern Commercial Convention at New Orleans," *DeBow's Review* 1 (New Series) (April, 1855): 520-528.

Faulk, Odie B. "The Controversial Boundary Survey and the Gadsden Purchase," *Arizona and the West* 4 (Autumn, 1962): 201-226.

Fong, Lawrence M. "Sojourners and Settlers: The Chinese Experience in Arizona," *Journal of Arizona History* 21 (Autumn, 1980): 227-256.

Kubista, Bob. "Tucson's Feast of the Jugly Smust," *The West* (October, 1968): 10-13 and 55-56.

_____. "The Railroad Comes to Arizona," *The Real West* (September, 1971): 31-34 and 60-61.

Kupel, Douglas E. "Roadside Rest: From Stage Station to the Space Age in Gila Bend," *Journal of Arizona History* 40 (Winter, 1999): 345-376.

Rippy, J. Fred. "A Ray of Light on the Gadsden Purchase," *Southwestern Historical Quarterly* 24 (January, 1921): 235-242.

_____. "The Boundary of New Mexico and the Gadsden Treaty," *Hispanic American Historical Review* 4 (November, 1921): 715-742.

Roman, Art. "Southern Pacific and Santa Fe Railroads: A long history in Deming," *Desert Winds Magazine* (September, 1997): 6-7.

Sacks, B. "The Origins of Fort Buchanan: Myth and Fact," *Arizona and the West* 3 (Autumn, 1965): 207-226.

Schmidt, Louis B. "Manifest Opportunity and the Gadsden Purchase," *Arizona and the West* 3 (Autumn, 1961): 245-264.

Tipton, Gary P. "Men Out of China," *Journal of Arizona History* 18 (Autumn, 1977): 341-356.

Wang, Wensheng. "The First Chinese in Tucson: New Evidence on a Puzzling Question," *Journal of Arizona History* 43 (Winter, 2002): 369-380.

Williams, Eugene E. "The Territorial Governors of Arizona—Anson Peacely-Killen Safford," *Arizona Historical Review* 7 (January, 1936): 69-83.

Wyllys, Rufus Kay. "William Walker's Invasion of Sonora, 1854," *Arizona Historical Review* 6 (October, 1935): 61-67.

Newspapers Cited

American Railroad Journal (New York)
Arizona Weekly Citizen (Tucson and Florence)
Arizona Republic (Phoenix)
Arizona Weekly Star and Arizona Daily Star (Tucson)
Arizona Sentinel (Yuma)
Charleston (Daily) Courier
Charleston Mercury
Chicago (Daily) Tribune
Daily Alta California (San Francisco)
Daily Arizona Citizen (Tucson)
Daily Picayune (New Orleans)
Dallas Weekly Herald
Deming Sun (Deming, New Mexico)
Detroit Free Press
Frank Leslie's Illustrated Newspaper (New York)
Illustrated London News
Lone Star (El Paso, Texas)
Lordsburg Liberal (Lordsburg, New Mexico)
Mesilla News (Mesilla, New Mexico)
Newman's Thirty-Four (Las Cruces, New Mexico)
Newman's Semi-Weekly (Las Cruces, New Mexico)
New York (Daily) Times
New York (Daily) Tribune
New York Herald
Pinal Drill (Pinal City, Arizona)
Public Ledger (Philadelphia)
Railroad Gazette (New York)
Railway Times (London)

Rio Grande Republican (Las Cruces, New Mexico)
St. John's Herald (St. John's, Arizona)
Thirty-Four (Las Cruces, New Mexico and El Paso, Texas)
Weekly Arizonan (Tucson)

Congressional and Federal Administration Records

U.S. Congress: House of Representatives

House Reports, "Railroad to the Pacific." 31st Cong., 1st sess., August 1, 1850, No. 439.

Appendix to the Congressional Globe, "Speech of Hon. V.E. Howard of Texas in the House of Representatives, July 6, 1852." 32nd Cong., 1st sess.: 776-781.

Congressional Globe. 33rd Cong., 1st sess., June 28, 1854: 1562-1565.

Congressional Record. 43rd Cong., 1st sess., April 8-13, 1874: 2896-2905, 2946-2958, 2987-2997, 3028-3042.

Congressional Record. 43rd Cong., 2nd sess., January 12, 1875: 404-407.

U.S. Congress: Senate

Senate Document, "Memorial of A. Whitney." 29th Cong., 1st sess., February 24, 1846, No. 161.

Senate Executive Document. 30th Cong., 1st sess., May 31, 1848, No. 52.

Senate Executive Document, "Treaty of peace, friendship, limits and settlement between the United States of America and the Mexican republic, concluded at Guadalupe Hidalgo, on the 2nd day of February, in the year 1848." 30th Cong., 1st sess., May 31, 1848, No. 52.

Senate Reports, "Report on the Memorial of Robert Mills for a Railroad Connection with the Pacific Ocean." 32nd Cong., 1st sess., August 18, 1852, No. 344.

Senate Miscellaneous Documents, "Memorial of a Committee Appointed at a Railroad Convention." 32nd Cong., 2nd sess., December 27, 1852, No. 5.

Senate Miscellaneous Documents, "Memorial of the Legislative Assembly of New Mexico." 32nd Cong., 2nd sess., February 10, 1853, No. 36.

Senate Executive Journal, 33rd Cong., 1st sess., March and April, 1854.

Senate Executive Document, "Report of A.B. Gray to the United States Senate." 33rd Cong., 2nd sess., February 8, 1855, No. 55.

Federal Administration

U.S. Department of State. Diplomatic Instructions of the Department of State, 1801-1906: Mexico. Vol. 16: November 10, 1845—April 6, 1854. Microcopies of Records in No. 77, Roll 112.

U.S. Department of State. Diplomatic Instructions of the Department of State, 1801-1906: Special Missions. Vol. 3: September 11, 1852—August 31, 1886. Microcopies of Records in No. 77, Roll 154.

U.S. Department of State. Dispatches from United States Ministers to Mexico, 1823-1906. Vol. 18: May 19, 1853—December 18, 1854. Microcopies of Records in No. 97, Roll 19.

Statutes

"An Act supplementary to an Act entitled 'An Act to incorporate the Texas Pacific Railroad Company, and to aid in the Construction of its Road, and for other Purposes'," 42 Cong., 2 sess., Statutes at large, chap. 132, 17 Stat. 59, May 2, 1872.

"An act granting to railroads the right-of-way through the public lands of the United States," 43rd Cong., 2nd sess., Statutes at large, chap. 152, 18 Stat. 482, March 3, 1875.

Other Sources

Anonymous. "A short history of the Gadsden Purchase of which Gadsden, Arizona is a small part." n.d. Gadsden, Arizona file, Arizona Historical Society—Yuma.

_____. "Deming in 1882." Photocopy. Deming Luna Mimbres Museum, Las Cruces, New Mexico.

_____. "Sketch of part of the march & wagon road of Lt. Colonel Cooke, from Santa Fe to the Pacific Ocean, 1846-7." Library of Congress, Geography and Map Division, Washington, D.C.

Arizona Territorial Legislature. "An Act to secure the construction and operation of certain railroad and telegraph lines, and to provide for other matters relating thereto," approved February 7, 1877 by A.P.K. Safford, Governor. History and Archives Division, Arizona Department of Library, Phoenix.

Corbett, J. Knox. Letter to his father dated 14/80. Corbett family papers, file 1, Arizona Historical Society Library, Tucson.

Crocker, Charles. "Facts gathered from the lips of Charles Crocker regarding his identification with the Central Pacific Railroad, and other roads growing out of it." 1888 oral history, Bancroft Library, University of California-Berkeley.

Drachman, Harry Arizona and Florence E. Transcript of oral interview AV 0003, Arizona Historical Society Library, Tucson.

Drachman, Mose. "Reminiscences, 1870-1935." File MS 225, box 2, Arizona Historical Society Library, Tucson.

Freudenthal, Samuel J. "Narrative of Samuel J. Freudenthal." n.d. New Mexico State University Library, Las Cruces.

Gadsden, Philip. "Gadsden family papers." 1854-55 letters. South Carolina Historical Society, Charleston.

Gadsden, James. "James Gadsden papers." Various dates. Manuscripts and Archives Division, The New York Public Library, Astor, Lenox and Tilden Foundations.

Goodwin, John N. "Speech to the first Arizona Territorial legislature." History and Archives Division, Arizona Department of Library, Phoenix.

Historical Data Committee of the Centennial—1949. "A History of Las Cruces and the Mesilla Valley." New Mexico State University Library, Las Cruces.

Hughes, Samuel. *St. Johns Herald*, February 1, 1894. Bio file of Sam Hughes, Arizona Historical Society Library, Tucson.

_____. "Interesting Reminiscences Indulged in by Sam Hughes." Tucson: *Arizona Daily Citizen*, September 8, 1899. Hayden file, Arizona Historical Society Library, Tucson.

Huntington, Collis P. "The Collis P. Huntington papers, 1866-1901." 1978. Sanford, North Carolina: Microfilming Corporation of America, a *New York Times* Company.

Kirkland, William. "Turning over the Gadsden Purchase to United States government by withdrawal of Mexican soldiers on February 20, 1856." File MS 1102, box 1, file 3, Arizona Historical Society Library, Tucson.

Lockwood, Frank. "Don Estevan Ochoa." 1940. Bio file of Estevan Ochoa, Arizona Historical Society Library, Tucson.

McCormick, Richard C. "Message of Governor McCormick to the Fifth Legislative Assembly of Arizona—Delivered at Tucson November 16, 1868". History and Archives Division, Arizona Department of Library, Phoenix.

Norwood, Thomas. "The Texas Pacific Railway Contrasted with a Real Southern Pacific R.R.—A Letter to the People of the South." December 1, 1878. Included in the Huntington Papers.

Parke, John G. "From the Pima Villages to Fort Fillmore," 1854-1855. Map. No. 2. Library of Congress, Geography and Map Division, Washington, D.C.

Romero, Mrs. Cruz Tellez. Reminiscences as told to Mrs. George F. Kitt in 1928. Bio file, Arizona Historical Society Library, Tucson.

Schmidt, Louis B. "The Gadsden Purchase and the Southern Pacific Railroad," a paper read at the first Arizona History Convention, March 26, 1960. Arizona Historical Society Library, Tucson.

Stanley, F. "The Deming, New Mexico Story." n.d. Deming Public Library.

Toole, James. Letter to George Gray of July 24, 1879. Bio file of James Toole, Arizona Historical Society Library, Tucson.

Tucson, City of. Minutes of 1877, 1879 and 1880 Meetings of the Common Council of the Village and City of Tucson. Tucson City Clerk's office.

Wheeler, C.C. "History and Information of Hotels in Tucson of Early Days." n.d. Manuscript file 853, Arizona Historical Society Library, Tucson.

Yuma, City of. Minutes of 1876 and 1877 Meetings of the Yuma Village Council. Yuma, Arizona, City Clerk's office.

0-595-32913-6

40512812R00175

Made in the USA
San Bernardino, CA
23 October 2016